MAO'S
HARVEST

MAO'S HARVEST

Voices from China's New Generation

Edited by Helen F. Siu
and Zelda Stern

New York   Oxford
OXFORD UNIVERSITY PRESS
1983

Printing: 9 8 7 6 5 4 3 2 1

Printed in the United States of America

Foreword

To many in the United States and Western Europe, the Chinese Revolution appears stymied. An intensely violent and visionary movement—led to victory by members of the Chinese Communist Party in the 1940s—which pushed through radical land-reform programs, expelled foreign armed forces and foreign investors, nationalized internal commerce, banking, and industry, and sought to transform the entire superstructure of education and artistic expression, finds itself now without clear direction. Inevitably, unanticipated problems complicated the solution of traditional ones dictated by China's geography, natural resources, and population, so that the newly emerging leaders, without the natural prestige of their predecessors, have to juggle and reassess their inheritance if they are to retain it at all.

Major bouts of doubt and self-questioning resulting in pressures for change, even under authoritarian regimes, have been common enough in the China of this century. As far back as the last years of the Qing Dynasty, after the Boxer Rebellion of 1900, scholars (many already in exile), applying newly acquired perceptions of Social Darwinism, sought to graft onto an archaic governmental structure foreign ideas of representative government. Then again, in the period between 1918 and 1925, warlord governments in Beijing and elsewhere were confronted by a demand for cultural change and an outright rejection of China's Confucian heritage, which was branded as sterile and self-deceptive. Another took place in the fugitive wartime universities, based in Kunming in southwest China in the early 1940s, when cosmopolitan cultural insights were used to criticize the limitations on all personal freedoms imposed by Chiang Kai-shek; yet another occurred in the Hundred Flowers movement of 1957, when the limitations of behavior and ideology of the Communist

Party of China were held up for scrutiny, analysis, and even ridicule by Chinese teachers and intellectuals.

To see some continuities between the clamors that have emerged during the years 1978 to 1981 and those of earlier periods is not to deny in any way the sensitivity or the desperation of these newest voices. The selections assembled here by Professor Helen Siu and Zelda Stern are a tribute to the range and sincerity of a new Chinese generation. In many ways "dissident," these voices are not exactly underground, for the government did let them speak in certain magazines and did let them post their pronouncements in certain areas. One can say that when permission to be spontaneous is necessary, there can be no true spontaneity—but that may be too hasty a judgment. The Chinese writers of 1978 to 1981 have seized the opportunities open to them and made of them what they can.

If sentiments that surface in these passages often seem maudlin, and the preoccupations localized, that may well be because modes of expression in China have been crimped for so long that a great deal needs to be said afresh. There is a splendid lack of self-consciousness in the desire these Chinese writers show to re-enter a world literary dialogue, where Tolstoy and Chekhov speak as individuals of genius and sympathy rather than as Russians and can be invoked in a context that includes Shakespeare, Thomas Hardy, Baudelaire, and Edgar Allen Poe. And there is extraordinary agreement among these writers about the loss of dignity that afflicts all Chinese denied privacy, in housing as in thought, forced forever to jostle and bargain and plead until the shouts become cries and the cries blows.

Throughout these selections one can find flashes of insight that illuminate the society of modern China more vividly than one might have expected. Sometimes these flashes are conveyed by the authors' depictions of objects: a tight and much darned palm-green sweater that a sister inherits, a pile of washing boards beside a railroad track, the toilet that no one can be bothered to clean, the overpass that never gets built. At other times they are conveyed by action: a young woman who vomits after her own desperate attempt to have a party and asks, "You had fun, right?" or the old worker, about to be summoned to a "struggle meeting" who shaves his skull so that no one will be able to pull his hair.

"It looks as if my generation is losing ground," writes Gu Gong of his talented poet-son Gu Cheng, and of course he is right. Those who make revolutions can never understand why their children don't appreciate the suffering their parents endured. "Between you and me stand the gunsmoke-filled / Thirties and / Forties" writes the poet Ye Wenfu of the Communist general, once so bold yet now "lamed by the weight of honors" and Ye Wenfu is also right. The Chinese of the 1980s must adapt to a world in which old struggles are over or forgotten and new ones presented in unexpected guises. Maybe they will get their overpass, their road to the future that will make relocation possible, but as a character in the novella with that title observes, it will need "a contract with the Japanese. Their money, their designs. We do the work. Just you wait and see." But the waiting is hard and the solution ambiguous; as Gu Cheng puts it "I am willful," and Bei Dao echoes him, "I don't believe the sky is blue." Helen Siu and Zelda Stern have given us a wondrously subtle group of selections from a world in flux.

Yale University   Jonathan D. Spence
June 23, 1982

Acknowledgments

This book could not have been completed without the generous help of many people. We owe special thanks however to Lee Yee, the editor of *Qishi Niandai*. Lee Yee not only introduced us to China's New Realism literature, but was also a constant source of invaluable material, information, and encouragement throughout the long task of selection, translation, and editing. We are also grateful to *Qishi Niandai* and its staff for access to research materials.

Unless otherwise noted, all of the selections included in this anthology were translated by us. We thank Michael Crook for his superb translations of *Overpass*, "Trust," "At The Denunciation Meeting," and "Proletarian Dictatorship is a Humanitarian Dictatorship." We edited his translations to conform to our style; any errors introduced during this process are solely our responsibility.

Sauling Wong helped us polish our poetry translations; whatever grace they may have is largely due to her. Her many suggestions also improved our prose translations. Cheng Chouyu supplied us with some of the material for this book, elucidated much that was obscure to us in the poetry, and was a constant source of information and enthusiastic support. Jonathan Spence was generous with encouragement and advice. Hong Yung Lee enlightened us on several aspects of the Cultural Revolution, and assisted us greatly in the analysis of that event contained in our introduction.

Bi Hua and Wei Ming supplied us with background information on the Chinese literary scene. Mark Sheldon helped us locate photographs to illustrate the themes of this anthology and went out of his way to assist us in other ways. Carole Rosen assisted us with the translation of "The Foundation." Helen Foster Snow read through the entire manuscript and made many valuable suggestions that improved the quality of our translations.

To Ralph M. Bradburd, we owe a special debt for his unwavering support and enthusiastic interest, as well as for his clearheaded comments, advice, and suggestions.

Others who helped us by supplying material, information, comments, advice, or criticism were Chuang Yin, Margery Wolf, Emily Honig, Gail Hershatter, Carl Crook, Tam Luen Fai, Deborah Davis-Friedmann, Howard Goldblatt, Leo Ou-fan Lee, Chen Jo-hsi, Yue Daiyun, Wang Yaping, Janet Yang, Karl Kao, Gene Bell-Villada, Ilona Bell, Leo Cawley, Carma Hinton, Michael Katz, Myril Filler, Maurice Filler, Perry Link, Florence Stickney, and Meg Dodds. We are grateful to Naomi Schneider for her patient editorial assistance.

We thank Rosemary Lane, Liz Kyburg, and Lorraine Fiondella for typing the translations. Their eagerness to find out what happened next spurred us on.

Finally, we wish to thank our editor, Susan Rabiner, for her belief in the book and in us, and for her enthusiasm, judgment, and unflagging support.

Most of the translations for this book were completed while Helen F. Siu held a Culpeper Postdoctoral Fellowship at Williams College. The Hoover Institute provided access to research materials.

We thank the authors whose works we have included for the use of their material. None of them had any part in the preparation of this anthology. We are solely responsible for all introductory material contained in this book.

Contents

Foreword   Jonathan Spence   v

Acknowledgments   ix

Introduction   xiii

Authors' Biographies   liii

I. Faith   3

Why Is Life's Road Getting Narrower and
Narrower? (letter)   Pan Xiao   4
The Two Generations (essay)   Gu Gong   9
A Generation (poem)   Gu Cheng   16
Shooting a Photograph (poem)   Gu Cheng   16
I Am a Willful Child (poem)   Gu Cheng   16
Reply (poem)   Bei Dao   19

II. Family   21

Remorse (story)   Zhang Jie   23
Overpass (novella)   Liu Xinwu   29

III. Love   91

Love Cannot Be Forgotten (story)   Zhang Jie   92
The Corner Forsaken by Love (story)   Zhang Xian   106
Longing (poem)   Shu Ting   125

IV. Work   127

The Foundation (story)   Jiang Zilong   128
Trust (story)   Chen Zhongshi   146

V. Politics   157

General, You Can't Do This! (poem)   Ye Wenfu   158
Whom Are You Writing About? (essay)   Ye Wenfu   165
In the Wake of the Storm (poem)   Shu Ting   171
At the Denunciation Meeting (story)   Wang Peng   173
The Two Realms of Love (poem)   Gu Cheng   178
Epigraph (poem)   Gu Cheng   179
Second Encounter (story)   Jin He   179
The Get-Together (story)   Gan Tiesheng   198

VI. Appendix   209

Proletarian Dictatorship Is a Humanitarian
Dictatorship (essay)   Wang Xizhe   210
China's New Generation of Politicians
(interview)   Wei Ming   219

Introduction

In 1979, during a thaw in which the usual political controls on writers were relaxed, a new kind of literature appeared in the pages of China's official journals. The socialist realism of the previous three decades had extolled the bright future of Chinese socialism. The New Realism of 1979–1981 suggested its darker side, portraying a society struggling with social and economic problems; a political system caught up in corruption, opportunism, and bureaucratism; and a people emotionally scarred by political disruptions brought about by their leaders.

The Chinese have a long tradition of using literature to convey moral and political messages. Lyric poems protesting the hardships of the common people appear in the *Shi Jing*, or the *Book of Odes*, an anthology compiled—by Confucius according to tradition—around 600 B.C. By the eighth century A.D., many Chinese poets considered it their duty to voice the people's grievances. The renowned Du Fu (712–770), often referred to as China's greatest poet, satirized the luxury of the emperor's court and described the suffering caused the peasants by heavy taxes and military conscription. Another Tang dynasty scholar, Han Yu (768–824), criticized the emperor and was banished. In the modern era, Chinese writers have likewise used their pens to express their concern for the welfare of the country. Lu Xun (1881–1936), revered in China as the father of revolutionary literature, wrote penetratingly of his society's ills. Many of the authors included in this anthology display a similar commitment to the use of literature as a vehicle for social change.

Since Chinese literature so often serves to express social criticism and political protest, Chinese rulers have been very sensitive to it. Chinese writers and scholars have thus traditionally relied on the use of metaphor to communicate their most critical points and such precautions historically have been well-founded. "Wenzi Yu"—the brutal persecution of scholars (and their families) for writings that have offended emperors—is well-known to Chinese writers. In the thirty years since the founding of the People's Republic of China, debates within the leadership over certain writings have been at the heart of major political campaigns.* Sometimes a particular method of literary research has been condemned for implying dissenting ideological stands. At other times, plays and operas have been castigated by one political faction with the purpose of attacking the works' political patrons. For example, "Hai Rui Dismissed From Office," a play written by the vice-mayor of Beijing, Wu Han, was attacked by Mao's followers in 1965 for implying disagreement with Mao's radical rural policies.

This debate between Wu Han and Mao's supporters in fact marked the beginning of the political struggles of the Cultural Revolution. In the early seventies, the Maoist faction of the party launched a campaign to criticize the classic novel, *Water Margin*. The campaign was interpreted as an indirect attack on the moderate premier, Zhou Enlai. Only recently, the censure of Bai Hua's screenplay "Unrequited Love" was seen as a move by the conservative army factions in the Chinese Communist Party to suppress "bourgeois liberalism."

The New Realism literature of 1979–1981 has been particularly disturbing to the present Chinese leadership because it is extremely candid and critical—condemning not only particular events or individuals in the Republic's history, but also questioning the ideological foundations on which the socialist regime has relied. Furthermore, most of the authors of New Realism literature were members of the first generation of Chinese to grow up under socialism. Successors to the revolution that Mao and his generation had begun, they had been reared on Maoist ideology, had come of age during Mao's Cultural Revolution, and were not antagonistic to socialist ideals. Quite the contrary, more than any other force, Mao and his ideas had influenced and shaped their lives. However, their works now suggest a deep sense of disillusionment—a loss of absolute faith in the political ideals taught them in their youth. These writers are among the most educated, articulate and thoughtful members of China's younger generation, yet they look toward the future with trepidation. Though they may be temporarily silenced, the fact that theirs will be a major—if not the leading—voice of society for decades to come cannot be ignored. By 1981, New Realism was history and controls were once more imposed on China's official journals. But the literature pub-

* See "Why is China So Sensitive to Literature?," an essay written by Lee Yee for the Conference on Contemporary Chinese Literature: New Forms of Realism, May 28–31, 1982, St. John's University.

lished during this brief thaw stands as a clear window onto contemporary Chinese society, a singular view of socialist China through the eyes of its first-born.

This book is a representative collection of the stories, essays, and poems published during the 1979–1981 thaw by writers of the "Mao Generation."* Whatever their subject—romantic love, family tragedy, problems in the workplace or in the political arena—the authors in this collection use their writings to examine society and themselves— the outcome of Mao's bold revolutionary experiment. As a window on socialist China, this collection needs little explanation. For readers who wish to use this anthology to obtain a deeper understanding of the Mao Generation, however, it is useful to be acquainted with the roots of this generation's discontent. Students and scholars of contemporary China will automatically bring this information to bear when reading this literature. For those who may be unfamiliar with the background material then, we present a brief description of the political system under which the young people of the Mao Generation grew up and of the ideological education the Mao Generation received as well as a review of the most important historical events that have shaped this generation. This historical synopsis is followed by a brief discussion of some aspects of New Realism literature and of the Chinese literary scene.

Ideology and the Political System

Although the basic assumptions of Chinese Communist ideology derive from Karl Marx's dialectical view of history, it was Lenin, rather than Marx, who provided the Chinese Communist revolutionaries of the 1940s, led by Mao Zedong, with the theoretical justification for revolution in China. Whereas Marx had hypothesized that Communist revolutions would begin in highly industrialized societies in the advanced stages of capitalism, Lenin predicted that Communism would have its greatest appeal elsewhere—within those nations that were the weakest links in the world capitalist system, the impoverished, colonized countries that had been severely exploited by the imperialist powers. Pre-revolutionary China was clearly one such nation.

It was also Lenin who first suggested the value of a vanguard party of revolutionary professionals to provide leadership for such revolutionary movements. He argued that through such a group of men and

---

* Our term. For the purposes of this book, we define this generation as those born roughly within the decade prior to or the decade after 1949, the year of "liberation."

women, who had the political consciousness to lead and the dedication to transform society in the interests of the working class, would
come the revolutionary commitment necessary to bringing about last-
ing political change.

Armed with the ideology of Marx and the political theories of
Lenin, Mao Zedong fathered a revolutionary new society in postwar
China, one that embodied and furthered the ideas and dreams of both
Marx and Lenin. But even more than Marxism-Leninism, modern so-
cialist China would come to reflect the ideas of Mao Zedong—practi-
cal strategies for creating a socialist society on China's agrarian base
guided by philosophical teachings both zealously Marxist and uniquely
Maoist.[1]

By 1949—the year of the Communist liberation—Mao had succeeded in bringing about this peasant revolution. He would spend
the remainder of his life—nearly three decades—until his death in
1976, working to bring about a more complete socialist transformation.

In 1949, when the Chinese Communists set up their government,
they established a "people's democratic dictatorship" and declared
that China had embarked upon a socialist road. Today, the Chinese
government still officially considers itself a dictatorship of the proletariat,* a dictatorship whose existence is required while society under-
goes the transformation that will allow China to move into the ulti-
mate Marxist stage of communism.†

The function of the state during this first, socialist stage is to protect the people from internal and external enemies—from subversion
by the reactionary classes and from possible aggression by foreign
powers. The methods that the state may employ to carry out its func-
tions depend upon the object of its attention. Towards the enemy
class it may employ the methods of compulsion and suppression.
Towards the people, it is supposed to employ democratic methods—
education or persuasion. Thus it is a "democratic dictatorship."

The backbone of the state—the administrative and policymaking
center of the people's democratic dictatorship and the highest moral
and ideological authority in the land—is the Chinese Communist

* The Chinese use of the word "proletariat" is ambiguous; usually it refers to the
"alliance between workers and peasants."
† According to Chinese Communist ideology, the transformations that must take
place during the socialist stage are 1) the elimination of inequality in society (of
particular concern to Mao were "the three disparities" that lingered on from pre-
revolutionary China: the gaps in power, status, and wealth between mental and
manual labor, city and country, industry and agriculture); 2) advances in production (economic development); and 3) the raising of the political consciousness of
the people.

Party.* Guided by Marxism-Leninism-Mao Zedong Thought, the party leads the masses in their revolutionary activities.

While Chinese Communist ideology maintains that the success of the revolution depends on the party, it also emphasizes that the activity of the party is fruitless unless combined with the activity of the masses, who are perceived as the motive force of the revolution.† For if the party cadres become alienated from the masses, Mao argued—if they begin to formulate policies unrelated to the needs and wishes of the people, or to use their positions of power to seek privileges for themselves—the party is in danger of becoming a new ruling class. To guard against this potential for corruption and elitism, Mao and the top Communist leadership launched periodic rectification campaigns, in which criticism and self-criticism sessions, and other forms of ideological education were created to help party cadres purge themselves of "degenerate tendencies" and rededicate themselves to the cause. Mao, in fact, was unique among his peers in the international socialist community in the extent to which he concerned himself with issues of party corruption. The most famous of these rectification campaigns, as well as Mao's last before his death, was the Cultural Revolution of 1966–1969.

Education: The Training of Revolutionary Successors

Under Mao's leadership, particular attention was paid to the ideological training of the young. There were two reasons for this: first, with no (or very little) memory of pre-liberation China, the young were the least corrupted by the old society and therefore the most promising subjects for transformation;‡ and second, after the first genera-

---

* In theory, the state and the party are separate. For every state organization, from a local work unit to the highest government body, there is a parallel organization in the party; the party unit is supposed to guide and advise its government counterpart. In fact, especially after 1966, many parallel government and party posts have been held by the same person.

† The principle by which the party and the masses are supposed to interact and by which the party fulfills its leadership role and the masses participate in political decisionmaking, is called the "mass line." With the concept of the mass line, Mao attempted to overcome the elitist implications of Lenin's theory of the vanguard party and to break away from the Soviet model's emphasis on centralization and top-down policymaking. See Mark Selden, *The Yenan Way In Revolutionary China* (Cambridge, Harvard University Press, 1971), pp. 274–76.

‡ In attempting to imbue the Chinese people with the socialist spirit, the Chinese Communist leadership had to overcome persistent remnants of Confucianism, a 2000-year-old ideology that is fundamentally antithetical to socialist goals. In contrast to socialism's insistence on egalitarianism and struggle, Confucianism fostered inequality, sanctioned class differences, and advocated the avoidance of conflict. For a comparison of Confucian and Chinese Communist ideology, see Donald J. Munro, *The Concept of Man in Contemporary China* (Ann Arbor: University of Michigan Press, 1977).

tion of revolutionaries was gone, the second generation would have to keep the flame alive.

One of the most important qualities Mao sought to foster in this generation of heirs was the "collective spirit"—a willingness to subordinate one's own interests to the good of the collective. In traditional Chinese society, the individual had also been expected to identify his own interests with those of the group—the family, the clan, the village, etc. But in Communist China, the local collective units tend to be primarily economic/political (production teams, brigades, communes, etc.) rather than familial/social, and the greatest emphasis is placed on serving the largest collective unit, i.e., the people. The pursuit of self-interest, which Western society with its tradition of individualism considers an unvarying attribute of human nature, is regarded in Chinese Communist ideology as a manifestation of a lower order of political consciousness characteristic of human beings in the (pre-socialist) capitalist stage; self-regard is considered a negative quality.

The primary responsibility for producing revolutionary successors imbued with this new socialist awareness has rested not with the family but with the schools,* where ideological transformation has been part and parcel of the curriculum. Under Mao, along with learning about the topography of their homeland in their geography texts, for example, Chinese students read about "liberating Taiwan" and "defending the coastline."[2] Mathematics textbooks were liberally sprinkled with questions asking "the distance of enemy ships from China's shore, the rate of unemployment in America, and the compound burdens on the peasantry of rents in pre-liberation China."[3] Primary school reading texts often contained illustrations of children doing good deeds for elderly representatives of the proletariat.[4]

In the literature classes, students read stories about the revolution-

* The methods of inculcation described here were used in the mid-sixties, when most of the Mao Generation were in senior middle school. Although the level of ideological content in the Chinese Communist curriculum has always been relatively high, it has fluctuated, reflecting a fundamental conflict at the top levels of party leadership. When Mao's political influence was greatest—during the Great Leap Forward (1958–60) and especially during the decade of the Cultural Revolution (1966–76), educational policy gave priority to ideological training and the redress of traditional inequalities in the educational system. During the period of Soviet influence (1953–57), again in the very early 1960s, and at the present time, educational policy downplayed ideological content in favor of academic/technical training, concentrating resources on the most advanced students in order to promote technical expertise. The latter approach stems from the belief that the creation of a technical elite is necessary in the short term in order to bring about the rapid increases in production essential for China's modernization. See Suzanne Pepper, "Chinese Education After Mao: Two Steps Forward, Two Steps Back and Begin Again?" in *The China Quarterly* 81 (1980):1–65.

ary martyrs who had died in order that they might grow up under socialism and about the deeds of model children who had exposed the plots of class enemies to sabotage the revolution.[5] Teachers assigned essays on such themes as growing up under the party's care and encouraged students to keep diaries in which they were to record their efforts to improve their political attitudes and isolate their ideological faults.[6] And lest they forget their obligation to serve the masses, students were continually reminded how many bushels of grain produced by the labor of the peasants were required to finance their education.

During the Socialist Education Campaign of 1963–1966, the schools held "recall bitterness" sessions in which peasants recounted to the students their bitter experiences before the Communist liberation. Such sessions were supported to reinforce the correct class feelings of the children of workers and peasants and help the children of the former ruling classes dissociate themselves ideologically from their parents.

In order to be able to better identify with the proletariat, contribute to economic transformation of the country, and bridge the gap between mental and manual labor, students were also sent out of the schools to participate in production. In the cities, workshops were built on the school grounds so that the students could manufacture things: in the rural areas, they did farm work with the peasants.

Peer pressure and competition were powerful catalysts for ideological transformation. In the early 1960s, student groups were expected to hold evaluation meetings in which classmates would assess each other's political attitudes and behavior: behavior that conformed to the ideal was praised, while incorrect actions were criticized.[7] Although competition for grades was officially discouraged (as being too self-seeking), competition to prove political superiority was encouraged, and students vied with one another to do activist deeds and display the correct attitudes in order to gain admittance to the party youth organizations (the Young Pioneers, and, when they were older, the Party Youth League), which were stepping stones to membership in the party. At the same time, those who became leaders in the student and party organizations learned organizational skills.

Inside and outside the classroom, students were presented with model figures for emulation. These exemplary persons, chosen from every level and age group in society, were singled out for their outstanding contributions to production or for their advanced levels of socialist consciousness. The names and deeds of national models were described in textbooks and newspapers and known to every schoolchild. Local models, including students who displayed exemplary socialist behavior, received honorary titles and certificates of merit. On the national level, negative models were sometimes presented to illustrate wrong thinking; students were advised to avoid their mistakes.[8]

Socialist culture and art reinforced what the students learned in the classrooms; under Mao, the arts became a vehicle for furthering the revolution. Posters, stories, plays, ballets, and operas presented near-perfect revolutionary heroes and, with glowing optimism, portrayed the Chinese people's march on the socialist road.

To Mao, the activist, however, correct thinking was the result of correct practice. Culture and art were important tools of ideological transformation, but experience remained the best teacher; society, not school, the best classroom. The most useful way to learn about revolution was to take part in revolutionary struggle. "Successors to the revolutionary cause of the proletariat come forward in mass struggles," Mao wrote, "and are tempered in the great storms of revolution." From 1966–69, Mao would provide the students with a Cultural Revolution in which to put their ideological education to practice.

The Conflict Between Ideals and Reality*

As Jonathan Unger points out in *Education Under Mao*,[9] it was becoming apparent well before the Cultural Revolution that the Chinese educational system was not equipped at its higher levels to meet the increased demand for higher education or professional training that the Revolution itself had sparked. This set the educational system at odds with the revolutionary goals of egalitarianism, selflessness, and cooperation, for at each stage of the educational system a fierce competition set in among the many candidates for the few spaces that existed. Even as late as the early sixties, resources set aside for education were still very limited. Only a small number of junior middle-school graduates, for example, could even think of moving on to senior middle school and an even fewer number might think of entering a university. However, the number of young people desiring to receive such specialized training at existing institutions of higher learning was increasing rapidly, because the higher a student was able to climb on the educational ladder, the better his or her chances for a prestigious, well-paid, professional career. For these reasons, at each stage in their education, students had to pass selective admissions procedures.

In general, students were admitted to institutions of higher educa-

* Much of the analysis in this and the following sections on the Cultural Revolution was provided personally by Hong Yung Lee.

tion on the basis of three criteria: academic achievement, class status, and political behavior, but the relative weight given to each changed according to the prevailing political atmosphere at a given time. School grades, the quality of the school one attended, and scores on entrance examinations determined one's level of academic achievement; over these factors, the student had some control. Students had no control, however, over their class status. Class labels had been assigned to everyone in China in the 1950s according to the occupation of the heads of household before liberation: children inherited their parents' class status. Broadly speaking, the class labels used by the Chinese Communists may be grouped into three categories: the red classes, also called the "five red kinds"; the ordinary classes; and the bad classes.* In deciding whether a student would be selected to advance in the educational system, the school authorities gave preference to those from red-class backgrounds and discriminated against those with bad-class backgrounds.

Good political behavior could improve a student's career chances. It was, however, extremely difficult for the school authorities to judge whether a student was putting on a good political performance out of selfish motives—that is, in order to advance his own educational

---

* Class labels were ranked more or less as follows. (Starred items are political labels, assigned according to political or criminal errors of the family's head rather than on the basis of economic standing prior to liberation.)

Red- or good-class origins also referred to in China as the "five red kinds"
   a. Politically red inheritances (the families headed by pre-liberation party members, plus the orphans of men who died in the revolutionary wars):
      1. Revolutionary cadres
      2. Revolutionary armymen
      3. Revolutionary martyrs
   b. Working-class:
      4. Pre-liberation industrial workers and their families
      5. Former poor and lower-middle peasant families

Ordinary-class origins
   a. Non-intelligentsia middle class:
      Families of pre-liberation peddlers and store clerks, etc.
      Former middle-peasant families
   b. Intelligentsia middle-class:
      Families of pre-liberation clerks, teachers, professionals, etc.

Bad-class origins
      Families of former capitalists (the bourgeoisie)
    * Families of "rightists" (the label denoting those who were too outspoken in The Hundred Flowers Campaign of 1956–57—usually intellectuals)
      Pre-liberation rich-peasant families
    * Families of "bad elements" (a label denoting "criminal" offenders)
      Pre-liberation landlord families
    * Families of counterrevolutionaries

   Based on Unger, *Education Under Mao* (New York: Columbia University Press, 1982), pp. 13–14.

opportunities—or out of genuine commitment to the regime's values. Undoubtedly, many young people were hypocritical and calculating in their displays of "selfless" political dedication. Under normal circumstances, the party leadership was willing to tolerate such posturing in the belief that even the performance of the correct sentiments and actions would help the students to internalize the correct values. To a certain extent, the assumption proved to be correct. After conducting extensive interviews with students who were in the school system in the early 1960s, Jonathan Unger concludes that at least up to the time of the Cultural Revolution, the political-activist competition encouraged by the educational system was quite effective in instilling idealism in the students and imbuing them with official values.*

So long as the school authorities were not compelled to interpret the motivation behind good political deeds, all student activism was accepted without question. Whenever political campaigns made it necessary to infer real motives, however, the party leadership often relied on class background to make the distinction: if a student was from a good-class background, his or her selfless motive was accepted; the motives of students with bad-class backgrounds were viewed with suspicion. This practice of evaluating motives by class background became one of the most controversial issues of the Cultural Revolution.

The combined use of academic and political criteria for academic selection represented the regime's effort to maintain academic quality in the higher educational institutions while correcting the inequality of educational opportunity that had existed before liberation. There were political considerations behind this policy as well: the regime reasonably assumed that the children of the former exploited classes would feel more grateful for the revolution and therefore would be more loyal to the socialist road than the children of the former ruling classes, who might harbor dreams of a bourgeois restoration.

Under this system of evaluation before the Cultural Revolution, two student groups did well: the children of the former bourgeoisie and intellectuals, and the children of party cadres and military men. The offspring of the bourgeoisie and the intelligentsia tended to be the most highly motivated students academically, and given their

* A few of the students Unger interviewed were bothered by the hypocrisy present in the schools. A purer idealism, rather than cynicism lay behind these students' scorn of self-seeking activism: Unger writes of these students: ". . . the net result of the party activism was that they yearned all the more for an opportunity to act out their commitment in a genuine manner—and grandly, in counterpoint to the trivialized acts at school." (Unger, *Education Under Mao*, p. 99)

family influence, were also the best prepared. If they were politically active as well, these students could look forward to being well placed. The children of the cadres and army men received preference in the selection process because of their class status, which was backed by the high social standing of their parents. Having gained enormous political power, high incomes, and a high degree of social respect, the party cadres and the army men (who were also often cadres) had become the most prestigious social group in Chinese society.

In contrast to these two groups, the children of workers and peasants did not particularly benefit from the evaluation system. Unlike the cadres and the military, the peasants and the workers held a low position in the social hierarchy, and so, although their class status as one of the "five red kinds" supposedly gave them an edge in the competition for upward mobility, these students were not in fact in a position to compete with the other students.

The student competition was made more intense by the fact that career opportunities from the time of the Great Leap Forward (1958–60) had been shrinking because of economic pressures. By about 1962, the tensions among student groups had begun to build up. The ability of the children of the bourgeoisie and the intellectuals to get ahead despite their class origins was resented by the other students, who felt that the same class that had been favored by China's traditional educational system was still rising to occupy the top positions in China's new socialist society. The higher status of the cadres' and military men's children was also resented by the students of lower status, who felt that a new, unduly privileged elite was forming. This antagonism among the children of different social groups was to have far-reaching consequences in the Cultural Revolution.

Events: The Cultural Revolution Decade 1966–76

The Cultural Revolution* that Mao launched in 1966 was a bold effort to cleanse the nation of pernicious bourgeois influences. Mao

---

* The Cultural Revolution was a complex social, economic, and political event that involved debates over culture and art, educational reforms, economic policies, the nature of political institutions, and, ultimately, the proper road to socialism in China. This section is not an analysis of the Cultural Revolution, but a description of some events during that turbulent decade that directly affected the Mao Generation. For a more thorough analysis of the Cultural Revolution, see David and Nancy Milton, *The Wind Will Not Subside: Years in Revolutionary China, 1964–1969* (New York: Pantheon, 1976); Hong Yung Lee, *The Politics of the Chinese Cultural Revolution: A Case Study* (Berkeley: University of California Press, 1978); William Hinton, *Hundred Day War: The Cultural Revolution at Tsinghua University* (New York: Monthly Review Press, 1972); Stuart Schram, ed., *Chairman Mao Talks to the People: Talks and Letters 1956–1971* (New York: Pantheon, 1975).

spoke of his concerns regarding bourgeois attitudes in culture and the arts, but what alarmed him most was the emergence of new social inequalities—in particular, the formation of a privileged social group connected with the Chinese Communist Party. In Mao's view, the revolutionary vanguard had become entrenched—bureaucratized, rigidified, conservative—a governing elite whose members had distanced themselves from the masses and were often more concerned with maintaining the status quo than with revolutionary change. Mao was also worried that the party's growing reliance on technical experts to bring about modernization would accelerate the formation of a new privileged group composed of the party cadres and experts. Claiming that his opponents had formed a bourgeois dictatorship within the party—in effect, a new ruling class—Mao called on the masses to rise up and purge the nation of "capitalist roaders" and bourgeois thinking, even if these existed at the highest levels of the party bureaucracy. The party, which had hitherto been the agent of struggle, was now to be the target. In its place, Mao designated a new vanguard: the young. In 1966, the year the Cultural Revolution was launched, a youth born in the year of liberation, 1949, would have been just seventeen years old.

As the Communist Revolution had been the definitive event of their parents' generation, so the Cultural Revolution was to become the event that politically defined the Mao Generation. China's first revolutionary successors came of age in that tremendous upheaval and the events of those years caused many to re-examine their commitment to the political ideals they had learned in school. Because of its central importance to the generation, we cover the Cultural Revolution here in some detail.

The First Phase: The Red Guards

The involvement of China's young people in what was to become the Cultural Revolution began in the early spring of 1966, when Mao asked students in the cities to participate in a campaign he was launching against some of his party critics.* The task he gave them was to write wall posters defending his political line. The students

---

* The first target of the campaign was Wu Han, then the vice mayor of Beijing. Wu Han had written a play in 1961 about an imperial governor in the Ming Dynasty who had been unfairly dismissed by the emperor. The play was widely interpreted as an attack on Mao for his having dismissed the defense minister Peng Dehuai in the late 1950's because he had criticized Mao's Great Leap Forward policies. In November of 1965, Mao commissioned Yao Wenyuan to write a critical attack on Wu Han's play, but had great difficulty getting the article published in party-controlled newspapers.

responded enthusiastically, forming poster-making groups that plastered the city walls with their handiwork.

In June, the campaign took a new turn as Mao hailed a wall-poster attacking the Beijing University administration. The children of party cadres in other major cities, who heard about the event, read Mao's endorsement of the poster as a sign to begin a general attack on all teachers and school authorities. Eager to show their revolutionary initiative, these red-class students began to criticize their teachers, accusing them of slighting politics and of placing too much emphasis on academic achievement.

The red-class students charged their teachers with having reinforced pre-liberation class divisions and with not showing the proper class concern toward the children of cadres, workers, and peasants. Encouraged by the schools' party committees, who hoped thereby to divert attention from themselves, the students intensified their "class-line" charges.

At this stage in the campaign, Mao supported the class-line arguments of the red-class students. At their request, he suspended all university entrance examinations and replaced them with new admissions criteria stressing class background.

At the same time that Mao was instigating the student campaign at the mass level, he was also seeking to tip the balance of political forces at the highest levels of government in order to redirect the attack against his primary target: top party "reactionaries." With the support of the army, Mao reorganized the Beijing Party Committee, the Propaganda Department, and the Ministry of Culture, placing them under the control of a group of loyal Maoists—the "Cultural Revolution Small Group,"—headed by his wife Jiang Qing and three party leaders from Shanghai (these four individuals would later be dubbed the "Gang of Four"). Mao's action effectively transferred control of the national organs of communication from the party to Mao and his supporters.[10]

In response to this step, the party sent work teams of party cadres to the schools to guide the student campaign. The work teams, under the national direction of Liu Shaoqi, represented the party's attempt to make an outward show of cooperating with Mao, while actually making sure that the campaign stayed on the class-line track. So long as the labels progressive and reactionary described one's class status and not one's politics, party cadres, as one of the five red-classes, were safe from attack.[11]

It was under the direction of the work teams that the students began to focus their attack on the older bad-class teachers and to employ systematic violence. Often one of the first steps taken by the work teams was to release the official dossiers of the teachers to the students, giving them access to their instructors' political histories. Confronted with information that often identified their teachers as former Guomindang members, political "rightists" who had participated in the (now illegitimate) Hundred Flowers Campaign, and other types of "dangerous elements," the students began to look on these bad-class teachers as enemies of the people and therefore no longer worthy or deserving of personal respect. Students subjected these "ghosts and demons" and "stinking intellectuals" to bouts of hard labor and abusive struggle meetings. At some of the schools, the targeted teachers were jailed in classrooms converted for this purpose by the work teams. Often, it was only the red-class cadres' children who were allowed the glorious task of meting out such punishments.

By the end of July, the red-class students had firmly positioned themselves as the leaders of the student campaign. In early August, high-level cadres' children at several senior middle schools in Beijing began forming their own youth groups, to which only young people of pure class origin might belong. They called their groups the Red Guards. As soon as they received word of this development, high-level-cadre youth in other cities began forming their own Red Guard organizations.

Mobilization of the Student Masses

As the first Red Guards were forming their organizations in Beijing, Mao, realizing the party had been deliberately diverting the student campaign away from an examination of party excesses, ordered the withdrawal of the work teams from the schools. He then initiated a series of measures designed to simultaneously mobilize the students and weaken the control of the party.[12]

One of his first steps was to set forth a sixteen-point program for the Cultural Revolution that defined the principal purpose of the campaign as the overthrow of "those power holders in the party who are taking the capitalist road." The document identified a second objective as the destruction of the "four olds": the "old ideas, culture, customs, and habits of the exploiting classes," which the bourgeoisie, though overthrown, were still "trying to use . . . to corrupt the masses, capture their minds, and endeavor to stage a comeback." Previous rectification campaigns had relied on the party to reform itself, but in the Cultural Revolution, Mao called on the masses to take the lead. The Sixteen Points directive declared that the liberation of the masses could be accomplished only by the masses, and Mao designated the Red Guards—a mass organization—as the new vanguard in place of the party.

On August 18, ten days after the promulgation of the Sixteen Points as the charter of the Cultural Revolution, Mao reviewed a mass rally of hundreds of thousands of Red Guards in Beijing's Tiananmen Square and was photographed donning a Red Guard armband presented to him by the daughter of a high-level cadre. With that symbolic gesture, Mao publicly sanctioned the Red Guards' vanguard role and established his own role as their "Supreme Commander."

Further emboldening the students were the actions of the official press, which had been under the control of the Cultural Revolution Small Group since June. Under this group, a radicalized version of Mao Zedong Thought was being spread. Mao's thinking had always stressed contradictions, maintaining that socialist transformation required both democracy and centralism, enthusiasm and discipline, destruction and construction, change and order. The new Mao Zedong Thought, however, by which the young people were to judge the correctness of their actions, emphasized the disruptive, decentralizing elements of these pairs: democracy, enthusiasm, change, and destruction. The new radicalized thought, and Mao's slogan "It is justified to rebel" gave the young people almost unlimited political freedom.[13]

The Red Guards were now allowed free travel on the nation's railways so that they could meet Red Guards from other parts of the country to "exchange revolutionary experiences" and attend rallies in the capital to hear Mao. Mao encouraged them to bring their complaints directly to him in Beijing or to write to him, postage-free. In this way, Mao established a line of communication between himself and the masses that bypassed the party; in effect, he took over the party's leadership role.

The Red Terror and the Movement to Destroy the Four Olds

Despite Mao's attempts to refocus the campaign, the Red Guards, whose parents for the most part were party cadres, ignored the Sixteen Points directive to root out capitalist-roaders in the party and continued to focus on the reactionary classes. With Mao's endorsement of their red-class organization, they began turning on their classmates from ordinary- and bad-class families, as well as continuing their attacks on their bad-class teachers. During this phase of the campaign, which the Red Guards themselves titled the Red Terror, the Red Guards subjected these students to humiliating struggle meetings, and sometimes, to physical abuse.

Towards the end of August, the Red Terror merged with the Destroy-the-Four-Olds movement, the latter referring to Mao's Sixteen Point directive to destroy the "old ideas, customs, culture and habits of the exploiting classes." In this new phase of the student campaign, anything old or foreign was considered reactionary and targeted for destruction: Confucian texts, recordings of Beethoven, Buddhist relics, translations of Shakespeare, traditional art, even Western-style furnishings and clothing. The Destroy-the-Four-Olds movement took the campaign out of the schools and into the streets. Bands of Red Guards roamed the countryside, vandalizing museums, knocking down old temples, ransacking bad-class homes to confiscate revisionist literature.[14] They were living up to the original Red Guard manifesto, in which they had vowed to "turn the old world upside down, smash it to pieces, pulverize it, create chaos and make a tremendous mess, the bigger the better."[15]

The Rise of the Rebels

Since the beginning of the campaign, the situation of the ordinary- and bad-class students had been difficult. When the party work teams had first entered the schools most of the ordinary- and bad-class students had joined in the attack on the bad-class teachers in order to prove their "progressive" class stand; some, under pressure from the red-class students, had even denounced their own parents. But because of their class status, they were never considered for any leadership role in the Cultural Revolution and, when admission to the universities became solely dependent on class standing, they were, in effect, denied the opportunity to continue their education by attending a university. Finally, during the Red Terror, the ordinary- and bad-class students became themselves the target of attack.

In the fall of 1966, however, having apparently decided that the activities of the Red Guards were no longer leading the Cultural Revolution in the right direction, Mao ended the reign of the red-class students by denouncing the class-line theory of redness as counterrevolutionary. By doing this, he shifted his support away from the cadres' children and opened the way for the ordinary- and bad-class students to take over the campaign and redirect the attack against the party. Immediately, ordinary- and bad-class students in Beijing began forming their own Red Guard units. In October, Mao closed the schools to allow students to engage in the revolution fulltime, and by the winter of 1966–67, the Rebel Red Guards (as they called themselves in order to distinguish their own groups from the original Red Guard organizations) had formed units throughout the country. Like the first Red Guards, they were granted free travel and other privileges.*

With the support of Mao and his allies in the party (the Cultural Revolution Small Group), the Rebels turned the focus of the movement away from the bad classes and aimed the attack at top-level government and party leaders, a group that included many of the parents of the original Red Guard. Their attacks pushed the Cultural Revolution into a new phase of power seizure. The movement was now polarized into two factions: a radical faction, led by the Rebels, which wanted a radical restructuring of the Chinese political system, and a conservative faction, led by the original Red Guards, who wanted to maintain the status quo. As the waves of the Cultural Revolution rose higher, engulfing every factory and commune as well as every school, all of China was awash in a sea of chaos. The policy of allowing the Chinese masses to seize power further aggravated the situation at every administrative level.

Restoration of Order

Eventually, Mao had to order the People's Liberation Army (PLA) to step in and unite all the factions in a "grand alliance." However, as part of the established elite in China, the army's sympathy lay with the conservative Red Guards—their children and the children of other red-class families. Thus, despite the wishes of the top Maoist leaders, the army discriminated against the radical Rebel groups. The result was the intensification of factional struggle and armed violence. By now, the members of each faction had come to feel that they were the only true defenders of the Maoist line: the opposing faction was the enemy, to be overthrown at all costs. The most idealistic youths willingly risked their lives and even killed for the sake of the cause (See Jin He's "Second Encounter" in this anthology).

Nonetheless, the People's Liberation Army eventually established firm control, and the Cultural Revolution entered the demobilization stage. The Rebel factions, now beaten back by the combined strength of the PLA and the red-class factions, encountered one difficulty

* Unless otherwise noted, our account of student involvement in the Cultural Revolution to this point is derived from Jonathan Unger's description of student participation in *Education Under Mao* (Columbia University Press, 1982) pp. 110–33. Unger's account is based on extensive interviews he conducted with young people from Guangzhou who were in junior- and senior-middle school during the Cultural Revolution. Student involvement in other cities may have followed a slightly different course.

after another. Because of their suspicious class background, many suffered in the campaign to "investigate class enemies" that marked the last phase of the Cultural Revolution. Some of them were arrested.* In contrast, the conservative Red Guards, although officially condemned for having deviated from the Maoist line in their support of Liu Shaoqi and the party, resumed the favored position they had held in the initial phase of the movement.

In April of 1969, the Cultural Revolution was officially called to an end, and a restructured party was restored to its vanguard position. By its close, the Cultural Revolution had undergone so many twists and turns that almost every participating group had suffered. Chinese society was polarized by all the latent tensions and contradictions that had surfaced when Mao removed or weakened the control exercised by the party, and the governing elite (the party, the government, and the army) had split into conservative and radical factions over social, economic, and ideological issues. Three contending power groups emerged from the struggle: the radical Maoists led by Jiang Qing and the Shanghai group; the moderates, led by Zhou Enlai and his protégé, Deng Xiaoping; and the army under Lin Biao. The army retained control until the purge of Lin Biao in 1971. Between 1972 and 1976, the moderates and the radicals were engaged in a power struggle in which the radicals led by the Gang of Four made steady gains; as the Maoists rose to dominance, the party's policies grew increasingly radical.

By this time, Chinese youth, whether they belonged to the conservative or rebel Red Guards factions, began to realize that they had been used as instruments in a power struggle between top-level politicians. More importantly, the former radicals felt threatened by the veteran cadres whom they had attacked in the preceding stage and who were returning to positions of power in the government. Many activists in the Cultural Revolution thus sought protection from radical Maoist leaders. However, when the Gang of Four were purged in 1976, these activists' connection with the Gang turned out to be a political liability. Many of them lost their positions. Some were even targeted by the new leaders for prosecution as "disruptive elements during the Cultural Revolution" (see Jin He's "Second Encounter").

* The position of the Rebel Red Guards improved somewhat in 1971–72 when Lin Biao, the commander of the PLA, was officially declared a traitor. Lin was widely viewed as Mao's closest comrade-in-arms during the Cultural Revolution (replacing Liu Shaoqi, who had become the party's "leading capitalist-roader"). With the purge of Lin Biao, many former Rebel Red Guards, who had been persecuted by the army under Lin, demanded rehabilitation. Quite a number of them were vindicated and obtained minor administrative posts in the party and the government.

Those who managed to survive may lose their jobs in the forthcoming party rectification campaigns.

Impact of the Cultural Revolution on the Mao Generation

The Cultural Revolution was the first political drama in which the Mao Generation played a major role. Within that role, experiences differed. Urban youths were more involved than rural youths since the cities were the centers of political action. The red-class children of high-level party cadres and the ordinary-class children of the intelligentsia and the bourgeoisie were, by turns, the leaders of the campaign. The children of the workers divided themselves between the two factions, some remaining loyal to their red class, others—resentful of the privilege of the cadres' children—deserting their class to join the Rebels. Of all the students, those from bad-class families suffered the harshest treatment.

Certain experiences, however, cut across the factionalism and were witnessed even by those who were not intensely involved in the campaign. On both sides, the motives behind student participation in the Cultural Revolution ranged from outright opportunism to the most fervent idealism and often consisted of a complex mixture of these two extremes. Both radical and conservative students inflicted violence in the name of political ideals; indeed, the most dedicated students on each side came to see violence as a measure of commitment. Finally, throughout the Cultural Revolution, the students who were assigned the vanguard role exercised almost unlimited political power; but it was power granted, and ultimately revoked, by Mao. Mao set the Cultural Revolution in motion, terminated it, and remained the dominant influence on events throughout.[16]

As the director of the drama, Mao had neither absolute power nor a script. He improvised as he went along, exploiting existing social contradictions and adjusting to changing political conditions, hoping to maintain a balance of political forces that would ensure the revolutionization, but not the overthrow, of the ruling structure. As Hong Yung Lee summarizes:

> He relied on the masses to criticize the elite and to break the coalition of reds and experts within the elite. But at the same time, he continued to recognize the need for leadership from the top and actually used the organizational capability of the PLA to maintain control from the top. He mobilized the radicals to attack the powerholders and to compel the privileged social groups to renounce their privileges. On the other hand he

depended on the conservative mass organizations to put pressure on the bourgeois experts and to check those with bad family backgrounds from directly challenging the Marxist class line.[17]

To the young people who looked to Mao for guidance however, Mao's one-hundred-and-eighty-degree shifts must have seemed at best confusing and at worst, manipulative.

Even before the end of the Cultural Revolution, many young people seemed to have become disillusioned, perhaps cynical. In March of 1969, for example, Guangzhou's *Southern Daily* bemoaned the fact that a large proportion of the student population not only had lost interest in the Cultural Revolution, but had stopped caring about China, the Chairman, politics, or even their own futures.[18]

The Cultural Revolution was thus a political education for China's revolutionary successors, but not quite the kind Mao had anticipated. Today, looking back, many of those who were its most active participants see it as a turning point in their lives, marking both the peak of their idealism and faith and the beginning of their disaffection with the political system that had shaped them (See Pan Xiao's letter, which begins this anthology). Mao himself had begun this process: when he gave the young people a mandate to criticize the party, that political body lost its cloak of infallibility. The generation learned to question and challenge authority in the Cultural Revolution; it was a lesson not easily forgotten, even when the right to rebel had been revoked.

If the Cultural Revolution was a political education for the Mao Generation, it taught them politics at the expense of their academic futures. Those who were older than seventeen when the campaign began were not much affected: most had already completed senior middle-school and some even held a college or university degree. For tens of thousands of students under seventeen, however, the Cultural Revolution effectively ended their schooling before they had acquired basic skills. Each of these students had missed out on a year of schooling at Mao's orders, in order to be able to take part in the struggle. When they were called back to the schools in the late summer of 1968, a few of the red-class students were permitted to continue their schooling for a year; the rest were informed that they were now considered junior or senior middle-school graduates. There was now a new generation to educate and there were not enough places in the schools for those who had lost out.

Most of the ordinary- and bad-class urban youth were sent to live in the countryside after the upheaval and would never again have the opportunity to resume their education. Others were eventually al-

lowed to return to school, but, under the educational policies of the
Gang of Four, their schooling stressed ideological more than academic
issues. As a result, the oldest members of the Mao Generation were
hurt far less than those younger members whose educations were
truncated. The educational differences between these two groups were
to have important consequences years later, when the "experts" rather
than the "reds" held sway.

Sent to the Countryside

Toward the end of the Cultural Revolution, as order was being restored, the state was faced with the problem of what to do with all
the young people who had spent the past two years engaging in mass
struggle. The schools had no room for them: there was a younger
generation to educate. The factories could not absorb them; in the
chaos of the Cultural Revolution industrial production had at times
come to a halt. The state's solution to the problem was to send the
displaced youths to work with the peasants in the countryside.[19] The
massive relocation had an ideological basis as well; the transferred
city youths would "learn from the peasants" and help to bridge the
"three disparities"—between town and country, mental and manual
labor, industry and agriculture—that still impeded socialist transformation.

Before the Cultural Revolution, urban youths had been encouraged
to settle in the rural areas, and some had volunteered. Now most had
no choice, and those assigned to the countryside went not knowing if
they would ever be able to return. In the decade following the beginning of the transfer program, 17 million young people—nearly the
entire generation of urban youths—were sent to the rural areas.[20]

Although some of the most idealistic youths went willingly, most
of the transferred youths looked on their assignments as a life sentence. A professional career had been the unspoken goal of most
students before the Cultural Revolution; now the sought-after prize
was a job—any job—in a city. Class origin and, to some extent, political behavior, determined the winners of this prize, with the city jobs
going to the sons and daughters of the revolutionary cadres and after
them, to the children of the working classes. Almost all the ordinary-
and bad-class youths were assigned to the countryside. The few from
this group who escaped rustification were largely those who had sided
with the conservative faction in the Cultural Revolution.[21]

Once the urban youths were settled in the rural areas, the state
more or less abandoned them, and they were dependent on the good-
will of the peasants and the rural cadres in order to survive. Relations

between the educated city youths and the peasants were usually strained. The farmers commonly viewed these inexperienced city youths as an extra burden and many rural cadres resented the time and effort required to help them adjust to rural life.[22]

Many of the city-bred youth could not accustom themselves to the physical demands of agricultural life. Since rations were apportioned according to one's productivity, they were unable to make an adequate living and had to rely on money sent to them from their parents in order to live. Even those who were able to do the work were often discriminated against in the assignment of work points. It was not uncommon for the villagers and the local cadres to take unfair advantage of the urban youths, who, far from their families, had no one to protect them.[23]

Although their life in the cities could hardly had been called affluent or luxurious, the urban youths were often shocked at the poverty and harshness of rural life and horrified that such backward conditions could still exist after more than two decades of socialist transformation. For many, the lack of stimulation and diversion—of books, news, movies, school—was as hard to bear as the physical rigors. (The Shanghai-born writer Zhang Xian, who spent many years in the countryside, touches on this aspect of rural life in "The Corner Forsaken by Love," included in this anthology.)

Trapped in the countryside, not knowing when or if they would be able to return to the cities and their families, many of the urban youths who had been given great power by the state in the Cultural Revolution began to feel helpless and abandoned—betrayed by the leaders and the system they had fought for. Former Red Guards began to question deeds they had committed in defense of the socialist cause and to wonder at the true purpose of the Cultural Revolution and their role in it. Had they been heroes, agents of a revolution that had brought the nation closer to communism? Or had they been the pawns of the power holders—used to further the political ends of a few?

Almost as soon as they were settled in the countryside, many of the urban youths began looking for ways to escape. Some simply went back to the cities and to their families without reporting to the authorities. Without proper registration, they were not entitled to ration cards or legal employment. These dropouts depended on their families or odd jobs in order to eat. After a few years, some of the rustified youths with senior middle-school or college degrees were allowed to return home. Others pulled strings if they had connections, or tried to curry favor with the few cadres who had the power to grant exit permits. Their own competitive, manipulative behavior in the scramble to get back to the cities was yet another source of disillusion. (Gan Tiesheng's "The Get-Together" describes the plight of those who were forced to remain behind in the countryside long after most had been allowed to return.)

Even when the urban youths were allowed to return home legally, most had difficulty finding jobs in the cities, and under the new, anti-expert educational policies, those fortunate few who were allowed to go back to school received an education that did not really prepare them for technical positions.

As they watched successive campaigns and sensed the underlying political struggles among the leadership, their anger and frustration mounted, the young people of the generation that had been displaced by the Cultural Revolution became more and more alienated. Any Chinese youth who looked back on the chain of events since the beginning of the Cultural Revolution could not but reach the conclusion that there was little justice in the system.

Yet the young people could not speak of their grievances openly. The radical Maoists who had been brought to power by the Cultural Revolution would tolerate no criticism of that upheaval or of their policies, and until Mao's death in 1976, the official Chinese press continued to hail the Cultural Revolution as a great success.

Protest

In January of 1976, Zhou Enlai, premier of China since liberation, died of cancer. As a voice for moderation and as an advocate of expertise for modernization, Zhou was viewed as an opponent by the ultraradicals in power since the Cultural Revolution. When he died, an official memorial service was held for him, but any demonstration of mourning by the masses was forbidden.

Zhou was greatly admired and respected by the Chinese people, and the suppression of their natural desire to mourn a beloved leader provoked a strong reaction. In early April, tensions that had been building since the sixties exploded in a spontaneous demonstration of grief for Zhou that became a mass protest against the excesses of the Cultural Revolution and the radical leadership of the past decade.

The demonstration began a few days before the Qing Ming Festival, a national day for remembering the dead, when crowds of people began coming to lay wreaths and poems eulogizing Zhou at the base of the Revolutionary Martyr's Memorial in the center of Beijing's Tiananmen Square—the same square where, almost a decade earlier, the first Red Guards had been ceremoniously appointed the vanguard of the Cultural Revolution. On April 4th, the day of the Qing Ming

Festival, public security forces were called in to remove everything from the memorial and on the morning of April 5th, the square was cordoned off to the public. These security measures incensed those who had come to lay new wreaths and poems in memory of Zhou: angry crowds broke through the lines and ran across the square, setting several official vehicles on fire and shouting denunciations of the Gang of Four.

The demonstration continued all day. Even after appeals made by the mayor of Beijing, the crowds refused to disperse. That night, public security officials were sent in to clear the square. Several hundred demonstrators were arrested on the spot, and some demonstrators were reportedly killed.[24] In a matter of days, the demonstration had been crushed. The crackdown continued for a few months, however, as security officials tracked down more demonstrators for interrogation and arrest.

On April 7, the Tiananmen Incident, which later came to be known as the April Fifth Incident, was officially declared counterrevolutionary. Deng Xiaoping, who had been restored to power after having been ousted in the Cultural Revolution, and who was generally considered Zhou's choice as a successor, was blamed for the incident and once more dismissed from his posts.

A huge number of the demonstrators in the Tiananmen Incident were from two groups within the Mao Generation: the ordinary- and bad-class returnees from the countryside and the good-class children of revolutionary cadres. By now, these former Red Guards were no longer youths; those born in 1949, the year of liberation were twenty-seven.

The returned children of the ordinary and bad classes had obvious reasons for taking part in the April Fifth demonstrations, but on the surface the cadres' children had little cause for becoming involved: they after all had benefitted from the class-line policies of the Gang of Four. Yet these privileged young people were also critical of the nation's leadership and its political twists and turns. Many of their parents had been persecuted in the Cultural Revolution and even those whose families had emerged relatively unscathed had witnessed the suffering caused others by those years of turmoil. There was another reason as well: although many of these good-class children of revolutionary cadre had been assigned jobs in the cities and had not been sent off to the rural areas, typically, they did not hold professional positions, and since most of them had been unable to complete their education, they had little chance of ever moving up. The children of the intelligentsia and the children of the cadres who had been enemies in the Cultural Revolution were united by their discontent.

In time, April 5, 1976, became associated in the minds of many Chinese with May 4, 1919, a day that marked in its time and for its generation the beginning of a broad political and intellectual movement, one that would change the course of China's history. On that date over half a century earlier, another generation had demonstrated in the same square; their protest had been against their government's ceding of Shandong province to the Japanese. Humiliated by the carving up of China by foreign powers, the May Fourth students and intellectuals had blamed their country's weakness on traditional Chinese culture and a government that did not concern itself enough with the needs of its people. They had sought solutions in the West, and their search had led ultimately to Marxism, the Chinese Communist Revolution, and the establishment of China as a socialist state.

Like the May Fourth Movement, the April Fifth Incident came to symbolize resistance and regeneration.[25] It was not long before the Chinese looked back on April 5, 1976, as the day they had voted out the Gang of Four, expressed their desire for new leadership, and heralded the coming of a bright new era.

Reaction: The Post-Mao Era

A Second Liberation

In September of 1976—nine months after the death of Zhou Enlai— Mao Zedong died. The April Fifth Incident had made clear that popular sentiment was against the radical policies that had characterized Mao's last decade. With Mao gone, the moderates moved quickly. On October 6 and 7, members of the Politburo placed Mao's wife Jiang Qing and the three other top leaders of Mao's inner circle (Zhang Chunqiao, Yao Wenyuan, and Wang Hongwen) under house arrest. The Gang of Four had been routed.

The smashing of the Gang of Four was greeted with euphoria by the majority of Chinese who hailed the event as the nation's second liberation. Almost immediately, the party relaxed controls and began to reverse the radical policies of Mao and the Shanghai Gang. Deng Xiaoping was reinstated and began his rise to the top position in the party. Many of those who had been sent to the countryside almost a decade earlier were now allowed to return to the cities. Economics supplanted politics (the class struggle) as the nation's first priority, and the "Four Modernizations"—of agriculture, industry, science and technology, and defense—emphasized as national goals by Zhou Enlai—became China's new central policy.

In the new push for rapid modernization, technical specialization was now valued over political or class background. Thousands of intellectuals and scientists who had been struggled against and removed from their positions in the Cultural Revolution were now restored to positions of power so that they could help speed up China's economic development. Intellectuals who had been branded rightists in 1957 were rehabilitated and those who had been in prison were released. The older members of the Mao Generation—those who had been able to complete most of their education before the Cultural Revolution—were given good jobs and encouraged to pursue further technical training, and the schools once more emphasized academic subjects and the acquisition of expertise.

On November 15, 1978, the party re-evaluated the April Fifth Incident. Called counterrevolutionary two years earlier, it was now labeled "a completely revolutionary event." It was not until the following year, however, that the party officially reversed its verdict on the Cultural Revolution. On October 1 (National Day), 1979, an official spokesman for the Central Committee declared that Mao's last campaign had been "an appalling catastrophe suffered by all our people."

"Scar" Literature

During 1977–78, in the liberalized atmosphere following the fall of the Gang of Four, a new kind of writing emerged in China that criticized events that had taken place during the previous decade and revealed the suffering caused by the Gang of Four. Called the "Scar" literature* (after a story called "Scar"), the new literature was written mostly by the older, more-educated members of the Mao Generation, who by now were in their late thirties and early forties. Though given positions of influence as salaried writers and editors in the new regime, these intellectuals were still angry at past mistakes and wanted to express the anguish of their own "scarred" generation.

The Scar stories, which were published in the state-sponsored literary journals, marked a new phase in Chinese socialist literature. Before this, writers had been expected to portray only the shining achievements of socialism in order to inspire the masses. Now, for the first time, they could admit that all had not been perfect under socialism. The criticism was always limited to the past, however,—specifically to the excesses of the Cultural Revolution. All of the Scar

* Also known as the "Wounded" literature. See Lu Xinhua, Liu Xinwu and others, *The Wounded: New Stories of the Cultural Revolution 77–78*, trans. by Geremie Barmé and Bennett Lee (Hong Kong: Joint Publishing Co., 1979).

stories carried an obligatory tag line in which the author expressed his or her confidence in the new regime: now that the four villains had been vanquished, the whole nation could look forward to a "bright future" under the new party leadership.

Disillusion with the New Regime

As early as the end of 1978, however, it had already become apparent that not all of China's problems had vanished with the downfall of the villainous four. In pursuit of its new policy or rapid modernization, the new government had made some huge economic blunders that revealed technical incompetence, bureaucratic mismanagement, and corruption at the highest levels. Attempting to root out party corruption, Deng Xiaoping and his moderate supporters in the party brought some of the individuals responsible to trial and made their crimes known to the public. By mid-1979, the exposure of negligence involving the loss of billions of yuan and many lives led to the resignation of one top-ranking oil minister, the arrest of other officials, and an official call for economic retrenchment. (Shu Ting's "In the Wake of the Storm" was written in memory of those who died in the disaster that brought down the oil minister.) Despite these efforts, however, the abuse of power and privilege in the party persisted (See Ye Wenfu's "General, You Can't Do This!").

The Mao Generation in the Post-Mao Era

From the perspective of the Mao Generation, the change of leadership after the fall of the Gang of Four had benefitted mainly the older, more-educated men and women who had graduated from middle school or universities before the Cultural Revolution. Prospects for the rest of the generation, who could offer no technical skills to accelerate modernization and who were now considered too old (most were in their thirties) to be retrained, were no better under the new regime than they had been under the Gang of Four. They were qualified only for ordinary factory work, and after the economic chaos caused by the Cultural Revolution and the retrenchment necessitated by the overambitious development plans and blunders of the new leadership, there were not enough of these jobs to employ them all. Those who had suffered for nearly a decade in the countryside returned home to find a society that had no place for them. Former Red Guards were now told that they had risked their lives and forfeited their futures in a political campaign that had been a gigantic mistake.

Even the official press began referring to the problem of the "lost generation." The Mao Generation felt doubly cheated—first by Mao and the ultraradical Gang of Four and now by Deng Xiaoping and the moderate party leadership.

Those who looked beyond their own personal grievances saw a society that appeared to have come no closer to the socialist ideal; corruption, inequality, and severe economic problems persisted despite major policy reversals. In the April Fifth Incident, activists of the Mao Generation had blamed the party leadership for the ills of China's socialist society. Now some went beyond criticizing the leadership to question the political system itself.

The cumulative effect of the events of the past ten years on China's first generation of revolutionary successors had been to erode their faith in the revolution. In the winter of 1978–79, many began to openly express their discontent. Their protest took three forms: semi-underground political activism (the democracy movement); political activism allowed by the system (running for election); and officially tolerated literature that was critical of the system and the leadership (New Realism). (Many, however, did not question the system; these young people responded to the political vicissitudes they had experienced with pragmatism, cynicism, and self-interest. Liu Xinwu's novella *Overpass* vividly describes this phenomenon.)

The Democracy Movement

The new outbreak of political activism was triggered by the re-evaluation of the April Fifth Incident. If a demonstration that had been considered counterrevolutionary could be relabeled completely revolutionary, perhaps other protests would be tolerated as well. A spontaneous movement began in Beijing in late November, 1978. As in the April Fifth Incident, its leaders were the sons and daughters of revolutionary cadres, and returnees from the countryside.

The leaders of the new movement demanded democracy and legality. The lack of these, they declared, had permitted the Gang of Four to rule the Chinese people like emperors. They criticized the state and the party for not observing the state constitution which guaranteed the people such rights as freedom of speech and assembly.[26]

What came to be called the democracy movement began with some posters attached to a well in the Xidan district of Beijing. The posters called for reforms ranging from more housing for newlyweds to freedom of speech, democratic elections, and an end to corruption in government. They also described the suffering caused by the Cultural

Revolution, protested the policy of sending young people to the countryside, attacked Mao, and criticized the privileges of the cadres. The Xidan wall became known as Democracy Wall.

As the democracy movement became more organized, semi-underground journals sprang up. Published after work hours on hand-lettered stencils and sold by activists at the Xidan Wall, these were filled with critiques and analyses of Maoist policy, calls for legal reforms that would guarantee human rights—even appeals for Western-style democracy.[27] (An essay by Wang Xizhe, one of the leading theoreticians of the democracy movement, is included in the Appendix.)

Strikes and demonstrations around the country were another manifestation of the democracy movement. In Shanghai, 10,000 people gathered on the waterfront in December to demand democracy and human rights. At the end of January, some young people who had been allowed to return from the countryside to Shanghai for the spring festival refused to return. When the official press called on people to report past wrongs for redress, thousands came to Beijing to petition the highest party authority, the Central Committee. Peasants came to the capital to protest hunger and political suppression. City-bred men and women who had been living in the countryside for a decade traveled to Beijing to demand legal means of redress against the maltreatment they had received at the hands of local authorities or to petition the authorities to allow them to return home. Small demonstrations also took place in provinces far from the capital.[28]

Elections

In the eyes of those who participated in the democracy movement, the party leadership had lost its legitimacy; they therefore felt justified in using unofficial or semi-official means to voice their discontent. Another group of activists worked for change within the system by running for office.

In late 1979, the revolutionary committees that had been set up in the Cultural Revolution were abolished and replaced by people's governments and people's congresses. Delegates to the people's congresses up to the county level were to be chosen by direct elections; this would be the first time in the history of socialist China that the state had allowed genuine elections. (In all previous elections, voters had been asked to ratify a list of party-appointed officials.) Many of the candidates who ran for office in the new elections were young people of the Mao Generation who were among the fortunate few who had passed the rigorous entrance examinations that allowed them to receive a university education. At Beijing University, the elections provoked fierce debates among the candidates over issues of democratic reform within a socialist framework (See Wei Ming's interviews with some of these young politicians in the Appendix).

New Realism Literature

While the young politicians were trying to get themselves elected to office in order to bring about change within the system, and the democracy-movement activists were organizing a variety of semi-underground activities, another group from the Mao Generation was writing stories and poems calling attention to the need for reforms. The authors of the new literature were often the same writers who had produced the Scar literature—the older, well-educated intellectuals who were now in their late thirties and forties. Like the Scar stories, the new writing was published in state-sponsored literary journals. The new literature was more daring, however, exposing problems and corruption in post-Mao China as well as revealing past abuses, and usually omitting the formulaic expression of faith and optimism that had ended every story in the Scar literature. The new writing, sometimes called "exposure" literature in China, has been named the "new realism" by overseas Chinese readers, who are impressed with its candid portraits of contemporary Chinese life.

Unlike the student-politicians or the democracy-movement activists, the exposure writers for the most part refrained from specifying reforms or pressing for solutions either within or outside the system. The differences in the degree of militancy of the three groups may have been a reflection of their different prospects in a regime that has chosen to reward expertise. The state gave the writer-intellectuals relatively good jobs and the student-politicians the opportunity to complete their education and become professionals; these members of the Mao Generation may therefore have had a stake in the success of the new regime. The democracy-movement activists, who at best could look forward to holding jobs as ordinary workers, had the least to lose by their activities.

Despite their common desire for reform and some overlapping membership, therefore, the three groups never solidly joined forces. Perhaps if they had, these separate voices of discontent might have formed the nucleus for a broad-based movement. As it was, all three groups were doomed to frustration. Towards the end of March, 1979, the party began to restore controls.

Clampdown

The clampdown was gradual. Throughout the winter of 1978–79, the party had permitted the activities of the democracy movement. Much of what the activists were protesting—the Cultural Revolution, past class-line policies and corruption—were also targets of the new regime. By April, however, the party's tolerance had been strained to the limit by demands for democracy and individual rights. The official press, which at times had encouraged the democracy movement, now condemned the activists for promoting bourgeois freedom and individualism, desiring to eliminate class struggle, and wanting to get rid of the leadership of the party. In December, the state revoked the right to put up posters on the Xidan Democracy Wall. The semi-underground publications and organizations were searched, their equipment confiscated, and their leaders interrogated; some of the leaders were arrested. In January of 1980, Deng Xiaoping announced that the democracy movement was disrupting the stability and unity of the country and that the right to put up wall posters would be withdrawn from the constitution because the privilege had been abused by the ultra-individualists. Scattered protests continued into 1981. In April of 1981, however, security officials arrested the movement's leading activists, and the party denounced the mass journals, pronouncing them illegal. "Spring in Beijing" was over.

Like the democracy-movement activitists, the young politicians also met with failure. The change in the election laws, which had aroused so many hopes, had little effect. When the elections were held, factions within the party saw to it that their own officials won. In October of 1980, there were demonstrations at Hunan Normal College protesting the college officials' violation of the election laws.

The exposure writers enjoyed a longer respite from controls than the activists. As late as the fall of 1979, China's leaders were still allowing and even encouraging the new freedom in literature. At the Fourth National Congress of Writers and Artists in Beijing in October of that year, Zhou Yang, the president of the National Federation of the Arts, condemned the artistic policies of the Cultural Revolution and encouraged artists to "liberate their thinking" and "attack careerists, bureaucrats, and feudal types as well as more traditional targets of anarchism, extreme individualism and bourgeois liberalism." Deng Xiaoping said that the party should lead, but not control the arts. At the same time, writers were asked to consider the social impact of their work.

The first significant tightening of controls occurred in April of

1981, when the *Liberation Army Daily*—an official organ of the army—came out with an article denouncing "Unrequited Love," a screenplay by Bai Hua about a nationalistic artist who was cruelly persecuted during the Cultural Revolution.* As a result of the paper's accusations Bai Hua was forced to write a self-criticism and make a public apology.

In December of 1981, the official ideological journal *Red Flag* published a long article on literature and the arts by one of the party's leading theoreticians. While assuring writers that they need not fear another Cultural Revolution, he warned that "bourgeois liberalism" in literature would not be tolerated. Since then, China's writers have had to tread carefully.

During the clampdown, some of the democracy-movement activists accused Deng Xiaoping of having permitted the thaw because criticism of previous policies would help strengthen his own power within the party; when Deng no longer needed this support, they claimed, he once again tightened controls. It seems more likely, however, that Deng and his moderate supporters were sincere in their desire for reforms but that they met with resistance from within the party—particularly from conservative factions in the army—which forced them to slow the pace of liberalization. Since 1981, the party has announced major bureaucratic and legal reforms, but it is still too early to tell whether these reforms will result in significant changes.

Literature:

The New Realism vs. Socialist Realism

The selections in this anthology are representative of literature published in China from 1979 to mid-1981, that is, from the end of the post-Gang-of-Four period of optimism that had produced the Scar literature to the tightening of official control over liberal expression in the spring of 1981.† Artistically, these works are characterized by

---

* The controversial line in the play was a question by the artist's daughter to her father: "You love our country . . . desperately . . . but does this country love you?"

† Because of our focus on the Mao Generation, the themes we wished to stress, space limitations, or the fact that we were unable to obtain biographical information in time, we were regrettably forced to omit some very fine literature of this period, by writers such as Liu Binyan, Gao Xiaosheng, Liu Shahe, Jiang He, and Shi Tiesheng.

Twelve of the authors included in this anthology can be considered representative of the Mao Generation. Two authors (Gu Gong and Wei Ming) describe actual members of this generation in their essays; the two older authors (Zhang Jie, Zhang Xian), are included in this collection because they write sympathetically about the Mao Generation.

their defiance of orthodox Maoist doctrine concerning the role of literature in a socialist society. At the Yanan Forum on Literature and Art in 1942, Mao declared that art, literature, and culture were instruments of the proletarian revolution: tools for uniting and educating the working people, and weapons for attacking and destroying their class enemies. Since the establishment of the People's Republic in 1949, China's writers have been expected to subordinate their own individual artistic visions to the collective interests of the working people. The socialist realism that was born of Mao's guidelines sings the virtues of the proletarian masses, extols the glorious changes wrought by revolution, and expresses faith in the bright future awaiting the Chinese people at the end of the socialist road. The characters of this literature tend to be class stereotypes: exemplary workers and peasants, and villainous reactionaries. Mao's last decade—1966–76— saw the most extreme application of his Yanan guidelines; writers during this period were severely restricted in their choice of subject matter and artistic treatment.

The restrictions on what writers were allowed to write were accompanied by a tightening of controls over what publishers were allowed to publish, what bookstores were allowed to sell, and what everyone was allowed to read. In 1960, 1,300 official periodicals were published in China. In 1966, at the beginning of the Cultural Revolution, the number was cut to 648, and by 1973, this number had been further reduced to about 50. During this period, not only almost all foreign literature but traditional Chinese literature as well as modern Chinese classics (written during the "golden age" of Chinese socialism in the 1950s and during the May Fourth period of ferment in the 1920s and 1930s) were barred from publication, distribution, and library circulation. About the only works widely available were political tracts, technical manuals, a few novels, and the collected works of Marx, Lenin, and Mao. The Mao Generation was particularly hard hit by this tightening of controls. Just as these young people were reaching maturity, they were denied access not only to foreign literature but to their own literary roots—to traditional Chinese classics as well as to the works of China's modern writers.[29]

The extent and significance of the liberalization of 1979–81 can be measured by the fact that the number of literary journals was allowed to increase to about 3,000. During this thaw, traditional and modern Chinese literary classics, as well as translations of foreign works, were reissued and made available. Authors who had been condemned in the antirightist campaign of 1957 were allowed to write again and even to travel abroad, and new translations of Western works were begun. Access to this sudden wealth of literature after the deprivation of the previous decade must surely have been a heady experience for the Mao Generation.[30]

Against this backdrop of broad access to a wide range of sophisticated literary works, writers of the New Realism literature in 1979–81 broke into restricted areas of literary discourse. First, many writers pleaded for literature to serve humanity rather than politics; even those essays published in official literary magazines called on artists to recognize the existence of human nature as distinct from class nature and to infuse their works with humanism and humanitarianism,[31] claiming that the absence of both had made previous literature sterile.*

Based on their philosophical assumptions about human nature, these writers rejected the black-and-white absolutism of socialist realism under the Gang of Four and replaced it with a vision of the world that included shades of gray. Instead of presenting models for the masses to emulate, these writers attempted to create characters with whom their readers could identify—individuals who were neither heroes nor villains, but often victims of the system. Moreover, characters in this new literature often responded to political and social situations in China's complex and changing society with ambivalence, confusion, doubt, or despair—emotions that had never been acknowledged in socialist realism because they implied less-than-total faith in the political system. By focusing on the emotions and moods of individuals, writers of the new realism also affirmed the validity of the inner self—a highly unorthodox notion in the Maoist literary tradition, in which the expression of inner feelings had typically been viewed as the unhealthy moanings of bourgeois individualists seeking to undermine the collective spirit.

By insisting on the validity of the inner self and the existence of compassion, questions of why these qualities had been suppressed and why human dignity had been violated naturally arose in literary discussions. Ultimately, the questions led to an exploration of wider social and political issues—what kind of institutions systematically

---

* Orthodox Maoist thought dismisses humanism and humanitarianism as bourgeois ideas brought to China by imperialist missionaries. The notions of the universal dignity of man and of human compassion are excluded from orthodox socialist literature because they contain dangerous implications for the class struggle, in which certain individuals are considered enemies of the people and are to be struggled against without compassion. In socialist realism the concept of dignity is conferred by class origins; stories often speak of the innate dignity of the workers and peasants. Similarly, the notion of compassion is present in socialist realism, but almost always in the form of class concern, i.e., concern for the working classes.

generated the above contradictions? What was the nature of the socialist system in China? Could there be alienation under socialism?
If it were possible, what were the sources of alienation? Concretely,
the writings in this period tried to pinpoint the causes of the devastating events of the Cultural Revolution; they revealed the disastrous
consequences of rural economic policies in the late 1950s; they exposed the abuse of power by party cadres; they demanded justice for
those victimized in past political campaigns; and they protested the
lack of color in lives spent almost exclusively in the pursuit of political goals.

To a certain degree, it can be said that by producing literature that
was critical of the system, writers in 1979–81 were merely following
the party line of the post-Mao regime, which fostered expressions of
discontent in order to discredit the old regime under the radicals and
win the support of intellectuals. While some writers played it safe by
limiting their criticism to acceptable levels, others daringly tested
the limits of the liberalization by extending their criticism beyond
what the party sanctioned. Having lived through so many reversals
of policy, few writers could have believed that the relaxation of controls would continue indefinitely. Even as they wrote, the most outspoken of them must have known that they were making themselves
vulnerable to persecution when the political wind shifted again. To
produce such literature under these circumstances required integrity
and courage. The candor of these works affords us valuable insights,
not only into this generation's turbulent coming of age, but also into
socialist China's three decades of trial and error.

A Note on Writing and Publishing in the PRC

The years 1979–81, which produced New Realism literature, have
been called the most liberal and encouraging period for China's writers in the history of the People's Republic.[32] Liberal policies should
not be confused with liberty however: all of the writers who published their works in official literary journals in China between 1979
and 1981 were directly or indirectly under party control. It may help
readers approaching Chinese socialist literature for the first time to
know something about how writers function and how works get published in China.[33]

All professional writers in China are paid a salary by the state. In
order to qualify as a professional writer, an aspiring writer must be
approved or recruited by the national Chinese Writers' Association or
by one of the Association's provincial branches. If accepted, writers

are paid according to a fourteen-grade pay scale. Higher-standard writers, who belong to the national association, receive between $80 and $200 a month; lower-standard writers, who are members of the provincial branches, receive less. (The level of membership—national or branch—of writers in this anthology is included in the authors' biographies.) In addition to their salaries, writers may receive money from publishing houses when their works are published. In China, where the average worker makes about $50 a month, writing is a well-paid occupation.[34]

A writer does not have to be salaried, however, in order to have his or her works published. Anyone can submit his or her work to a journal; if it is accepted, the writer will be paid for its use.

Writers provide material for two main types of publications: party organs and mass journals. The most important publications of the first type are the *People's Daily* and *Red Flag*, which are under the control of the Central Propaganda Department; the *Liberation Army Daily*, an organ of the army; and *China's Youth*, an arm of the Communist Party Youth League. These newspapers and journals generally carry the orthodox party line, whose content is determined by top-ranking party leaders.

The second type of publication—the mass journals (in which most of the material in this book first appeared)—are under government control. Although these publications are not instruments of the party, the policies of the party are passed down to their editors by party members who sit on every editorial board. If a journal deviates from party policy on an issue, party members affiliated with that publication will usually call a meeting to discuss the problem with the editors and to criticize those responsible. Occasionally, party members organize another publication and initiate a campaign of criticism to pressure the editors of the original journal to refuse controversial articles.

Many mass journals also have subsidiary journals attached to them—small publications which publish more "off the line" articles. Major mass journals receive a budget from the state while the subsidiary journals are partially self-supporting and partially funded by major mass journals with which they are associated.

Occasionally—as took place during the democracy movement in 1977—writers print their own underground or semi-underground journals, which receive no funding from the state. The publication of such journals depends on access to paper and printing supplies, the distribution of which are controlled by the state.

Both writers and editors may or may not be party members. If they do belong to the party, it does not necessarily mean that they adhere strictly to the party line. Some of the most politically outspoken writers are party members.

At the Yanan Forum on Literature and Art in 1942, Mao encouraged artists and writers to produce literature for the workers, peasants and soldiers. The largest readership for literature in China, however, are urban youth, who constitute only about ten percent of the population.[35]

Notes

1. For information on Maoist ideology, see John Bryan Starr, *Continuing the Revolution: The Political Thought of Mao* (Princeton: Princeton University Press, 1979) and Franz Schurmann, *Ideology and Organization in Communist China,* 2nd ed. (Berkeley: University of California Press, 1970).

2. Donald J. Munro, *The Concept of Mao in Contemporary China* (Ann Arbor: University of Michigan Press, 1977), p. 125.

3. Frank Swetz, *Mathematics Education in China* (Cambridge: MIT Press, 1974), pp. 276–77; reprinted in Jonathan Unger, *Education Under Mao* (New York: Columbia University Press, 1982), p. 84.

4. Unger, *Education Under Mao,* p. 86.

5. Ibid., pp. 85–86.

6. Ibid., p. 87.

7. Ibid., p. 89.

8. See Munro, *The Concept of Mao,* Chapter 6, "The Use of Models," pp. 135–37.

9. See Jonathan Unger, *Education Under Mao* (New York: Columbia University Press, 1982).

10. Hong Yung Lee, "Mao's Strategy for Revolutionary Change: A Case Study of the Cultural Revolution," *The China Quarterly* 77 (1979): 62–63.

11. Ibid., 63.

12. Ibid., 58.

13. Ibid., 59.

14. Maurice Meisner, *Mao's China: A History of the People's Republic* (New York: The Free Press, 1977), p. 315.

15. From "Long Live the Revolutionary Rebel Spirit of the Proletariat," *Peking Review,* Sept. 9, 1966, pp. 20–21; reprinted in Meisner, *Mao's China,* p. 315.

16. Lee, "Mao's Strategy," 50–51.

17. Ibid., 70.

18. From *Nanfang Ribao (Southern Daily),* March 7, 1968, in *Survey of the Chinese Mainland Press Supplementary Series;* reprinted in Unger, *Education Under Mao,* pp. 132–33.

19. For a more thorough analysis of the rustification program, see Thomas Bernstein, *Up to the Mountain and Down to the Villages: The Transfer of Youth from Urban to Rural China* (New Haven: Yale University Press, 1977).

20. Roger Garside, *Coming Alive: China After Mao* (New York: Mc-Graw-Hill, 1981), p. 223.

21. Unger, *Education Under Mao*, p. 135.

22. Bernstein, *Up to the Mountains and Down to the Villages*, pp. 132–43.

23. Ibid., pp. 139–40.

24. David S. G. Goodman, *Beijing Street Voices: The Poetry and Politics of China's Democracy Movement* (London and Boston: Marion Boyers, 1981), p. 32.

25. Ibid., p. 33.

26. For more information, see James Seymour, *The Fifth Modernization: China's Human Rights Movement, 1978–1980* (E. M. Coleman Ent., 1980); Roger Garside, *Coming Alive: China After Mao* (New York: McGraw-Hill, 1981); Gregor Benton, ed., *Wild Lilies, Poisonous Weeds: Dissident Voices from People's China* (London: Pluto Press, 1982); David S. G. Goodman, *Beijing Street Voices: The Poetry and Politics of China's Democracy Movement* (London and Boston: Marion Boyers, 1981).

27. See Goodman, *Beijing Street Voices*.

28. Garside, *Coming Alive*, pp. 226–36.

29. Leslie Evans, *China After Mao* (New York: Monad Press, 1978), p. 28.

30. Leo Ou-fan Lee, "Recent Chinese Literature: A Second Hundred Flowers," in Robert Oxnam and Richard C. Bush, eds., *China Briefing* (Boulder, Co.: Westview Press, 1980), pp. 65–73.

31. See Zhu Guangqian, "Guanyu Renxing, Rendao Zhuyi, Renqingwei he Gongtpongmei Wenti," ("Concerning Human Nature, Humanitarianism, Human Compassion, and A Common Standard of Aesthetics") in *Xinhua Yuebao*, February 1980. See also essays published in *Xinhua Wenzhai* and *Shikan* in 1980.

32. See W. J. F. Jenner, "1979: A New Start for Literature in China?" in *The China Quarterly* 86 (1981): 274–303.

33. See introduction to Perry Link's *Stubborn Weeds* (Bloomington: Indiana University Press, 1983) for a detailed and insightful analysis of the mechanics of the political control of literature in the PRC.

34. John Hersey, "A Reporter at Large: China–Part III," *The New Yorker*, May 24, 1982.

35. See Perry Link, "Fiction and the Reading Public in Guangzhou and other Chinese Cities," a paper presented at the Conference on Contemporary Chinese Literature: New Forms of Realism, May 28–31, 1982, St. John's University.

Author's Biographies

Bei Dao was born in 1950. He is a graduate of senior middle-school and has worked as a forger of iron tools. At present, he is an editor in the Foreign Language Bureau of the Chinese Reporting Editorial Department in Beijing.

Chen Zhongshi was born in 1942 in a village near Sian, Shanxi province. His family have been farmers for generations. He was graduated from senior secondary school in 1962 and taught village school for six years. He then worked outside the commune for ten years. In 1979, he joined the National Chinese Writers' Association. He has published about thirty stories, many of which focus largely on rural themes. He is at present working at the Cultural Center, Baqiao district, Sian. "Trust" won an award in the National Awards for Short Stories in 1979.

Gan Tiesheng was born in 1946. His father, a Taiwanese, has been missing since 1947. After graduating from Qinghua University Secondary School in 1968, he was sent to the countryside in Shanxi province, where he farmed and worked as a carpenter, stonecutter, and shepherd. In 1975, he returned to Beijing and worked in a food factory. He is at present a carpenter in the Trademark Printing Factory No. 3. He writes in his spare time and started publishing stories in February, 1980. "The Get-Together" is his first work.

Gu Cheng was born in 1957. His parents were cultural workers with the army before liberation, and have remained in the literary and arts fields. During the Cultural Revolution, the whole family was sent to the countryside. Gu Cheng has a junior secondary school education and now works as a carpenter in a street-repair station in Beijing. Since 1977, he has published over a hundred poems in established journals and has aroused wide attention in Chinese literary circles as one of the foremost young poets in China today.

Gu Gong is the father of Gu Cheng, whose poems follow "The Two Generations." Born in 1928 in Shanghai, he was educated in Beijing. At the age of fifteen, he joined the underground and the People's Liberation Army as a cultural worker. After liberation, he was stationed in Nanjing as a professional writer. In 1969, he and his family were sent to an army farm in Shandong to tend pigs and he suffered a breakdown there. In 1974, he returned to Beijing, and since then has published over two hundred poems and stories.

Jiang Zilong was born in Hebei province in 1941. He has been an ordinary worker and a workshop director as well as secretary to a factory manager. He started publishing his work in 1962, and has written over thirty short stories, seven novels, and numerous essays and reviews. In 1979, he joined the National Chinese Writers' Association and has been an executive committee member of the association. He has won many awards. His best-known story is "Manager Qiao Takes Office," which won first prize in the National Awards for Short Stories in 1979.

Jin He was born in 1943. He was graduated from the Chinese department of the University of Inner Mongolia in 1968. Since then, he has worked as a journalist and done administrative work. He began writing in the early 1970s, and has won awards for his work. Since late 1978, he has been a professional writer in the Liaoning Province Writers' Association.

Liu Xinwu was born in 1942 in Chengdu, Sichuan province. He was graduated from Beijing Normal College in 1961 and taught secondary school for fifteen years. In 1976, he joined Beijing Chubanshe (Beijing Press) as an editor. In 1979, he was elected a member of the third executive committee of the National Chinese Writers' Association. He is also a member of the committee on young writers' work and editor of *Ertong Wenxue* (*Children's Literature*). His stories have won national awards.

Pan Xiao is a pseudonym for two young people who were the authors of "Why Is Life's Road Getting Narrower and Narrower?" Xiao, the major author of the letter, and the one who appeared on Chinese television as "Pan Xiao," is a twenty-four-year-old woman worker. After graduating from junior middle-school in 1972, Xiao was unemployed for a year. In 1974, she got a job working at the Beijing Wool Sweater Factory No. 5.

Pan, the other author, is a twenty-year-old male university student. He graduated from senior middle-school in 1978 and is now enrolled in the Beijing Economics Institute.

Shu Ting was born in Fujian province in 1952. When she was a child, her father, a bank official, was accused of being a rightist, and sent to the countryside. Intellectual relatives stimulated her interest in literature, and she was exposed to foreign literary works at an early age. She was in junior secondary school when her education was disrupted by the Cultural Revolution. In 1969, she was sent to the countryside in Western Fujian. She returned to Xiamen in 1972 and was unemployed for a time, working at odd jobs when she could get them—as construction worker, cook, clerk, and the like. In 1975, she finally found a job in a collective factory making light bulbs. She has interacted with the poetry circles in China since 1970, and she has friends among the young poets in Beijing, such as Gu Cheng and Bei Dao.

Wang Peng was born in 1949 in Sian, Shanxi province. Because of his father's "problematic" political background, the family was sent to settle in a rural brigade. He was ten years old at the time. In 1964, he was graduated from junior secondary school but could not continue his education because of his father's label. He also suffered similar discrimination when he looked for work. Now he is working in the countryside as an ordinary commune member. He has been writing since 1973. His stories are full of the rural flavor of southern Shanxi. He was recruited in 1979 by the Shanxi branch of the Chinese Writers' Association.

Wang Xizhe was born around 1948 and is a native of Sichuan. He was graduated from Guangzhou Number 24 Secondary School and participated in Red Guard activities during the Cultural Revolution. In 1968, he was sent to the countryside, in the Yingde area of Guangdong province. He later returned to Guangzhou and became a furnace worker in a cod-liver oil factory. In 1973–74, he coauthored a controversial big-character poster (the *Li Yizhe Dazibao*), which raised issues of socialist democracy and legality. The three authors were accused of being antiparty and were jailed as counterrevolutionaries. They were finally rehabilitated in 1978. After his release, Wang Xizhe participated in the democracy movement and edited the mass-based journal *The People's Voice*. He was also an editor of *Zeren*, a publication of the Federation of Mass-Based Journals, founded in 1980. He has written several very controversial theoretical essays on the nature of socialism and a critical evaluation of Mao Zedong and the Cultural Revolution. In the spring of 1981, he was arrested again, and in May of 1982 was accused of forming and leading counterrevolutionary organizations and sentenced to fourteen years in jail.

Wei Ming was born around 1957 in South America and subsequently moved to China. She spent three years (1978–80) studying at Beijing University.

Ye Wenfu was born in the mid-forties. Several of his poems exposing corruption in the party bureaucracy have been severely criticized by the Chinese government. Formerly a writer in the army, he has been transferred to a railroad bureau because he would not "admit his mistakes."

Zhang Jie was born in 1937 in Liaoning province. After being graduated from Renmin University, she worked in the Bureau of Machines. Since she began writing in 1978, she has won national awards for her short stories. At present, she is a scriptwriter for a movie company in Beijing. Her stories have created a stir in China for dwelling on melancholy inner emotions.

Zhang Xian was born in 1934 in Shanghai. After graduating from Qinghua University in 1953, where he had majored in metallurgy, he joined the An Shan Steelworks as a technician. In 1956, he joined the Beijing Metallurgy Design Institute. The year after, he was accused of being a rightist and spent the following three years in the countryside. In 1963, he joined the Ma An Shan Cultural Bureau in Anhui as a scriptwriter. During the Cultural Revolution, he was struggled against and sent back to the countryside. In 1978, he returned to the Cultural Bureau, and was fully rehabilitated in 1979. Since then, he has published many award-winning works. "The Corner Forsaken by Love" won the National Award for Short Stories in 1980. At forty-eight, Zhang Zian is technically outside the age range of the authors represented in MAO'S HARVEST, but he writes so sympathetically about the young that we feel he spiritually belongs to the Mao Generation.

MAO'S
HARVEST

I. Faith

In May of 1980, a letter entitled "Why Is Life's Road Getting Narrower and Narrower?" appeared in the Beijing magazine *China's Youth*. In it, a young person identified as "Pan Xiao"—a twenty-three-year-old Beijing factory worker and the daughter of Communist Party officials—confessed her loss of faith in the communist ideals she had cherished in her youth. Over the next few months, some forty thousand young people from all over China responded to the letter, echoing the author's disillusionment. Pan Xiao became a celebrity: in a later issue of *China's Youth*, Hu Qiaomu, the Chinese Communist Party's top-ranking theoretician, replied paternalistically to her confession, appealing to the older generation to have patience with China's "troubled" youth. Pan Xiao was even invited to appear on Chinese television.

"Why Is Life's Road Getting Narrower and Narrower?" is actually the work of two authors. Before its publication, the editorial board of *China's Youth* had organized a panel on the topic "Views of Life of Today's Youth." After the discussion, the board chose two of the participants—a woman worker and a male university student—whose views they felt were most representative of their contemporaries, and asked them to collaborate on a letter that would merge their attitudes and experiences. The surnames of the authors were combined to form the name "Pan Xiao."

Given the fact that *China's Youth* is a party organ, it is entirely possible that the publication of Pan Xiao's letter was a deliberate attempt on the part of the post-Mao leadership to elicit expressions of discontent. Whatever its intended purpose, the letter obviously struck a nerve. From the tremendous response it generated, it is clear that thousands in Pan Xiao's generation have traveled the same road, "from hope to disappointment to despair." The letter's central themes—the arbitrariness of China's political system, the destructive effects of politics on human relationships, the desire for recognition of the individual's worth in a collective society—recur again and again in the New Realism literature. And the larger issues Pan Xiao ponders—the fundamental characteristics of human nature, the ideal relationship between the self and society, the meaning of life—are very real and urgent concerns to the New Realism writers. Until the political thaw that permitted the publication of works like Pan Xiao's letter, such issues had seldom been open to question in socialist China.

The essay that follows Pan Xiao's letter, "The Two Generations," is an attempt by Gu Gong—the father of the young poet Gu Cheng and a well-known poet himself—to explain to his contemporaries why his son's view of the world is so dark and twisted, so unlike the optimistic vision of the poets of his generation. Quoting from his son's poems over the years, Gu Gong, like Pan Xiao, traces a journey from innocence and faith to doubt and despair.

While Gu Gong writes that there are many who are alarmed by the younger generation's loss of faith in communist ideals, Gu Cheng himself, in the three poems that follow his father's essay, sees his generation's disillusionment as an awakening—the end of a long period of darkness and the beginning of a search for light. In "I Am a Willful Child," he paints a picture of a different world; his longing for this other world is a protest against all that is lacking in his present reality.

Unlike Pan Xiao and Gu Cheng, Bei Dao, the author of the poem "Reply," is defiant, not despairing. Challenging the world and shouting his doubt, he believes only in his disbelief, has faith only in his loss of faith.

Why Is Life's Road Getting Narrower and Narrower?
PAN XIAO

Comrade Editor:

I am twenty-three. I should say that I am just beginning life, but already all of life's mystery and charm are gone for me. I feel as if I have reached the end. Looking back on the road I have traveled, I see that it was a journey from crimson to grey—from hope, to disappointment, to despair. When I began, the long river of my thought arose from a selfless source; now, at last, it has found its final resting place in the self.

I used to have beautiful illusions about life. In primary school, I heard the stories *How the Steel Was Tempered** and *The Diary of Lei Feng*,† and although I did not fully understand them, the heroic acts they described excited me so much that I could not sleep for days. I even neatly copied Pavel's‡ famous words on the first page of my diary: "So live life that when you look back on the past, you will feel no regrets over having let the years go by, no shame at not having achieved anything." When one diary ended, I copied the quote in the next one. This quote gave me so much encouragement! I thought: my father, mother, and grandfather are all party members. Naturally, I believe in communism. Someday, I will join the party too. I never had any doubts.

Later, by chance, I read a pamphlet entitled, "Who Are You Living For? How To Be Human." I read it over and over, completely captivated. I began to develop my first and most beautiful views about life: Men live to make the lives of others more beautiful; Men live, and so should have high ideals; When the party and the people are in need, without hesitating, one should give one's all. I lost myself completely in a kind of ecstasy of self-sacrifice. In my diary, I wrote paragraphs and paragraphs of bright and shining words, and in my every speech and action I imitated the model of a hero.

But often, I felt a lurking pain, and it was this: the reality my eyes saw always sharply contradicted what my mind had been educated to accept. Soon after I entered primary school, the waves of the Cultural Revolution began and grew more and more terrifying. I witnessed the following: the searching of homes and seizure of property; violence; human lives disregarded; whole days when there was no talk, no laughter in my family; Grandfather very carefully preparing for the inspections; young people a little older than me swearing, gambling, and smoking all day; everybody weeping terribly when my sister-in-law was sent off to the countryside. . . . I felt lost, because I began to realize that the world around me was not as beguiling as it had been portrayed in books. I asked myself, Shall I believe in the books

* A popular school text in the People's Republic at the time. It is a Soviet novel, written in the early 1930s by Nikolai Ostrovsky. Pan Xiao read a Chinese translation.

† Lei Feng was a soldier who died in 1963. The year of his death, the Chinese authorities made him a model hero and began a campaign in the schools that encouraged students to emulate his behavior. Lei Feng's diary, found posthumously, described the many small anonymous good deeds he had performed in his lifetime and revealed his wish to be a small but useful "screw" in the machine of socialism. The Lei Feng campaign emphasized that the performance of small, mundane acts to "serve the people" were as necessary to the advancement of socialism as the glorious deeds of the revolutionary guerrillas.

‡ The hero of *How the Steel Was Tempered*.

or in my eyes? Shall I believe my teachers or myself? I felt full of contradictions. But I was young then, and I could not analyze these social phenomena. After all, my past education had endowed me with strange abilities: I had learned to close my eyes, to talk myself into believing things, to memorize slogans, to hide inside my own pure and elevated spiritual world.

Later, however, it didn't work. Life's adversities pounced on me. The year I graduated from junior middle school, Grandfather died. My warm, supportive family suddenly turned cold and cruel. We quarreled over money. My mother, who was working elsewhere, refused to support me any longer. I had to leave school, and was reduced to being a street youth. I felt as if I had been clubbed on the head. Heavens, if relationships among family members were like this, what about other relationships in society? I fell seriously ill. When I recovered, I relied on the help of some schoolmates, who reported my case to the neighborhood office.* I was given sympathy, and a job in a small collective enterprise. There, I began an independent life. At the time, I still admired truth, goodness, and beauty. Maybe my family's misfortunes had been a special case. Now I was on my own. Life was tempting once more; it beckoned.

But once again I was disappointed.

I believed in the party organization. Nevertheless, a complaint made to my leaders blocked my entry into the Youth League† for years. . . .

I sought help in friendship. Once, however, I made a small mistake, and a good friend of mine went so far as to secretly write up all that I had confided in her and report it to the authorities. . . .

I sought love. I came to know the son of a cadre. His father had been persecuted by the Gang of Four, and they had been in a terrible situation. I rushed to the son with my most sincere love and deepest sympathy, soothing his wounds with my own wounded heart. People say it's a fact that women throw themselves completely into the pursuit of love, that only in love do they draw the strength to sustain life. You can't say there is no truth to this saying. Even though I met with adversity outside, I had love. Love gave me comfort and happiness. But I never thought that after the Gang of Four was smashed, his family would be reinstated, and from then on he would take no notice of me. . . .

I was devastated. For two days and two night, I couldn't sleep or eat. I was angry, irritated. My heart felt ready to burst. Man, you

* The office of the neighborhood committee, a local administrative body of elected representatives that runs neighborhood affairs in China's cities.
† The Communist Party Youth League.

truly revealed your vile, ugly face. Was this the intriguing mystery you wanted to show me?

Seeking the answer to the meaning of life, I observed people. I asked the white-haired old men, the inexperienced young men, the cautious masters, the farmers who rise in the dark to beat the dawn. . . . But not one of their answers satisfied me. If you say we are here for revolution, the idea is too abstract and farfetched. And anyway, I don't want to listen to dogma any more. If you say we live for fame, it is out of the reach of ordinary people. "Those who leave a good name for generations" and "those who are notorious for ten thousand years" are few. If you say we live for mankind, it doesn't match with reality. We break heads over a few work points; we argue furiously over the most trivial things. So how can life be for mankind? If you say we live to eat, drink, and be merry, then we are born naked, and we die an empty shell. But coming into the world for one go-round seems meaningless too. Many people try to persuade me not to be so troubled, saying, "Life is for living. Many don't understand it, but they still go on living all right, don't they?" Not I. Life, meaning— these words tumble around in my mind. I feel a rope strangling me, forcing me to make a choice right now.

I sought help from the treasury of man's wisdom. I read desperately, hoping to find comfort and explanations. I have read Hegel, Darwin, Owen's social science. I have read the works of Balzac, Hugo, Turgenev, Tolstoy, Lu Xun, Cao Yu, and Ba Jin.* But reading does not free me from my problems. These masters cut open layer after layer of human nature with pens like knives, enabling me to penetrate deeply all the ugliness of this human world. I am stunned to see how closely reality resembles what these masters described. It doesn't matter whether I immerse myself in books or return to reality, all I see are characters like Galathée and Nekludov.† I lie in bed tossing and turning—thinking, furiously thinking, laboriously thinking. Gradually, I become calm, cool. Social Darwinism gave me a deep revelation: man is human! No one can escape life's underlying laws. In crucial moments, everyone chooses according to his instincts. No one can religiously follow the high morals and convictions he preaches. Man is selfish; there is no such thing as a selfless, noble person. The propaganda of the past was exaggeration or fiction. Ask the great saints, the distinguished scholars, the noble teachers, the well-respected propagandists. If they dare confront themselves, I dare ask how many of them can say they have escaped the underlying law

* These last three are well-known Chinese writers of the modern era.

† Galathée is a character in one of Balzac's short stories. Nekludov is the major character in Tolstoy's last novel, *Resurrection*.

of selfish struggle! In the past, I believed fanatically that "Man lives to make the lives of others more beautiful," and "Don't hesitate to sacrifice your life for the people." When I think of it now, it seems ridiculous!

Having seen through life, I feel schizophrenic. On the one hand, I denounce this vulgar reality. On the other hand, I ride with the waves. Hegel once said: "Whatever is real is rational, whatever is rational is real." This has almost become a motto with which I comfort myself and soothe my wounds. I am human. I am not a noble person, but I am a rational one, just like all other rational beings. I fight about wages; I calculate bonuses. I learn to flatter, to lie. . . . Doing such things, I feel terrible inside. Then I remember Hegel's words and I become calm.

Of course, I am not content to go through life simplemindedly eating, drinking, and seeking pleasure. I have my own career. I have liked literature ever since I was young. Especially since I have gone through such difficulties in life, I want to use the pen of literature to write all this out. You might say that everything I do now is for this—literature.

But nobody seems to understand me. My co-workers at the factory are family-oriented: young women who concern themselves with nothing but perming their hair and wearing nice clothes. I find it difficult to communicate with them. They think I am aloof, strange, and ask me if I want to be single forever. I pay no attention to them, because I think they are vulgar. My inability to fit in makes me melancholy and lonely. When I am terrified by loneliness, I want to join the crowd and the laughter; but as soon as I move closer to their vulgar conversations, I would rather withdraw into my own loneliness again.

I know I don't want to write for the purpose of making a contribution to the people or for the Four Modernizations* but for myself, for my own personal needs. I am not content to let society treat me as if I were nothing. I am determined to use my writing to express my existence. Desperately, I hold onto this spiritual support, as if clinging to a small boat in a sea that threatens to swallow me up.

I have come to understand this principle: whether one lives to exist or to create, everybody works for others by working for himself. It is like the sun giving off light: this is, first of all, an inevitable phenomenon of the activity of its own existence; its shining on the world is nothing but a kind of incidental result deriving from this. Therefore,

---

* The modernization of agriculture, industry, science and technology, and defense. First presented as goals for China to work for in a speech given by Zhou Enlai at the Fourth National People's Congress in 1975, the Four Modernizations became China's central policy under Deng Xiaoping.

I feel that if everyone strives to improve the value of his own existence, human society must move forward. This is, generally speaking, the law of man, and also a law of biological evolution—a law that no dogma can drown or deceive.

It is said that when you have a career, you feel strong, happy, and content. But I am not like this. It seems to me that I am suffering, struggling, torturing myself. Everywhere I want to show that I am a strong person, but I know that inside I am weak. My wages are low. Since I have to buy a lot of books and paper, I have no choice but to count pennies and dimes. . . . Sometimes I suddenly ask myself: Why should I torture myself to begin a career? I am human; I should have a warm, happy family, become a good wife, a kind mother. And, furthermore, what can I write anyway? Even if I produce something, can a few pages of writing stir up life, influence society? I really don't believe it will. People say the era is marching forward, but I cannot feel its strong arms; others say the world has a grand design, but I do not know where it is. Life's road—why is it getting narrower and narrower? I am already so tired. It is as if, were I to let out one more breath, it would mean utter destruction. I confess, I have gone secretly to watch services in the Catholic church. I have thought of becoming a nun. I have even thought of dying. . . . My heart is so confused, so contradictory.

Comrade Editor, I write this letter to you in a very troubled mood. I do not reveal these feelings expecting a prescription from you. If you dare to publish this letter, I hope youth all over the country will read it. I believe that the hearts of the young can communicate with one another. Maybe from them I can get some help.

from *Zhongguo Qingnian* (*China's Youth*)
May, 1980

The Two Generations
GU GONG

A Discussion Arising from "Not Understanding" Poetry

I am finding it increasingly difficult to understand my child Gu Cheng's poetry. I am getting more and more angry. . . .

In front of me is a new poem of his entitled "Love Me, Sea." I force myself to read it line by line:

Love me, sea,
I say silently
As I walk toward the high mountain. . . .

In the curving trough of the wave,
There is only doubt.
The instant a drop of water falls
Does it magnify the setting sun?

When I come to a poem like this, "there is only doubt" in the trough of the wave of my mind. Brows knit, I continue to read line by line:

My shadow
Is twisted.
I am trapped in a landmass.
My voice is covered with
Glacial scars,
Only the line of my gaze
Is free to stretch.

The more I read, the angrier I get. It is too depressing, too terrifying!

Who is moving in the distance?
It is the clock's pendulum,
Hired by the god of death
To measure life. . . .

I have never read this kind of poetry. When I marched and fought in the war, the lines of poetry we chanted were bright and exalted, like bomb shells bursting, like flaming bullets. Not like this! Not like this at all!

I begin to tremble for my child, for our younger generation. Why? Why in the depths of their souls are there such "glacial scars," such "doubt"—or, even worse, such thoughts as "Who is coming—the god of death."

Angry and worried, I put down these scattered drafts. I recall Gu Cheng—his childhood, his youth. When he could barely write, he was already writing poems (or at least thinking up poems). At the time, he was only eight or ten years old.

Every day, he would come home swinging his schoolbag. From the stairway entrance at the far end of the corridor, he would run toward me, toward home, happily shouting, "Daddy, daddy, I thought of another poem!"

Once, panting, he recited:

Withered leaves are scuttling in the street,
Withered branches are wailing in the wind,

The land has shed its bright fall clothes,
And changed into a silver-white snow robe.

This poem moves me, makes me ponder: yes, winter came, the season of blooming was over! Oh, Cultural Revolution, you have made so many leaves fall, made so many branches howl with sorrow. I do not know what the child was thinking. He was still so young then, and knew so little. Could he have had such subtle premonitions? At the time, I could only keep my musings to myself. I would not have dared reveal even a hint of what I was thinking.

A few years later, "the red storm"* blew down our door and windows. Our whole family was driven out of Beijing and sent to a desolate place where the river drained into Bohai.

The country folks here extended their warm hands,
But here there were also the gleaming green eyes of wolves.

I and fourteen-year-old Gu Cheng were sunbathing our tanned bodies on the river bank. With his finger, he scribbled "A Fantasy of Life" in the sand. I am still pleasantly surprised by these beautiful lines:

Let the waterfall of sunlight
Wash dark my skin. . . .

The sun is my boatman.†
It pulls me,
With ropes of bright light. . . .

The sun warms the earth
Toasting it like a piece of bread. . . .

How beautiful! I was surprised that his slender little fingers could write such grand, strong lines. But, at the time, those lines could not be made public or shown to anyone. The word "sun" alone could have caused our downfall or even death.‡

Hurriedly, I helped him cover up the lines with sand.

Today, he is grown, and so has history. The poems he writes need not be covered with sand. Poetry can bloom with the flowers or fly

* The Cultural Revolution.
† When a river gets too narrow for a boat to navigate on its own power, "boatmen" are employed to drag the boat along with ropes from shore.
‡ At the time, any use of the word "sun" referred to Mao. To use the word without explicitly glorifying Mao might have been interpreted as a serious sign of disrespect.

with the swallows' wings. Why, then, has his poetry become so obscure, so depressing, so hard to understand? I am angry!

I thought: maybe his young heart still has too many "glacial scars." I shall think of ways to brush away these "scars." I shall make his heart a smooth lens.

I thought: I should tell him more about the revolution, the war, and the difficult roads the older generation covered with footprints of blood and tears. I should make an effort to drive the shadows from the depths of his heart so that it will always be filled with waterfalls of sunshine.

I thought: I should guide him—I should guide him in this way!

Last spring, I set out to do some journalistic research, and Gu Cheng hurried to join me.

Father and son wandered around the mountains of Sichuan and floated along a vast river. I grabbed every moment to feed him revolutionary thinking I thought he should be fed. Thirty years ago, in these lush mountains, his mother and I marched with the troops, bags on our backs. We camped, and chased bandits. We passed through the newly liberated mountain city* and Bai Gongguan and Zhazi Dong outside the city,† strewn with dead bodies and dying embers.

I led Gu Cheng up Gele Mountain and looked down onto the remaining traces of those years.

I sat with Gu Cheng beside the Jialing River and gazed far off at the thin mist and light sails. . . .

And all the time I talked about the footprints of battle. . . .

Such constant guidance, I thought, would at least turn around this child's mind and poet's spirit so that he would also sing the battle songs that we had loved to sing in the days of our youth.

But no . . .

On the river boat, I watched him lean on the rails, writing poems. Again these poems went beyond my expectations; they shocked me and scared me.

Look what he wrote about the bustling mountain city:

This is a piece of unflattened land,
Is it an outdated will?‡

Look what he wrote about the rugged stone cliffs:

* Chongqing.
† Nationalist concentration camps. When the Nationalists fled Chongqing, they burned the camps with prisoners still in them.
‡ May refer to plans Mao had for the province of Sichuan—plans that had not yet been implemented at the time of his death.

What searing hatred,
Burnt crooked, the iron-black bodies.

Look what he wrote about people who died for their principles:

Yes, I need go no further,
The road has come to an end.
Though my hair is still black,
The daytime of life has not yet begun.

Look what he wrote about the meandering Jialing River:

The landslide has stopped,
High up on the river bank rear giants' heads.

Sailboats in mourning
Slowly pass by
Unfurling drab yellow shrouds.

I kept reading his poetry. I was disappointed, lost in thought. Finally, I exploded. I bombarded him with incessant lectures and questions:
   "What kind of eyes are you using to observe life?"
   "The world you write about, is it real or fictitious?"
   "Why can't the giant rocks high above the river be swan's eggs instead of heads?"
   "Is poetry the study of beauty or the study of ugliness?"
   But the son was no longer an obedient tool. He began a vigorous defense of his poems and his generation's poems:
   "I use my eyes, the eyes of human beings, to observe."
   "The world I feel, within the realm of art, is more genuine than the world of matter. Artistic feeling is not tape measures, spectrographs, or flash cameras lens."
   "I am not conscious of the world, I am conscious of human beings—the existence and value of humanity in the world."
   "The purpose behind portraying the world is to portray 'the self.' Your generation sometimes wrote about 'the self,' but this 'self' was always described as 'a pebble used to build roads,' 'a gear valve,' or 'a screw.' Is this 'self' human? No, it's only machinery!"
   "Only if 'the self' participates, resists life's alienating forces, and reforms the world, will art emerge, will a great torrent of schools pour forth, will beautiful planets and the Milky Way come into being. . . ."
   Oh, I want so much to convince him, to conquer him—in spite of myself—even to suppress him!

Oh, I want so much to return him to our generation's way of thinking, to have him orbit in our poetic path. . . .

But it looks as if I am losing ground.

It looks as if my generation is losing ground.

Here I recall a commentary on poetry by Gong Liu, entitled "A New Subject for Study—Discussing a Few of Comrade Gu Cheng's Poems." I was very excited after reading this commentary, and completely agreed with it, especially this paragraph:

> Nowadays, parents everywhere are saying that they do not understand their own children. Yes, there appears to be a gap between us and the young people. Frankly, I am very shocked by the thoughts and feelings in some of their poetry, as well as by the methods they use to express themselves. But we must try to understand. The more we understand, the better; this is a new subject for study.

Yes, this *is* a new subject for study!

How can we understand, how can we penetrate the heart of the new generation, the pursuits of the new generation, the poetry of the new generation?

What has formed Gu Cheng's thoughts, sounds, sense of beauty and ugliness, his feeling for the outer shells and inner tensions of people and poetry? Are they inherited from the new schools of thought that arose after "May Fourth?"* Have they been strongly influenced by modern schools in the West? No, no, Gu Cheng has grown up in a cultural desert, in an archaic age in the arts. In the past he never saw—and today he has seen little of—symbolism, futurism, expressionism, stream of consciousness, the school of the absurd. He is not imitating, is not searching for the past or for a foreign crescent;† he is truly going his own way.

These poems are the spring and oasis his generation has found in the wasteland.

These poems are the refracted light of their spirits, a display of images.

Are these poems similar to the modern poetry of the West and the modernism that once appeared in China? Is there a spiritual communion in their soul searchings? There is definitely something to this.

Let's look into it. How did the modern schools in foreign countries

---

* On May 4, 1919, Chinese students demonstrated against their government's ceding of the province of Shandong to Japan. The demonstration was part of a political, literary, and intellectual movement that rejected the old Confucian tradition and sought new models for China in the West.

† Probably refers to the Crescent Society, a literary group during the May Fourth Movement that sought inspiration in Western literature.

come about? The first time, before and after the Second World War, there were a series of historical events that imperiled and cruelly injured human beings and their spirits. They made many people lose their traditional confidence and spiritual pillars. Many people could not find a solution for existence and for society; they became the "confused generation," the "lost generation," the "angry generation." People were searching for a way to exist in such a turbulent world.

Let's look into this. Are there any similarities between the historical experiences of foreign societies and present-day China, which has gone through ten years of utter confusion and destruction?* If there are, and if today we have produced our "exploring generation," our "confused generation," our "pragmatic generation," then why should we be shocked or surprised? And if they are beginning to use their own generation's patterns of thinking, observation, and artistic expression (including poetry)—patterns shaped by history—to reveal and unburden themselves, what is so strange or abnormal about that?

Are our generation's patterns of observing and feeling things really so perfect, so flawless? Is the theory of reflection† that we are used to the most precise, the most impeccable method for reflecting reality? Can we absorb some new light and heat from other schools of thought?

The forerunner of the modern school, America's Edgar Allen Poe, emphasized poetry's symbolism and beauty of sound; France's Baudelaire emphasized that one must express the intersensitivity of the five organs, changing hearing into sight, the sense of smell into touch. At this moment, I remember some lines of Gu Cheng's that I cannot stand: "My voice is covered with / Glacial scars." The "sound" of hearing, has it not been transformed into "scars" of sight and touch? Isn't this also symbolic allusion?

The American symbolist poet Pound believed that poetry "is not the jet engine of human moods" but "the formula (*i.e.*, symbols) of human moods." From then on, the stream-of-consciousness technique made the poetry of the abstract images school delve deeper, from expressing "a moment" to expressing all of modern society—the grand panorama of human life.

Poetry should have different kinds of antennae.

Poetry should have all kinds of tentacles.

In the process of understanding my child, I am understanding poetry.

In the process of understanding poetry, I am understanding my child—the new generation.

* The decade of the Cultural Revolution, 1966–76.
† Socialist realism.

My pen and my child's pen—the pens of two generations—should dash and charge together in the runway of poetry.

Poetry will not be like comets, which flash once and are gone.

Poetry will rise up each day with the morning light.

from *Shikan* (*Poetry*)
October, 1980

A Generation
GU CHENG

The night has given me dark eyes
But I use them to look for light.

Shooting a Photograph
GU CHENG

Sunlight
Flashes in the sky
And is covered by dark clouds again.

Violent rains develop
The negative of my soul.

both from *Xingxing* (*Sparks*)
March, 1980

I Am a Willful Child
GU CHENG

I want to paint windows all over the earth to let all
eyes accustomed to darkness grow accustomed to light.

Maybe
I am a child spoiled by his mother
I am willful

I wish
Every moment
Could be as beautiful as color crayons
I wish
To be able to paint on treasured blank paper
Paint awkward freedom
Paint a never
Tearful eye

A patch of sky
A patch of feathers and leaves belonging to the sky
A light green evening and apple

I want to paint the morning
Paint the smiles that morning dew can see
Paint all the youngest
Painless love
Paint in imagination
My lover
She has not seen rain clouds
Her eyes are the color of the clear sky
She is forever looking at me
Forever looking
She will never suddenly turn her head away

I want to paint distant views
Paint the bold horizon and ripples
Paint many many happy streams
Paint rolling hills—
Covered with light downy grasses
I will let them lean close together
Let them love each other
Let every tacit promise
Every quiet wave of spring's excitement
All become a small flower's birthday

I also want to paint the future
I have not seen her, and cannot
But I know she is very beautiful
I will paint her autumn jacket
Paint the flaming candlelight and maple leaves
Paint the many hearts that
Were extinguished for loving her
Paint a wedding
Paint many wake-up-early festival days
Pasted on them are cellophane candy wrappers
And illustrations of fairy tales from the north

I am a willful child
I want to wipe out all misfortune
I want to paint windows
All over the earth
And let all eyes accustomed to darkness
Grow accustomed to light

I want to paint the wind
Paint higher and higher mountain ranges
Paint the longings of the Eastern race
Paint the vast sea—
Endless happy sounds

Finally, in a corner of the paper
I also wish to paint myself
Paint a tree bear*
Sitting in Victoria's† dark forest
Alone sitting on a branch
In a daze
He has no home
He has no heart left in a distant place
He has only many many
Berry-like dreams
And very very big eyes

I am hoping
Thinking
But I do not know why
I have not received any crayons
Have not had a colorful moment

I only have myself
My fingers and painful wounds
I can only tear to bits those pieces
Of treasured blank paper
Let them go look for butterflies
From today on let them vanish

I am a child
A child who has been spoiled
By Mother Illusion
I am willful

from *Xuangua De Pingguo* (*Hanging Apples*),
a collection of the author's poems, 1980

* Probably a koala bear.
† A province in Australia. Here, implying exile.

Reply
BEI DAO

Baseness is the safe-conduct of the base;
Nobleness is the epitaph of the noble.
Behold, in the gold-plated sky
Flutters a host of snarled reflections of the dead.

The Ice Age is passed,
Why are icicles still covering the earth?
The Cape of Good Hope has been found,
Why are sails still jostling in the Dead Sea?

I came to this world with nothing
But paper, rope, and a shadow
In order to declare the voices of the sentenced
Before judgment.

Let me tell you, world,
I—don't—believe!
Even if a thousand challengers are at your feet,
Count me as the thousand-and-first.

I don't believe the sky is blue;
I don't believe in the echo of thunder;
I don't believe that dreams are false;
I don't believe in death without retribution.

If the ocean is destined to burst its dikes,
Let all the bitter water pour into my heart;
If land is destined to rise,
Let mankind choose anew the pinnacle of life.

New turns and sparkling stars
Stud the clear sky,
The symbolic words of five thousand years,
The gazing eyes of generations to come.

from *Shikan* (*Poetry*)
March, 1979

II. Family

Pan Xiao's letter describes how, after her grandfather died, her "warm, supportive" family suddenly turned "cold and cruel" and began to quarrel over money. Her family, which might have been a refuge from political upheavals and personal anguish, instead became merely another source of disillusionment. The deterioration of family relationships is one of the most common themes of New Realism literature, which almost always holds the political system responsible.

"Remorse," by Zhang Jie, describes how the relationship between a father and his son is twisted by a political "crime" committed by the father over twenty years before. The crime consisted of having criticized the party leadership during the Hundred Flowers Campaign—a brief period in 1956 when, with the slogan "Let a hundred flowers bloom; let a hundred schools of thought contend," China's intellectuals were invited to challenge and debate party programs and policies. When the blooming and contending exceeded expectations, those who had spoken out were accused of having tried to undermine the revolution, were denounced as "rightists," and were forced to make public confessions. Like the father in "Remorse," many were also removed from their administrative posts and, if they had been party members, stripped of their party affiliation. For more than two decades, those who had been denounced in the 1957 antirightist campaign lived under a cloud of suspicion, and their children, like the son in "Remorse," suffered from intense discrimination.

The target of criticism in "Remorse" is not the antirightist movement per se, but political labeling, a process common to many political campaigns in socialist China, in which the assignment of a label—"rightist," "counterrevolutionary," "bourgeois intellectual"—has justified the ruthless treatment of individuals. Following shifts in the political wind, new campaigns have often reversed the verdicts of previous ones; in "Remorse," the father's label is ultimately removed and he is reinstated. While labels can be removed and campaigns can be reversed, "Remorse" portrays the effect of both on human beings as shattering and irreversible. No reinstatement can give the father back his son: no political reversal can undo the damage done to this relationship. The ripples set off by such political crusades continue long after the political action has ended, touching the most private and intimate corners of people's lives.

In Liu Xinwu's novella, *Overpass*, the cause of the disintegration of family relationships is not a specific political process or campaign; it is the result of the system itself, and of the cumulative effect of all past political actions on society.

As the story begins, relationships among the members of the Hou family are strained by overcrowding. An overpass is to be built in their neighborhood. When construction begins, the three generation Hou family will be relocated—moved by the state from their three room apartment to more spacious quarters. While they wait and wait for work on the overpass to begin, however, family members plot against one another for more space, and the tensions become unbearable.

The most successful member of the family—the second son, Hou Yong—is the most selfish. Hou Yong takes lessons on how to manipulate the system to his advantage from an expert wheeler dealer who tells him he must harden his heart to his family if he is going to get anywhere. Yet Hou Yong has a more noble side too: when his sister Hou Ying suffers an emotional breakdown and runs to cower beneath a table, it is Hou Yong who is the first in his family to rush to her.

Hou Yong is not—indeed, none of the characters in the novella are—fundamentally bad. It is just that the society the author depicts rewards the selfish behavior of Hou Yong and punishes the selfless idealism of the oldest brother Hou Rui. The day-to-day necessity of having to adapt to a terrible system has eaten away at people's lives and corroded their relationships—distorting, hiding and destroying that which is human.

Who or what then, is ultimately to blame for all of this? *Overpass* points offstage to two villains: a bureaucracy that is inefficient and insensitive to basic human needs; and a general decline in morality, a rise in selfishness, that is society's response to past political campaigns and all the failings of the system. In this story as in "Remorse", the ripples of past political actions are felt in people's lives long after the actions themselves are over.

Not the least of these lingering aftereffects are the chasms in education and experience that divide individuals in the same family because of slight differences in age at the time of the Cultural Revolution. Hou Rui, the eldest son, who graduated from college before the Cultural Revolution, is an intellectual and a teacher in a middle school; he is idealistic, widely read, familiar with Western classical music, the friend of a famous playwright. Hou Ying, the youngest in the family, who never graduated from junior middle school because the Cultural Revolution intervened, is a factory worker who isn't sure where Hong Kong is. Her life has been stunted, not by her own capacities, but by a cataclysmic political event.

Remorse
ZHANG JIE

—to the Unfortunate Child—

Finished.

The last bit of flame flickered and went out.

This was all that remained of his son. Sixty-five kilograms, one and four-fifths meters. A son of flesh and blood had become a thin thread of smoke, a handful of white ashes. Life won through thousands of years of evolution had been destroyed so easily it was scarcely believable.

After returning home from the crematorium, he instinctively wanted to recall his son's life—though it was an exaggeration to call twenty-seven years a lifetime. So short, so young! Yet it seemed as if he couldn't remember a thing. He had known too little about him. People say that it is harder for men to reveal themselves to each other than it is for women. Was this the only reason they had lived together like passersby in the street? But what kind of man had his son been? He had not even been in love; he had not enjoyed enough sunshine.

He looked at the things his son had left: a copy of *Andersen's Fairy Tales*, published before the Cultural Revolution; an old, broken iron pencil box; a one-inch portrait, "half-body, front-view, hatless"; an old book of abacus tables, its edges curling up.

The beautiful *Andersen's Fairy Tales* had been taboo in the family. The son had known this very clearly. Why, then, had he stubbornly held onto the book?

When he was thrown off life's normal tracks, the son was just at the age when he was playing with toy guns, and certain that his father was a great hero. This "hero" hardly understood how he had come to be such a low, vile thing!

But such a father, who knew very well that he himself was the hammer that had shattered his own son's dream, and who understood that there was no escape from this arrangement of fate, he would surely feel a sensation so painful it would feel as if he were choking, or being burned in a fire.

At the time, his son could still look at him angrily with a pair of round eyes filled with tears, and ask: "Father, why won't my little friends play with me anymore?"

He could not answer. How could he explain?

For some time, the anthill under the tree in the yard had been the lonely son's only entertainment. He would squat there for a long time, totally absorbed by the busy ants scurrying back and forth. Their animated, simple, fraternal life must have aroused envy and yearning in him. He had asked, "Father, why is it that ants always play with one another, and never desert each other?"

"I don't know!"

"You are a grown-up, why don't you know?"

But how could the son know that there are many questions that not even adults can answer?

One day, another child came over, and with a few stomps flattened the kingdom of ants that had not been doing anyone any harm. He knew he could not blame the child. He also knew how lonely his little son was. But he did not dare give him another little brother or sister for company, because he knew he no longer had the power to protect another innocent little soul.

When the son grew a bit older, as if he understood his position somewhat, he avoided his father as if the man were a plague, as if he would spread a disease. Whoever caught this disease would be forgotten by life, would become a solitary being.

Innocent son, he did not realize he was already contaminated.

The father could never forget the expression of yearning on his son's face when he looked at the red scarves* waving on other children's chests. It seemed like that of a person who had fallen into hell, and who, cherishing a devout wish to be reincarnated in a better life, looked hopefully toward heaven.

Once he heard his son ask his wife: "What crime has he committed?"

"Who?"

"Him!"

"Who is 'him?' "

"Him—father!"

He felt his wife groping for the right words: "Because he told an Andersen's fairy tale to a leader!" If the emotions contained in speech

* A sign that they were Red Guards.

could be weighed, there would be no scale that could measure the dignity she put in her voice, stung by the son's judgment of his father.

"Which one?"

"*The Emperor's New Clothes.*"*

"That's ridiculous! Why doesn't anyone call Andersen a rightist? He told so many of those tales!"

If Andersen—who had used beautiful, sincere feelings all his life to exert a good influence on people—heard this sentence in heaven, no doubt he broke into a warm, moving smile. There is such a difference between real life and children's tales!

From the "half-body, front view, hatless" portrait, the son looked at him with a pitiful expression. If it hadn't been necessary for a work permit, the boy would never have had his picture taken. He could imagine his son's thinking. He must have felt that there was no moment in his life worth recording. He wished so much that his child could have been like other children—mischievous, noisy, throwing temper tantrums, fighting. . . . But no, he always wore such a pitiful expression. What wrung his heart most was his son's face when it didn't wear this pitiful expression. When interacting with others, no matter whom, his son wore an anxious-to-please expression, like a dog wagging its tail, asking for pity. For the father, it was worse than if he had spit in his face. That sort of expression should have been buried with the old life!

In 1972, the son was assigned to a produce station to sell meat. Originally, his father had been a very open-minded person, and had never considered measuring a person's worth by his occupational position, high or low. Nor had he minded the differences among people in the social division of labor. But his common sense told him that he was the reason that his son was selling meat. How could he not look upon the relationship between moral character and occupation as a natural pattern of cause and effect? Was he not a materialist?

From then on, the curled-edged, frayed old abacus tables and an old abacus became the sole substance of the son's life after work. He either sat at the little table that was both a dining table and a desk, moving his lips, silently reciting the abacus tables, or he noisily practiced on the old abacus. When, from the window upstairs, there floated the sound of a Schumann étude being played on a neighbor's violin, the son would sigh lightly, inaudibly, and rise to shut the windows of the house, not caring that it might be the hottest part of July. . . .† His son's manipulation of the abacus had long been out-

* Implying criticism of the party leadership, and probably of Mao himself.

† As the son of a rightist, he was forbidden such privileges as going to a music school.

standing; for addition and subtraction, he was as fast and as accurate as a calculator. Yet as soon as he got off work, he continued to recite and to practice, as if the abacus had become a biological need like eating or sleeping, or a necessary outlet for his emotions.

The father also knew that the customers who did not know his son's background all liked him, and complimented him by calling him "Just One Chop."* Once, he had stealthily stood around the produce station, watching his son sell meat. He could see that the boy got satisfaction and enjoyment from the endless repetition of weighing the meat and calculating. A slight flush suffused his pale face, indicating excitement. At those times, he must have felt that there were many people who still wanted him, who had not deserted him.

But as soon as he left the meat counter, he would become a different person. At home or in the work unit, he avoided people. Except for reciting the tables and practicing on the abacus, squeezing into a corner was his only hobby. As long as nobody noticed him, he would sit in that corner for hours, staring blankly at the tips of his own shoes as if they were not his shoes, but the text of a volume of profound Hebrew scriptures that could solve the riddle of fate. He always tried his best to hunch himself up, as if his innocently fearless, excessively broad shoulders occupied a bit too much of boundless space, and thus might offend someone.

This son-who-was-like-a-stranger understood the difficulties of the family. The father could still remember his little son watching other children eating chocolate, only to turn away proudly. He had also seen this son who dreamed of being a hero press his nose tightly against the glass panes of shops filled with toy guns and cannons . . . yet he had not asked for anything. Even the old iron pencil box that was broken and worn at the edges had been bought only when the boy had started primary school. How could this son, who had once been so greedy, so eager to throw temper tantrums on the floor, and who would never get up until he got what he wanted, all of a sudden give up all demands? No one had given him a special warning. It was so strange!

In the last part of the Cultural Revolution, the father discovered the nobody-can-enter expression of his son's eyes gradually opening up toward him. Yet he had quickly pushed away this long-hoped-for understanding.

The night before the Tiananmen Incident,† the son had said to him, "Father, I want to go to Tian An Men!"

---

* His precision was such that he could cut the exact weight of a meat order with just one chop.

† A spontaneous mass memorial for Zhou Enlai in 1976 that was really a protest against the ultraradicalism of the Gang of Four.

For the first time he detected in his son's eyes what could be called a passionate yearning. He knew that he should—why not?—have given his pitiful, cautious, timid son a bit of sympathy or a hint of support. It would have given the boy tremendous encouragement and strength; maybe it would even have gotten rid of his pitiful expression. But he did not. He was so nervous, he felt breathless.

"What for?"

The son hesitated, wavering, and said, "I wrote a poem . . ."*

It was as if he had been stung by a scorpion. Instantly, nervously he had yelled, "No, you cannot go!"

His expression of extreme apprehension immediately made his son lose courage: "Will people die?"

"No, the terrible thing is not death . . ."

The light that had lit up his son's eyes a moment ago went out. He returned to his usual corner. No, it was he who had pushed the son back to that corner.

The son became ill. He was not sure whether it was because of his son's habit of not wanting to bother people or whether the boy had long hoped for something like this. Anyway, a common virus developed into a fatal urinary infection.

When, in a state of great agitation, he had brought the news of his total reinstatement to his son, the boy's gaze was unfocused. He could not have understood any sentence uttered to him. He was beyond happiness and sorrow.

He suddenly realized that even if his son had understood the news he had brought, the pitiful expression would not have disappeared from his face because it had already permeated his soul.

With remorse, he felt that his son would carry in him an unliberated soul when he died. Yet the day his soul flew to another world, a peaceful, relaxed expression returned to the boy's face—the same expression he had worn on the day he had been born. Apart from that, the face had an excited look, as if it were happily contemplating something.

The son had left him, carrying with him the emotions of a stranger. For more than twenty years there had been no love, no friendship or understanding, no heart-to-heart talks between father and son. It was as if the father had brought him life and had reared him without getting anything back—as if he had suddenly caught a handful of flowing water and then, right before his eyes, the water had leaked out through the cracks between his fingers.

He really could not even tell whether the boy had loved him. If he hadn't, it served him right. What right had he to demand his son's

---

* Thousands of people wrote poems of protest to lay at the foot of the Revolutionary Martyr's Memorial in Tiananmen Square.

love! Even the name he had given his son had not been deliberated over, just casually picked! Jianshe [Construction] had been the most common name given to children born during the fiery era of the early years of national construction. At the time, as the chief editor of a journal, he had been too busy; thinking of a name for his son would have taken him away from his work.

But perhaps the son had loved him after all. He remembered when the boy was four years old. One night, because of a meeting, he had returned home very late. He saw that on the chest of drawers beside the bed, there was a tray of peeled water chestnuts. Each water chestnut had a little bite taken out of it, as if a naughty, but not greedy, little mouse had taken a bite of each. His wife had said to him, "Your son left these for you."

Intrigued, he pointed to the little bite marks on the water chestnuts and laughingly asked, "What are these supposed to be?"

"He took a bite out of every water chestnut to find the young ones to be left for you; the tough ones he ate himself."

He looked at the water chestnuts that looked as if they had been bitten by a little mouse and his heart was filled with the blessings and satisfaction of being a father. He had hardly slept that night. Several times he had sat up in bed, holding that tray of water chestnuts, smiling, imagining what his son, who at such a young age had demonstrated such delicate emotions, would become when he grew up. An honest worker? A great hero? A romantic poet? No matter what he imagined, there was always a rose-colored mist before his eyes. Maybe this was how every father felt about his son. He had imagined everything, but somehow he had never imagined this—his son nakedly leaving the world!

It had been a few days since he had received the notice of complete reinstatement. After the initial excitement, he had calmed down, and gradually he began to feel an inexplicable thing charging toward him, tightly enveloping him, entangling him, pressing him, gnawing at his heart to the point where he couldn't totally immerse himself in longing for his son. Yet he wanted so much to obtain a little bit of tenderness and solace from the heartbreak of remembering. What he felt was not the sorrow triggered by the death of his son diluting the liberation he had longed for, because this feeling was not the same as sorrow. It was more solemn than sorrow, more profound, heavier. . . . When had it begun? Maybe it had begun on the day he had stopped his son from going to Tian An Men. Maybe it had been even earlier; maybe it had long been hiding somewhere in the past and had now come to settle an old account with him.

Why was it that when he had heard about recovering his party membership, his spectrographlike mind had shot out a range of emotions, including an empty, lost feeling? Strange, for twenty-two years* he had never formally accepted in his heart the decision that had expelled him from the party. But ironically, during the process of his reinstatement, he had begun seriously to question his own worth. An empty, lost feeling. . . . He had lost something more precious than life! Twenty-two years of party standing could be compensated for, but what could compensate for having relinquished the sacred responsibility of being a Communist Party member? Certainly he could still remember the oath he had recited under the hammer and sickle flag. Yet for more than twenty years, because of his family, because he had not wanted to add yet more sorrowful colors to his son's apparently joyless childhood and youth, he had lived timidly, just staying alive. He had stood to one side of life, watching the slow flow of dirty water, not wanting to move a finger. He had not even done the most basic thing: communicate to his dearest beloved son belief in truth, confidence in life, and the spirit to sacrifice for one's life's work. What else could one say?

When someone dies, people often think with remorse about the wrongs they have done that person in the past. Yet where was the wrong he had done his son for which he should really feel remorseful?

He was full of remorse! He would always be full of remorse! Not because he had done something, but because he had done nothing.

Was he not responsible for the pitiful expression that had penetrated his son's soul?

No other sentence or punishment could make him suffer as much pain or reproach as this remorse!

from *Beijing Wenyi* (*Beijing Literature and Art*)
November, 1979

A Note on the Abridgement of **Overpass**

The version of *Overpass* that follows represents slightly less than two-thirds of the entire novella. Many of the sections omitted develop the character of Erzhuang, a young neighbor of the Hou family who plays an increasingly important role as the plot develops.

Erzhuang is a very ordinary, honest, and innocent youth—a worker, with no great ideals or ambitions. Like Hou Ying, he has suffered from a poverty of experience: sent to the countryside during the Cultural Revolution, he never missed home because there was nothing

* Since the 1957 Anti-Rightist Campaign.

much to miss. Despite his lack of education and experience, however, the young man is curious. One chapter not included here describes how Erzhuang, who has never ridden in a taxi, secretly hires one at great expense just to see what it would be like.

Overpass
LIU XINWU

I reverently dedicate this to all who strive to open up new physical and spiritual space.

1

Is there anything new?

Every time he returned from the outskirts of the city and got off the bus to walk up to the crossroads at Dongdan, Hou Rui* looked eagerly for some sign that work was about to begin on the overpass.

However, he was always disappointed.

As ever, the old barnlike structure of Dongdan Restaurant, standing at the northwest corner of the crossroads, hit the eye. As usual, there were people lined up to one side of this ever-crowded restaurant, waiting to buy youtiao.† It had been thirty years! This ugly old restaurant had been whitewashed again and again but never torn down. How long would it linger on?

Hou Rui walked up to the iron railings at the junction, lit a cigarette, and turned to look across at the southwest corner of the crossroads. There, behind the pedestrian crossing, in the shape of an *L*, stood a never-ending line of billboards. He quickly noticed the latest change in the advertisements. One at the corner was now replaced by an advertisement for the Japanese electronics firm National Panasonic: a gigantic Monkey King‡ was leaping out of the screen of a color television. The background was made up of millions of little metal discs that fluttered in the air currents. When they caught the sun at dusk, they produced an optical effect of golden ripples. Looking at these colorful advertisements that had such an air of the artisan, Hou Rui exhaled a puff of smoke. He thought: Life does, after all, bring changes. Things long longed for—even if not to be had immediately—had, after all, come within the realm of possibility.

Hou Rui had graduated from Beijing Normal College in 1964. After

* Like Dickens, Chinese writers often choose names to reinforce character. *Rui* means "acute."
† Fried dough rolls popular mainly for breakfast in Beijing.
‡ A famous mythical character from Chinese lore.

graduation, he was assigned to a commune middle school in the distant outskirts of Beijing to teach Chinese language. This autumn of 1980, he was exactly thirty-nine years old. At college he had been widely acclaimed as dashingly handsome . . . .* but Hou Rui, now standing at the intersection by the pedestrian crossing, puffing on his cigarette, seemed old before his time. He was grey at the temples, and though the crows' feet at the corners of his eyes were not very noticeable, his tear glands had already become greyish and were clearly discernable. The skin that had been tight and ruddy was now brown and rough. But seen from a distance, he still looked to be an attractive, middle-aged man.

It was with a confused mass of emotions that Hou Rui leaned against the railing and gazed at the bustle of Dongdan Intersection. Changan Boulevard, running in the east-west direction was good and wide, but all the streets running across it—especially those north of Dongdan—were narrow out of all proportion, compared with Changan Boulevard. Obviously, an overpass should be built as soon as possible, and yet. . . . .

Hou Rui threw away his cigarette butt and propped himself up with his hands on the railings. Gazing at the heavy traffic rolling by, he let threads of despair and hope weave within his heart a net of all feelings.

Just then he was startled by a slap on the shoulder.

2

Hou Rui turned, and recognized the fat man standing before him as his classmate from college days: Ge Youhan.

Ge Youhan had taken the college entrance exams as a salaried cadre† and was five years older than Hou Rui. He had hoped to get into a famous college from which he would go to some research institution to "play the role of a dignitary." He never imagined he would end up in a mere normal college,‡ to be assigned, upon graduation, to teach in a most unremarkable middle school in the back streets. This was Ge Youhan's lifelong regret. To this very day, he was filled with nostalgia for his old organization, and the time when he was a clerk in an office. He would often say, "If only I hadn't been so intoxicated with the notion of going to college. I'd have wangled myself a position of department head long ago!" He despised everyone at the middle school, and they in turn practically all despised

* *Editor's note:* An ellipses of five dots indicates material omitted by the editors.
† A cadre is a party or government official.
‡ This is a teacher's college.

him, for he was useless at teaching. Later he became librarian and would frequently take sick leave on account of half-genuine, half-imagined kidney trouble. How had he got by all these years? Political movements, the Ten Years of Calamities*—while they had not left him unaffected—could hardly be used as clues to summing up his life. For many years now he had not read papers or listened to the radio, had not taken an interest in any gossip of a political nature, and, aside from furniture design manuals and cookbooks, had hardly read any books. And he a librarian! For five years he went from one Housing Exchange Office to another, making the acquaintance of countless housing department officials. Seizing on other peoples' crises—such as family disputes, or the fear following a death in the family, or hardship attendant upon the political fall of a family member—through all kinds of similar situations, by legal means, he exchanged his apartment for ever bigger ones. His family now occupied a most ideal three-bedroom apartment on the third floor of a new housing estate, and there were only three in his family—he and his wife and a son still in primary school. His apartment was impeccably furnished—the result of long years of going to and fro between all the second-hand furniture shops in the city, whereby, through meticulous, study, comparison, selection, exchange, selling off, and then buying back, he had completed his collection, item by item.

He now stood placidly before his old classmate, his stomach bulging out. His round face, his eyelids, his nose, his mouth, were all heavy laden with flesh—evidence of richness of diet and peace of mind. On one arm he carried an ample basket stuffed full of fresh goods just bought at Dongdan market. Hou Rui peeped at the basket and caught a glimpse of two moist fat fish tails sticking out.

"Hey! I recognized you from behind at a glance!" Ge Youhan said in a loud voice, his face beaming. "Well, what's up? Getting a charge out of watching cars go by?"

"I'm just back from school—only got off the bus a moment ago. Haven't even been home yet." Hou Rui said lazily. He had no wish to linger with his erstwhile classmate.

"So! You still haven't moved?" Ge Youhan countinued at the top of his voice.

Where could he move to? Hou Rui felt a stab. He was especially reluctant to discuss this matter with Ge Youhan. He was well aware what his classmate's present apartment was like, and he sensed the satisfaction and feeling of superiority oozing from Ge Youhan's very bones. From the expression in his eyes, Hou Rui could tell that, at

---

* This refers to the decade of the Cultural Revolution, 1966–1976.

this very moment, Ge Youhan probably had a vision of the one-room abode of their family of three generations.

"Don't worry." Just wait for the relocation—it won't be long now!" Ge Youhan indicated the intersection with his free hand. "They say work will begin in the next year or two—an overpass, a contract with the Japanese. Their money, their design. We do the work. Just you wait and see. Your folks will come into their own. . . ."

Not allowing Hou Rui to get a word in, Ge Youhan suddenly took a step forward. Gently prodding Hou Rui's chest with one stubby finger, in a low and extremely chummy voice, he cautioned, "When the time comes, don't let yourself be swindled by the Relocation Office. They're sure to offer to move you to Chuiyangliu,* but you mustn't go there! It's too close to the paper mill. If you drink the water there, it'll give you cancer. And don't go to the south side of Tuanjie Lake. The land there is low-lying. When it rains, it's just one great big "toad pond" all around. . . . No, you must hold firm: it's got to be Tuanjie Lake, north side, and it's got to be third floor with a wide entrance hall, and two built-in closets! I tell you, 'Where there's a will, there's a way . . . Fight to the last and be victorious.'† These two dicta are well attested!"

"How reliable is your information? There's not the beginning of a sign of an overpass!" Hou Rui continued lazily, "And anyway, I'm not smart like you—so good at trading apartments!"

Hou Rui had thought that, hearing these last few words, some sign of displeasure would appear on Ge Youhan's face. But not at all. He just looked even more sincere. Nodding several times in succession, he said, "True, true, you're not like *me*—reckless and shameless, running around, begging, and pleading. Besides, you're out of town most days, don't get back till Saturday, and first thing Monday morning you have to be off again."

Hou Rui had already turned, and was gazing at the dimming evening sun and the dust falling on Changan Boulevard, continuing his thoughts. But Ge Youhan good naturedly babbled on a little more before taking his leave.

3

Hou Rui's home was on a hutong‡ not far from the intersection. If an overpass were indeed to be built at Dongdan, the compound where they lived would certainly be demolished.

* The Weeping Willows—a place in Beijing.
† The first saying is old and literary; the second smacks of Mao and the Cultural Revolution.
‡ A side street in a neighborhood of compounds.

Hou Rui ambled along toward the hutong.

The hutong was a mass of grey: grey walls, grey tile roofs, grey road surface. As always, the moment Hou Rui turned into the hutong, he felt grey.

For some years now, Hou Rui had gone home every week without exception. Sometimes he would even go twice in a week. Actually, to go home from school, Hou Rui had to walk a couple of li,* catch the suburban bus, then change to a city bus—the whole trip involving a great expenditure of time and energy. But he still preferred to go home whenever he had the time.

There had been a time when Hou Rui's head had been filled with rosy pictures, and he had vowed to "sink roots" in the countryside and dedicate himself to the cause of secondary education among the peasants' children. When this spirit had been at its peak, he had once stayed away from home for six months. However, a mass of worldly events had, like so many pairs of scissors, cut to pieces the threads of ideals that had bound his heart. These past two years, more than ten teachers from the three commune middle schools had already been transferred back to the city—transferred, it was said, on account of family hardship, or poor health, et cetera. Actually, it was a well-known fact—and they themselves made no attempt to hide it—that, in actuality, they had almost all accomplished the transfer by plaguing officials, pulling strings, and going through the back door. Once back in the city, they enjoyed to the full all the material and intellectual comforts of city life. Few, if any, truly "took better care of aging parents," or seriously tried to "rest and recuperate." In the streets of the commune town, Hou Rui often came across his ex-students. They had become, for the most part, commune people who were well-informed, who "saw through it all." They would invariably come right out with "Sir! Have you still not got yourself transferred back to the city?" From their faces and eyes, Hou Rui could clearly discern a feeling of contempt or pity. Things had come to such a pass that a willingness to work for the people in a place of hardship was looked upon with suspicion or pity. Have you got yourself transferred to a cushier place? You are useless, you're a real jerk! Hou Rui could not bear this sort of treatment. Once he retorted, "No, I haven't been transferred back; I haven't got the pull. So don't just stand there and laugh at me. Help me! Do something on my behalf!" The ex-student had grinned and said loudly, without compunction—in fact with a gleam of satisfaction mixed with teasing and contempt—"Fine! But what can you do for *me*?" Hou Rui had turned and walked away. He

---

* A *li* is equivalent to three-tenths of a mile, or half a kilometer.

hated himself, he despised himself. He had nothing—no money, no power, no connections. All he could do was beg help from others, and he had nothing to offer in return. In this modern age, he felt himself to be simply useless. "Useless jerk!" he cursed himself, to vent his spleen.

He was coming up to the compound gate when, owing to some complex feeling, he paused. He stood beneath a power-line pole and lit a cigarette. He stood there watching the ancient gateway. It was said that a few decades ago the compound had been an inn, which is why it was crowded with several rows of rooms. Light now shone through the tiny window set in the back wall of Hou Rui's room. It shone through the pretty pink curtain with the blue flowers on it. This curtain stirred in him a feeling of profound gentleness: this was, after all, the only place that merited the name "home!" But at the same time, there arose in him a pain, a sense of injustice, for, on entering the gate, one saw on the left his home, but on the right was the men's toilet. The visitors from other parts of the country and foreigners who walked to and fro along Changan Boulevard would probably never have suspected that, less than a couple of hundred yards away, there existed toilets so primitive, so filthy. It has been said somewhere that the most reliable sign of the level of civilization in a place is the state of the toilets. Actually, the toilet in their compound was by no means impossible to clean. But strange to say, though in recent years the families residing in the compound had become more and more particular about furnishings in the home, they had become more and more careless of the public utilities there, such as the street light in the compound, the faucet, and this toilet. The toilet was now forever strewn with pieces of used toilet paper, so that one had nowhere to set one's foot. Hou Rui had once made a supreme effort, and cleaned the place himself, but this had immediately aroused the displeasure of some people in the compound, because the very act itself seemed to suggest a contempt for the long-term residents there; this they found insufferable. The next time Hou Rui returned home, the toilet was still in the same state, and he relinquished his great ambition to transform it.

Standing outside the compound gate, he actually pondered over this toilet for quite a while. How droll! Or perhaps this was just another sign of what a useless jerk he was. Hou Rui laughed bitterly.

Most unwillingly, Hou Rui recalled the chance meeting in the street a few moments before. Unwillingly—yet the fat face of Ge Youhan persisted in appearing in his mind's eye, proof that man is indeed unable to control his thoughts. Hou Rui had once been to Ge Youhan's place: every detail in the three-bedroom apartment had excited his greatest envy. It was not that Hou Rui was a boor—he had visited the army compounds outside Fuxing Gate, and they were far superior to that of Ge Youhan. But then they were the high and mighty. And Ge Youhan—what had he to rely upon?

Hou Rui often compared Ge Youhan's situation with that of Cai Bodu. The more he compared the two, the more indignant he felt.

Cai Bodu had been a classmate of his and Ge Youhan's. He was now the resident playwright at a theatrical company. For two years past, two of his plays had been highly successful: they were shown in theaters, made into films, published in book form, reviewed in export journals.* The newspapers printed more than one commentary; he was even invited to be on television. In Ge Youhan's words, Cai Bodu had become an "Immortal."† But what of Cai's accommodation? It was only two months ago that, in accordance with the policy of giving preferential treatment to artists who had made significant contributions, he had been assigned a small two-room apartment. This apartment was on the south side of Tuanjie Lake—precisely the location Ge Youhan had scoffed at. Furthermore, it was on the top floor. Of course, this was very much better than the four of them, from all three generations, crowding together in a single room on the ground floor. But once Cai Bodu had moved in, it did not seem in the least spacious. The state of Ge Youhan's and Cai Bodu's housing often aroused a great indignation in Hou Rui. It just seemed too difficult to remold society in such a way as to reflect distribution truly according to work. Cai Bodu could already count himself lucky to be assigned such an apartment, because all he had to rely upon was "the organization"; he was even less adept than Hou Rui at seeking out and utilizing "extra-organizational" personal ties, which in fact had more actual distribution power. For this top-floor apartment to materialize, it had taken the repeated deliberation of many a leading comrade; many a circle had been drawn‡ before Cai got the apartment. And what of the larger apartments on the second and third floors? Were they occupied by people even more brilliant and outstanding? No, strangely enough many of them were Ge Youhan types. Don't keep going on about cadres enjoying special privileges—it's time the Ge Youhan type of wheeler-dealer was exposed. Corrupt cadres and cunning wheeler-dealers exist in symbiotic union, like rotten wood and poisonous fungus.

* Journals meant for foreign readers in China and abroad.

† In Chinese folk religion an "Immortal" refers to someone who is so illustrious he is no longer an ordinary mortal.

‡ Documents sent to various departments may begin or end with "For the attention of Comrade John Smith." J. Smith would not initial the name, but would draw a circle around it.

Hou Rui threw away the extinguished half of a cigarette, yet he still just stood there beneath the power-line pole. The street lights lit up, turning the greys to a kind of dark silver. Somehow this added a touch of poetry to the hutong that had been so drab.

5*

When Hou Rui pushed aside the curtain and walked in, there was his brother Hou Yong sitting on the big bed facing the door, playing around with something in his hands.

Hou Yong was a full nine years younger than Hou Rui. He was a 1966 junior middle school graduate. He went through the period of transition from boyhood to youth precisely in the midst of the chaotic and strange time of the Great Cultural Revolution. During the tumultuous Red August of 1966,† he had charged about with a bunch of cadres' kids from his school, recklessly destroying the "four olds."‡ In the winter of 1967, he had again gone with a group of such kids, to join a rural team in Shanxi province. Actually, the house of Hou was a rather questionable one. During the movement to "purify class ranks," their father Hou Qinfeng had been drafted into the study class§ and was in the life class.‖ However, around a crowd of cadres' kids, one often comes across people of this sort, who could be openly contemptuous of his family because they were "dog's spawn"; they, for their part, often despised in their hearts those bloated, overnourished "high-born" youth. Yet they could somehow hang out together all day long, forming a kind of mutually dependent, mutually fulfilling bond. Hou Yong had observed firsthand, and upon occasion had even personally participated in, the experiences of many of these cadres' kids—experiences filled with vicissitudes, the rise and fall of honor and shame. He knew them best. Therefore, he felt the most respect for them, as well as the most contempt. He was able to discriminate clearly between those deserving respect and those deserving contempt.

In 1969, on the closing night of the Ninth Party Congress, Hou Yong and his crowd were in a poor village in Shanxi. When they

---

* Chapter 4 omitted.
† An early phase of the Cultural Revolution, when the Red Guards were allowed almost unlimited political freedom.
‡ The "four olds" include old ideas, culture, customs, and habits ("old" in the sense of feudal)—all of which were to be rooted out during the Cultural Revolution.
§ "Study class" here refers to Mao Zedong thought study class—an institution for remolding bourgeois ideology.
‖ A kind of detention, in which members are not allowed to go home.

heard the list of Central Committee members and Reserve Central Committee members over the village broadcast system, the reactions among these youth, these collective register card holders,* were many and varied. Some wept loudly from joy at finding his or her father named; others laughed wildly from grief upon discovering that his or her father had indeed been dropped. Some rejoiced to hear of the "reemergence" of a parent's old superior; others became worried that an old superior of a parent "went missing." Many a young face, tortured and distorted by a strange political life, flitted across Hou Yong's mind. The weeping, the laughing, the cursing, the shouting, the fractious, the vacuous. . . . He felt that this was a most telling and easily comprehended textbook of life. Of course, there were also the strangely calm, undistorted faces. They belonged to the one or two with ideas, who did not set store by being the children of cadres. Besides these, there were a few others who were commonfolk like Hou Yong himself. Alas, Hou Yong did not make a careful study of this book of life.

In 1974, Hou Yong and a few other "educated youth" were transferred to a local factory to be workers. Not long after, he married the daughter of an army cadre. At the time, of course, that particular army cadre was going through hard times, and was spending his day "reclaiming lakeland and turning it into fields" down at a cadre school in Hubei province. But Hou Yong had placed his bet with precision and patience. In 1977, the army cadre had sure enough been restored to his position; the whole family was relocated back to Beijing and went back to the old "four-bedroom and living room" accommodation in an army compound outside Fuxing Gate. From then on, to be transferred back to Beijing along with his wife became Hou Yong's most immediate and important purpose in life. However, on account of the factory's stubborn resistance, and his father-in-law's being unexpectedly "old-fashioned" and "useless," the transfer had still not come through. Nonetheless, the factory considered that Hou Yong had "connections" in Beijing and did not have to stay in hotels, and also had many potentially useful acquaintances there, so they made him a buyer. This way, he often took the plane from Taiyuan to Beijing. What he held in his hands at this moment were, in fact, plane tickets for which he would be reimbursed.

Seeing his elder brother come in, he merely looked up, nodded, and went on playing with his plane ticket, as though it were a serious matter. He was like this on purpose. His feelings for his brother were

* All Chinese must have a family registration card, which is used as an I.D., that shows one's legal place of residence (a town or village, et cetera). Single people— e.g., students at boarding schools—may be on a "collective register."

a mixture of respect and contempt. The people of his brother's generation had read a lot, seen many old films he himself had never seen, and they included famous people like Cai Bodu. What's more, after Cai Bodu had become a celebrity, he still saw him often. All this only made him feel respect for his brother. On the other hand, his brother was such a jerk, so useless! A mere middle school teacher in the country! Why, the school was not even walled: step out of the door, and you were in the fields—shrouded in the odor of manure! His brother had never left Beijing in his life—never ridden in a car, not to mention an airplane! Had it not been for the fact that he, Hou Yong, had married up into a cadre's family, thus enabling his brother to pay his in-laws an occasional visit, he would never even have had the chance to see the floor space in a "four-bedroom" apartment, never would have had the chance to see a snow white, enamel bathtub! What a jerk!

Hou Rui had not expected his brother to be back again. Actually he had come back on business only two months ago. "Nobody knows a man better than his elder brother": from the way Hou Yong fiddled with his airplane tickets and the sundry items strewn on and around the bed—the suitcase, the airline bag, the chewing gum and glossy foreign language magazines one gets free aboard airplanes—all signs of "worldly" man—Hou Rui could see at a glance what was going on in his brother's mind. He knew that this was a time when his younger brother most despised him. So he summoned all his self-respect, sat down on the folding chair next to the big bed, and said with an air full of the authority of an elder: "So how long are you here for? Where will you stay?"

Hou Yong did not even bother to raise his head. He put away his airplane tickets in a classy snakeskin wallet and said almost provokingly, "I shall stay precisely as long as I please, and precisely where I please."

This suggested he would not stay long, and further that he would, as usual, be staying here. Cai Bodu had once expressed surprise upon finding that every time Hou Yong came to Beijing on business, he would squeeze in with his overcrowded family in Dongdan and not go to enjoy the luxurious living space of the army compound outside Fuxing Gate. Cai Bodu had asked Hou Rui, "Why is this? After all, aren't his children also there with their grandparents? And it's easy to get to town from there by bus or subway. So why should he squeeze in with you?" Hou Rui felt a little ashamed of answering truthfully. He merely laughed and answered, "You're a playwright. Surely you'd know his simple lines. I was hoping you'd repeat them to me!"

In truth, Hou Rui knew very well that his brother could not feel comfortable there. His parents-in-law seemed to treat him quite decently. But his various brothers-in-law and sisters-in-law despised him with every bone in their bodies. They thought of him as an opportunist, one who had gained from their misfortunes. Not that they would say anything to his face, but the way they ignored him, the way they openly pitied their sister, and the reluctance they showed in introducing him to guests—in addition to the derision he brought on himself from time to time with faux pas that stemmed from an ignorance of their life-style—all these made him thoroughly uncomfortable. Over there he played a minor part at a disadvantage, whereas in the Dongdan home he played the leading role and in everything had the advantage.

Hou Yong tidied up his things. With his forehead wrinkled tightly, he headed for the mirror on the south wall. The room was cramped and messy. He impatiently kicked aside a cane chair that was in the way, leaned close to the mirror, peered at himself, then used both hands to squeeze a blackhead by his nose. The blackhead had become infected and had pus in it. In the crooked mirror, Hou Yong could see the whole outer room of this hateful home. He wanted to smash this mirror just as he was squeezing this blackhead. "What a dog den!" he muttered angrily.

To call it a dog den was, of course, wrong—a human den would be far more appropriate. Indeed, the word "den" gave the only accurate description of the cramped nature of his family's living space. What they lived in had originally been a room sixteen meters square. In Hou Yong's childhood not only had this room not seemed small, it actually gave one a feeling of spaciousness. When he was five and his sister Hou Ying three, they would get under the square dining table to play house, and would often play through a whole afternoon. In those days, they had felt that a world the size of a table was plenty. Yet, there exists in the world such a regrettable phenomenon: people grow bigger day by day, yet their rooms do not expand correspondingly. When Hou Yong and Hou Ying started senior primary school,* a curtain often had to be drawn across the middle of the room. But then a curtain was no proper solution to the problem. In this very room, in the heat of a summer's night, Hou Yong had wakened and been startled by the sight of an act that his parents, who were still not that old should rightfully have kept from him. That had been a fearful enlightenment. After that night, when Hou Yong got up in the morning, he seemed to be a different person.

---

* Grades five and six.

Before this, he had revered his parents, especially his mother. He had felt that every hair on her was sacred. But that day, when his mother reminded him as usual not to forget to check his school bag, he had, for no reason whatever, become disagreeable to her.

There were a few years when there had been less pressure on this room: Hou Rui had not often come home from the suburbs, Hou Yong had joined up with a rural team in Shanxi, and Hou Ying had gone off to the construction brigades in Inner Mongolia. Yet it was precisely in those years that the old couple's hair had turned white in large streaks. Later Hou Ying had come back from the construction brigades because of "poor health," and—through the agency of Cai Bodu—Hou Rui had finally met a girl he decided to marry. Thus the room became crowded once more. So that Hou Rui could marry, the Housing Office was called in to put in a partition, turning the one big room into two small rooms, each measuring less than eight meters square. Then Hou Rui's wife, Bai Shufen, had had Little Linlang. When Hou Yong brought his wife, Peng Xueyun, to see her parents-in-law, there would be as many as eight people in the two rooms.

The front room that was now reflected in the mirror had a double bed in it against the south wall. A small clothes closet just fit between the bed and the west wall. The top of the closet was crammed with sundry household items, but nonetheless was also decorated with glass vases and bunches of plastic flowers as well as porcelain objets d'art purchased at a reduced rate. In front of the closet stood a washstand. The space between the washstand and the door to the back room barely held the cane chair that had been stuck there. To the north of the bed, against the east wall, stood the square table that had been passed down from generation to generation. Over the table was spread a plastic tablecloth with a design of large orange flowers. Two folding chairs fit snugly on either side. On the table against the wall were thermoses and a teapot. This was where the family normally had its meals. Above the table was a picture frame containing photographs of members of the family in various permutations and combinations. What was strange—and yet not strange—was that the central spot was occupied by a picture of Hou Yong's parents-in-law in uniform. The remaining walls were rather fussily decorated with New Year pictures or cutouts from magazines—shots of scenery, portraits of film stars. Directly above the double bed hung the big glossy calendar that their father, who worked in the post office, proudly brought back from work each year. Such a rare privilege. Valued at over five yuan, the unit would sell them to their staff at a special price of two yuan.

Objectively speaking, everything in the room did not suggest poverty. In fact, one could say it abounded in a certain air of complacent well-being. Yet the cramping, even more than the poverty, gave one, somehow, an inexplicable feeling of oppression. While he was squeezing the blackhead, Hou Yong's face was covered with suffering—the suffering that resulted from being humiliated by others. Hou Rui, sitting on the folding chair by the table and gazing at his brother's face in the mirror, felt even worse. Hou Yong didn't look a bit like him: he had a long square face with dark eyebrows and long eyes that were slightly triangular. His nose was very straight, and he had a wide mouth. His teeth were very straight; however, one front tooth was grey, in sharp contrast to the surrounding teeth. Indeed, this was his most striking feature.

Gazing at his brother, Hou Rui felt sad. They coexisted in such a tiny space, yet their minds were so far apart. What could he say to his brother to bring forth a smile, a gentleness?

"So what business are you here for this time?" Hou Rui asked as kindly as he could.

Hou Yong had finished with his blackhead and had walked over to the washstand to wash his face. He said unfeelingly, "You wouldn't understand even if I told you!"

Hou Rui's hand, which was holding a cigarette, shook with anger. He raised his voice and said, "What's wrong with asking? You could tell me even if I didn't understand."

"I can't be bothered." Hou Yong, discovering that the water in the washbasin was dirty, picked up the basin and rushed over to the door. Pushing aside the door curtain, he emptied the water out into the yard just as their neighbor Er Zhuang* was walking by, pushing his bike. "Hey there! Watch what you're doing!" Hou Yong paid no attention. He turned around and grabbed a thermos. Picking it up, he found it to be empty. Impatiently he set it down and grabbed another. Finding that to be low in water, he grumbled, "Don't know what they do all day. Don't even have hot water ready! Just like pigs!" So saying he emptied the thermos into the washbasin.

"Can't you be a bit more civilized?" Hou Rui couldn't help saying. "Stop carrying on as though everyone owes you something!"

"Oh, shut up," Hou Yong said contemptuously. "Don't waste your energy bothering me. Why don't you use it to get yourself some housing. That would be more useful."

"You!" Hou Rui rose in anger. Just when they were about to fight in earnest, a woman came in. Sizing up the situation at a glance, she stamped her foot and said, "Quit fighting! You're brothers! What is there you can't talk over nicely?"

* *Erzhuang* means, literally, "second (child)" "strong (one)."

6

The woman who had entered was their mother.

She was fifty-eight—already a little overweight, and her hair had practically all turned white. Yet her skin was still rosy and soft. A close scrutiny would reveal that her elder son, Hou Rui, had her eyes. Hou Yong, on the other hand, was thoroughly unlike her. Yet these past years her favorite had been this second son who was uniformly rude and unreasonable with everyone in the family.

She had been a worker at a nearby neighborhood* mat-embroidery shop until she had retired two years before. Until her second son had so dramatically married the precious daughter of an army cadre, her knowledge of the world had been extremely limited. In fact, nothing out of the ordinary had ever added color to her everyday life. Aside from two or three semi-invalid men, their tiny shop, whose business was embroidering edges of table mats, consisted entirely of middle-aged or elderly women who had not entirely shed their housewife attitudes. Once the office of the Neighborhood Committee† got hold of a load of pears‡ from the countryside, and the strangest thing happened—they remembered their tiny embroidery shop, and for once gave the shopworkers a chance to buy something cheap too. This begot boundless gratitude in Mrs. Hou and her colleagues: it signified not only a certain political status but a certain welfare bene-fit. They finished work early and went along with their fellow work-ers to the compound of the Neighborhood Committee to stand in line and wait to weigh out their share. When it was their turn, they tried their best to pick the largest ones, and—totally ignoring the derision of the bystanders—begged to be allowed to buy some extra. After lug-ging the pears home, Mrs. Hou washed clean a large dish to serve as a temporary fruit bowl. She polished each pear and then piled them up on the dish, as if for an offering. That evening, having bathed their feet in hot water, she and her husband sat down together to enjoy their "leathercoat" pears. She thought they tasted just like the sacred peaches of the immortals.

It was when her son Hou Yong had married that she had come by what she had never even dreamed of. As the in-law of high cadres, she was invited to the four-bedroom-plus-living-room luxury apart-ment. The maid polished the bathtub, filled it with warm water, then asked her to bathe. The superior quality of the food went without

* "Neighborhood" not being the vicinity, but the social/administrative unit. A neighborhood enterprise is a kind of local cooperative enterprise.
† The Neighborhood or Street Committee acts as a branch of local government, a marriage registry, etc.
‡ Literally, "spotted pears"—a pear of low quality with a spotty, tough skin.

saying, and the Longjing tea she was served after dinner—well, it took getting used to. But what amazed her most was the huge dish of fruit that was brought out of the refrigerator. Such big apples. Such smooth pears! Such juicy grapes! But even these were not *that* extraordinary. It was the fresh lychees—skins so red you'd think they had been dabbed with chicken's blood, the insides so white you'd think they had been made from snow flakes. And the taste! They could beguile the spirit from you! Why in late summer, you could take one hundred yuan* to Wangfujing or Xidan† and you wouldn't get such lychees.

After watching the color television, which was just like watching the movies, her son's mother-in-law brought her a spare pair of terry cloth pyjamas and a pair of leather-soled brocade slippers, and invited her to rest on the full-size fold-out bed specially prepared for her. When all this happened to her, how do you suppose she felt?

Every time she returned from the western suburb, she felt her spiritual world had been enriched. All the old women in the neighborhood, and occasionally even Old Man Qian from the west room of the compound who was always drunk, would come and sit in her room and listen to her talk about their in-laws. About certain finer details they would inquire repeatedly, then join in with her in making noises of approbation.

However, there were also times—when their roof was leaking, or when Hou Rui had come back home with his wife and child and Hou Yong was also home resting—when the room would be in a state of chaos and one could not move without bumping into something. At times like this she could not stop herself from comparing their home with that of their in-laws! Then she would feel low. They had such a wonderful place, but one could not be visiting them forever, and though one could enjoy the luxuries there once in a while, one could not, after all, cart it all home. And once she had become aware that abodes infinitely more comfortable existed in the world, this rough, dreary life became all the more hard to bear. Whenever this state of mind took possession of her, she could not help thinking angrily: Why did we have to go and get such in-laws?

And yet, it was, after all, her second son who had brought something new to her life. Everytime he came back on business, the first thing she would do was march off to Dongdan Market with basket in hand. She had just now returned from the market; her basket was full to the brim.

* A *yuan* is a Chinese dollar.
† Wangfujing and Xidan are the two main fashionable shopping streets in Beijing.

"But Mother, you don't know! Yong is losing all his manners!" Hou Rui couldn't help saying. "I ask him something perfectly nicely, and he just keeps jabbing at me."

"Manners! Who cares a fig about manners!" Not letting his mother get a word in, Hou Yong continued, "It annoys me just to look at this place. And you want to bother about manners!" Then before Hou Rui, who was biting his lips with rage, could say a word, he grabbed the basket out of his mother's arms, took one look inside and said, "Who wants that horrible ribbon fish!* I've told you before, at Xueyun's they never eat these scaleless fish!"

The mother replied quickly and apologetically, "Oh, that's for the old man—you know how he likes to have sweet and sour ribbon fish with a drink or two. You don't have to touch it. I also have chicken. . . ."

But Hou Yong's brows knit yet closer, and his voice became even more unpleasant: "You're all so ignorant! You think if it's chicken, it's got to be good. But people aren't eating chicken these days. Chicken has cancer cells—it's dangerous!"

Now the mother despaired. "If even chicken is no good, what is there left to eat?"

Hou Yong gave the basket a shove and replied, "These days, duck's the thing to eat. Chicken is "hot"†—it makes you choleric; duck is "warm"—it builds you up!"

The mother hastily replied, "You should have told me so earlier. I'll get duck tomorrow. It so happens that's easier to get than chicken.

Hou Rui could not contain himself any longer. He finally exploded. His face taut, he slapped the table and said, as though it were a command, "Mother! What have you turned into—his slave? You shouldn't spoil him the way you do. What right has he to call the tune around here?"

The mother watched her second son, deathly afraid he would be angry. But surprisingly Hou Yong just smiled. He said with a glance at Hou Rui, "Oh, never mind him, Mother. You go about your business. He's just jealous of me." With this, he turned and went into the inside room.

Hou Rui was so angry he was ready to rush over and really confront him, but his mother put her basket down on the table and barred his way. She lowered her voice and said, "Don't be so hard on him, he is nine years younger than you."

Rou Rui also lowered his voice, "But still, he's an adult now!"

* Ribbon fish is a popular low-class specialty.

† Chinese science classifies things according to a five-element theory in which various "humors" are attributed to different foods.

The mother said sincerely, "Yong has done a lot for the home. Without him, would we have a television? Why, without him, we would not even have got the kitchen lean-to* built.

Hou Rui was left without a word to say. Indeed, these many years, those of the family who had stayed in Beijing had saved up enough money for a television. But neither the old man, nor Hou Rui and his wife, nor Hou Ying could get a television coupon from their units. The last time Hou Yong had come home on business, he had easily gotten hold of a twelve-inch set, thereby making the evenings in these sixteen meters much more lively. The "kitchenette" was also Hou Yong's doing: from getting the bricks to getting the manpower, he had done it all in the space of a few days. And the mother had omitted to mention the gas cylinder. That was also gotten by Hou Yong when he had been back on business. As for Hou Rui, it was not that he did not try, but he could not pull off a single feat of this kind. This being the case, how could he deny Hou Yong's special status in the home, and quibble about his manners?

Hou Rui just sat there, puffing on his cigarette, not saying a word.

Suddenly, there came from the back room a scream, followed by sobbing.

7

If the front room was cramped, then the back room was like a quaint storeroom, with very little space leftover. The room was furnished very cleverly with three large items, the first being a steel-framed double bed. The legs of the bed were raised with stacks of bricks. In this way the space under the bed became quite usable. It had been originally propped up in 1976 as an earthquake precaution.† Later, when the quake period was over, they could not bear to give up the advantages of this arrangement, so it had become permanent. Now people could sleep not only on the bed, but under it as well, for a place had been made up there. When not used for sleeping, the place was used for keeping overcoats and bags and the like. The second item was a single bed, also propped up high with bricks. Beneath this were trunk and baskets. The third item was a wardrobe made from self-supplied wood.‡ This belonged to Hou Rui and his wife. A pity that they had now been married eight years—their daughter Linlang

---

* Single-story dwellings often have a tiny shed or lean-to for cooking in order to save space.

† When people were advised to sleep *under* their beds.

‡ For many years there was a great shortage of wood, so furniture was very hard to come by. Thus when people could get hold of some wood, they would have a carpenter make it up into furniture.

was already six—and yet they still had no home of their own. But since they taught in the same county (even though their schools belonged to different communes), could they not make a home there? They had, indeed, resolved to get transferred to the same place and make a home for themselves at the school. But they had seen too many cases where honest middle school teachers had made their home at the school. With low income and a lack of welfare facilities, no one cared that these people had a hard time improving themselves professionally and suffered hardships. And besides all this, there were some commune cadres who, on finding that one's whole family's files, household register, and grain and oil connections were all in their control, would put on the airs of a superior and assign chores at the drop of a hat—now asking one to join some "propaganda team" or other, now getting one to draft some document or even to spend a morning writing double-happiness signs* and couplets for some relative of theirs who was getting married. For these and various other reasons, they decided they preferred it the way it was with the two of them teaching at different communes. They also hung on to their city household register, in obstinate pursuit of a nest of their own, even if only six meters square. In this way, they were able to maintain a modicum of necessary independence before the commune cadres as well as the middle school leadership.

For the past two years, every time Hou Rui came back from school he would go to the Housing Office and request housing. In theory, this family of six, spanning three generations (for though little Linlang normally lived at the school with her mother, she was also registered as part of her grandfather's household) and living in only sixteen square meters, undoubtedly qualified as a hardship case deserving the special consideration of the Housing Office. But they had completely despaired of the housing official. That puny, pallid official had the most remarkably good disposition: whether one begged repeatedly, demanded compellingly, cursed him roundly or threatened to report him to his superiors—whatever one did—he would just smile, hold his hands up, and say, "There's nothing empty in this area. But the moment an empty room comes up, I'll let you have it. How's that?" Thus it was that Hou Rui and his wife had engaged in eight years of "guerrilla warfare," and the wardrobe they had prepared for a home of their own had to be stuck in this room.

Besides these three large pieces, there was a sewing machine—also used as a writing table—that barely made it in, and two square stools that were stuck in the corner when not in use.

* Auspicious writings that are pasted on walls and windows at a wedding.

When Hou Yong had gone into the back room, it had been with the intention of lying down for a rest. Air travel was, after all, tiring, on top of which he was feeling confused. For all of these reasons he felt he had to recline and compose himself.

In the back room, facing the *hutong*, there was a small window with a pink curtain with a blue rose pattern strung across it. This made the room rather somber and quite stuffy. By now, Hou Yong was feeling quite miserable, and it startled him to see his sister Hou Ying spread out on the big bed, fast asleep.

When Hou Yong saw Hou Ying, he felt very mixed feelings. This sister, whom he had once happily played with under the square table, had now become the chief obstacle to the realization of his hope to return to Beijing. True, she was pitiable. Yet she had to be disposed of without delay.

Hou Yong had more or less given up hope that his parents-in-law could effect his transfer back. When he thought of the image of the cadre, as portrayed in the literary exposés of privilege—including that play of Cai Bodu's that had caused such a stir—he had to laugh. Those were mere caricatures. Cadres in real life were just like any other kind of people, each with his own idiosyncrasies. His parents-in-law were a thorough disappointment to him. They were totally incapable and timid. Why, the fact that the trumped-up case against them was overturned had been due solely to its being the unified policy of the higher levels and their children's involvement—they had had no hand in it. Hou Yong gradually perceived that though they were both fairly senior in rank and enjoyed good incomes and benefits, they were not among those in the compound that held actual power. The father-in-law was a vice-head at a ministerial level. However, in that ministry, there were as many as nine vice-heads. The mother-in-law was a department chief, but because she had often been absent due to poor health, the real power had fallen into the hands of the vice-chief who, in fact, did not get along with her.

True, they lived well, ate well, dressed well—but there was no denying it: it was all come by legally, in accordance with rank and income. Hou Yong had carefully gone into the source of each luxury they enjoyed and was forced to the conclusion that none had come "through the back door." For example, the twenty-inch color television, the 1900-liter refrigerator—even the fresh lychees whose taste his mother would never forget—all were bought from the shops in and around the compound, and were paid for with hard cash. As for the "back door," it was not so much that the old couple disapproved of it on theoretical grounds as that in this area they were utterly incapable, and also inexplicably timid.

Their eldest son (Hou Yong's elder brother-in-law), a graduate of a military academy, was married and had been assigned work in another army compound not too far away. On the rare occasions when he was home for a visit, he would lecture them—either tell them they were lagging behind, or that they were just plain feeble. On such occasions, the old couple would oddly enough remain perfectly amiable and sit through their son's chiding with an insufferable kindliness, as though they had not the least resentment. Their third child, Hou Yong's younger brother-in-law, was a typical hedonist playboy. Upon high school graduation, while awaiting a job assignment, he had on many occasions urged his parents to open a "back door" for him and get him into uniform. But with his parents it was a case of "The power is ample, but the guts are lacking." When he really made a scene, his mother actually broke down and wept and assured him that, if only he would not make trouble, they would support him all his life. Later, the school assigned him to be a worker in a state-owned factory not far from home. There he enjoyed the reverence and envy accorded him by quite a few people at the factory on account of his being from the "compound." These days he changed girl friends, on average, once a month, but had no intention of getting married and starting a family. The fourth child, Hou Yong's sister-in-law, had gotten good enough grades to get into a university, but could only qualify as a day student. She felt it was much more comfortable living at home, and did not mind cycling back and forth each day. The parents-in-law had enough children, and furthermore had Hou Yong's son living with them. This, and their firm belief in the aphorism "Better one less thing to do than one more thing to do," made them quite indifferent to their daughter and son-in-law's plea to help get them transferred back to Beijing.

Once when Hou Yong had been back on business, he had brought up this matter with his father-in-law, who was at the time standing in front of his special spirits vat, just about to ladle himself a drink. Hearing Hou Yong once again bring up the matter of transfer, he said lightly, "Well, after all, they *do* need people to build the place up. If you find the life hard, just ask your mother to send canned goods." Watching the vat, and his father-in-law drinking from the long ladle, a strange, inexplicable feeling came over him. The vat had been remodeled from a tropical-fish tank, and was fully a half-meter square. At the bottom were ginseng, deer antlers, the fruit of wolfberry, angelica,* and so on. The vat was always kept more than half full with spirits—maotai, wu-liangye, langjiu, and the like†—all

* Chinese medicines, thought to promote vigor and longevity.
† Most famous and expensive liquors in China.

good mixers. Whenever one entered his room, one could smell that particular fragrance of medicinal spirits, even though the vat was normally sealed tight with a thick sheet of glass.

Hou Yong had delved deep into the question, What did his father-in-law want? He obviously did not hope for further promotion; neither was he after power; and he did not even think about writing his memoirs. Nor did he, like some other cadres in the compound, exert himself to plan a brilliant future for his children. It seemed that after the ten calamitous years* he was extremely tired. He was no longer conscientious or enthusiastic about things. Yet he had a persistent yearning for a healthy old age, and all his spiritual vigor, creativity, and pertinacity were concentrated on this enterprise with the liquor vat. What use was there in pleading again and again with such a father-in-law! Besides, Hou Yong knew that sooner or later his younger brother-in-law would set up a family there. Even if his parents-in-law did not feel it as a threat, his brother-in-law would see it as a battle for space. For it was obvious that, even if Hou Yong and his wife were transferred back to Beijing, they had no immediate—or even long-term—prospect of being assigned quarters. And the parents-in-law's place certainly could not hold the families of two of their children!

Under these circumstances, Hou Yong decided to "use self-reliance."† It was not impossible in this case: Hou Rui, his wife, and daughter Linglang could be forced to relocate their household register to the distant suburbs. That would leave, besides the old folk, just Hou Ying on the register. Let her hurry up and get married! Once she had been married off—preferably in some far-away place—there would only be the two old folk left. Then their units could be asked to write a note certifying that they were old and poor of health, but had no children at hand to take care of them. Armed with this certificate, and given the manipulative skills Hou Yong had acquired over the years, it would not be difficult to cite some relevant policy and have himself and his wife transferred back to Beijing.

Hence the vital question: When would Hou Ying leave home? When he got home this time, and he asked his mother about this matter, all she could do was sigh. Hou Ying still had no one to marry, she would still be holding out here, day after day.

Thus it was that when he saw his sister lying on the big bed, Hou Yong was filled with annoyance.

Hou Ying was sleeping soundly. She had been washing clothes all morning. After lunch, she did the dishes, and at 2 o'clock or so, she lay

* The Cultural Revolution.
† Quote from Mao—a party slogan.

down on the big bed to sleep; she was on night shift that night. When Hou Yong came in she had not wakened. Now Hou Yong stood by her bed and she was still sleeping.

Actually Hou Ying's sleep was not peaceful. She had been dreaming all along—a chaotic, painful dream. It seemed to her that she was sleeping on the mud kang* of the construction brigade in Inner Mongolia. Suddenly she heard the bugle sound the reveille and a clatter of footsteps by her ear. Someone was shaking her, but try as she might, she could not open her eyes—it was as though her eyelids were glued together. She was a junior middle school graduate of '69. One could write a whole sociology work on the fate of this group of middle school graduates. Actually they could hardly be called middle school graduates. The chaos of the Great Cultural Revolution had prevented them from completing grade six of primary school and going on to middle school according to schedule. It was not until the second half of 1967 that they were asked to report to the middle school. But at that time it was "Back to classes and carry on the Revolution"—merely a matter of going to the wreck of the classroom every day for an hour of "Daily Reading."† The rest of the time they were herded together but given nothing special to do. When, in the winter of 1968, the large-scale movement to "go up to the mountains and go down to the village," swept through the land, their class was told to pack everything up and go en masse to the construction brigades. Thus it was that in 1969 Hou Ying ended up in a construction brigade in Inner Mongolia. This gentle, peace-loving girl from a common city family was like a shadow in the ranks of the brigade. People often forgot about her very existence—and she was quite willing to be forgotten. Her only friend was a girl called Li Wei who belonged to the same company but lived in a different dormitory. They would often go to each other's rooms and sit for awhile. Occasionally they would go to the edge of the grasslands. But when they sat together they did not have much to talk about. Besides recounting their letters from home, and showing each other what their families had sent them, they would often just sit there—sometimes for quite some time.

Hou Ying and Li Wei had very similar families. Neither was from a particularly good family—what they called "families with blemish" —but then their parents played no major roles—were neither "capitalist roaders" nor of the five black types.‡ Still less were they "reac-

---

* A sleeping platform, normally made from brick, with mats on it. People sit on it by day and sleep on it at night. It can be heated in winter.

† The reading of Mao's works.

‡ That is, landlords, rich peasants, counterrevolutionaries, bad elements (criminals), and rightists.

tionary authorities." They were merely clerical workers or petty artisans. During the turmoil of the Great Cultural Revolution, their families' fortunes had remained relatively stable. So they had no great sorrows and no great joys. Some of their comrades-in-arms threw parties with sweets and drinks to celebrate the "realization of party policy"* (with regard to their parents). Others beat their breasts on account of their parents' or siblings' "turning their backs on the people" or, having inherited knowledge from their parents, steeped themselves in study to improve themselves. Still others, through mental or emotional complications, took up romantic or even flippant life-styles. Their case was different. Like those puny weeds of the grassland, they went unheeded by pastor and sheep alike; yet they were so insignificant they could not bloom on their own anyway.

One day after work, Li Wei went down to the main irrigation channel to rinse her sandals, fell in, and drowned. Her disappearance wet unnoticed until practically everyone was in bed, and it was not until noon the next day that her corpse was discovered some ten-odd li away. As far as Hou Ying was concerned, this was the most significant event of her life. During the rather shoddy memorial meeting held at the company, Hou Ying attracted attention for the first time by crying passionately. People discovered for the first time that she, too, was capable of deep feeling.

Li Wei often appeared in Hou Ying's dreams. Poor Li Wei! Her mother and brother hastened to the brigade upon her death, but they shed few tears; instead, they embarked on a protracted haggling session with the brigade, all day, and every day for a long while. First they wanted five thousand yuan in compensation. Later, they lowered the claim to three thousand, but in the end the brigade cited some document, saying that, as she had not died in the course of duty, there was no case for compensation. So the mother and son went off with five hundred yuan. Hou Ying walked them all the way to bus station. It was only when they were several hundred li away that Hou Ying discovered they had not even taken her ashes. This was the first time she realized the cruelty of life.

At this moment, Li Wei had once again appeared in Hou Ying's dream. The squinted eyes on Li Wei's pale, gaunt face seemed incapable of ever opening. Hou Ying was clutching Li Wei's arm, begging her to accompany her to Zhongshan Park. Li Wei's face was utterly expressionless, but she finally agreed to go. Perhaps it was in the Tang Flower Gardens—or it might have been by the flower beds

* Meaning their parents had been rehabilitated.

in front of the concert hall—a man stood coldly surveying Hou Ying. Hou Ying kept thrusting Li Wei forward and hiding herself behind her, whereupon she heard Li Wei whisper in her ear, "I'm already dead. Dead people don't look for a husband. If you have to meet him, then go on. . . ." Hou Ying's body became drenched with cold sweat. She turned. Li Wei disappeared in a cloud of mist. She ran after her, shouting, "Don't leave me! I want to be with you—I don't want to look for a husband like this anymore!"

Indeed, Hou Ying was truly reluctant to go on any more dates fixed up by others in parks and such places. When Hou Ying returned to Beijing from the brigade in Inner Mongolia, she was assigned to be a worker in a collective enterprise. Her life now was actually even more monotonous than it had been in the brigade. She had neither her second brother's broadening opportunities to travel nor her elder brother's rich mental life, founded upon his wide reading. She just worked her three different shifts in turn, and, when she got home from work, she would do the laundry, cook, or do the shopping. Any time remaining she would drift along with the fashion and get a perm, or get some colorful new clothes, or see a few films— that was all. Before she knew it, she was of an age to start looking for a husband.

At first, on the basis of Hou Yong's success in marriage, her parents had great hopes for her. Her mother had openly expressed to Hou Yong's mother-in-law the desire that she might send some high cadres' sons her way. But before long their hopes were dashed. Hou Yong told them bluntly, "When the young master from the high cadre's family goes looking for a wife, if he's not after someone of his own class, then he's after a great beauty. As for our Ying, she's not of the right class, neither is she a beauty. She hasn't got a chance!" All this had been said in front of Hou Ying, who had had no very clear notion of the demands men placed on women's looks. Hearing this, she secretly looked at herself in the mirror and realized that she was not up to the standards required by young master from a high cadre's family, and immediately despaired of marrying into a family such as that of her brother's in-laws. But her parents did not despair. Especially her mother. She had had a taste of what it meant to have an alliance with a high cadre's family. Hou Yong's marriage gave her a rich daughter-in-law, but that was half as satisfying as having a rich son-in-law. She could not go with Hou Yong to live with the Pengs, but it would be possible to follow Hou Ying to a rich son-in-law to enjoy her old age. What a life that would be! So when she failed to get Hou Ying a high cadre's son, she started to work on the high cadres or high academics themselves. For were there not middle-aged widowers of that sort? "Our Xiao Ying* is of a good disposition. She's mature, virtuous—sure to get along with children from a previous marriage." She tried her best to seek out opportunities whereby Hou Ying could form an alliance that would benefit the family. Yet time flew by, no such opportunity was found, and Hou Ying was approaching her late twenties. What was more worrying was that Hou Ying began to turn noticeably fragile. Once when Cai Bodu came round to see Hou Rui, he ran into Hou Ying. This fairly renowned, yet nonetheless tactless playwright remarked within the hearing of the Hou parents, "Why, Xiao Ying looks like she could be thirty. How time flies! Why, the first time I came around, she was only so high and just like a flower!" These words sounded most unpleasant to the parents' ears. If she was like a flower *then*, what was she like now?

The standards her parents and elder brothers set for Hou Ying's partner were lowered as the months went by. At first they had sought engineers and technicians—then any professional, even a middle school teacher. After that, workers were okay. But they had to be from state-owned factories, without family burdens, decent-looking, and with no bad habits. Thus, Hou Ying came to be dated with increasing frequency. A number of times Hou Ying had returned from park meetings and clearly indicated her approval to her parents and the go-between,† but, incredibly, the go-between had returned not long afterward with apologies: the man had been dissatisfied with the meeting. This was an even harder blow for her parents than for Hou Ying herself. Indignantly, they thought: Why we'd even considered marrying her into a cadre's family. How dare you, mere workers, be so picky about such a girl!

Successive failures made Hou Ying's personality even more introverted. According to the go-between what the prospective partners had objected to was that she acted so old. They felt her conversation and her behavior to be dull. For that reason, her mother nagged at her almost daily, "Can't you be a little more lively? Why are you always scowling and looking so mournful? It's a good thing I'm your mother. Why, if I'd been your mother-in-law, I wouldn't like my son to bring home such a wife!" Only her sister-in-law Bai Shufen would say a few words in her behalf: "Don't torment her so. Cai Bodu says he saw this report. It said that in the city of Beijing, among young people aged twenty-three to twenty-eight, the number

* *Xiao*, or "little," is a term of endearment and is used by an older person addressing someone younger.
† Not a professional go-between, just a helpful acquaintance.

of girls exceeds the number of boys by tens of thousands. Xiao Ying isn't the only girl having a hard time finding a partner."

Not that there were none who aspired to Hou Ying. But what manner of people were they! One evening at sunset, when Hou Ying had been accompanied back from Tao Ranting* By Bai Shufen, they both looked downcast. It had obviously been another unsuccessful meeting. Hou Ying went into the inside room, took off her checked flannel overcoat, combed out the elm seed pods that had fallen into her curls, sat down on the bed, and went into a daze. At this moment, Old Man Qian from the west room of the compound came visiting, and started a rather one-sided conversation with Mrs. Hou. She was sitting at the table in the front room, stringing string beans. As Old Man Qian talked on, he got carried away. Emboldened by a drink or two, he squinted out of the corner of his bloodshot eyes and said, "So how is the business of your finding Xiao Ying a husband? Naturally it's not for my son Er Zhuang to play 'the toad who would eat of the swan,' but, after all, he grew up under your very own eyes, and you know in your heart whether or not he's a lazy layabout or a sneaky, back-street swindler. . . ." Mother was greatly shocked when she heard him talking like this. Old Man Qian was a retired pedicab driver; his son Er Zhuang was a laborer on a construction team. How dare they entertain such notions? Treating the Hous as if they were nobodies! She immediately put down the wicker dish with the string beans in it, and said, "Old Man Qian, you must have had a drop too much again!" Old Man Qian went off ashamed, but as for Hou Ying, sitting in the evening twilight in the back room, her heart was pounding.

Hou Ying, lost as she was in dreamland, could not, of course, know with what infinite annoyance her brother was surveying her sleeping form.

In the space of a few short seconds, all the resentment Hou Yong felt against Hou Ying gathered into a thundercloud. First he felt that Hou Ying's posture as she slept was inelegant. Seeing as there was bedding under the bed, why did she not go and sleep under the bed? Then she could draw the curtain and hide herself. Hou Ying's hair was now very messy, her eyes were half shut, her mouth was gaping; she displayed not the slightest bit of female elegance. Her body suggested a vulgarity of rigid joints; it lacked beautiful, soft curves. Her rigidity, her lack of style, her ignorance, her ineffectuality, her increasing frailty, and especially her inability even to find a decent

* Joyous Pavilion Park.

man—all this was already too much for Hou Yong to bear. Then, the last time he had come back, his mother had told him that her daughter seemed to be showing symptoms of hysteria, that when her mother was nagging her, she might be very quiet, then suddenly wail loudly, and then, again, suddenly cease and go into a reverie. . . . Oh, when would she get married and leave this home? How long would she keep him waiting?

The clouds were gathering closer and closer in Hou Yong's heart. Suddenly lightning struck, and thunder rolled. Hou Yong took a sudden step forward, jerked Hou Ying up and yelled, "Stop sleeping like a dead pig!"

Thus startled awake, Hou Ying dazedly opened her eyes; then, suddenly seeing Hou Yong's menacing face before her eyes and feeling his viselike grip on her wrist, she could only utter a fearful scream: "Aaaa—!"

When Hou Ying screamed, the expression on her face seemed to Hou Yong infinitely loathsome. He gave her a sharp prod, and said even more angrily, "What are you screaming for? Are you a pig being slaughtered?"

Hou Ying was more completely awake. She immediately perceived what an impediment she was in the eyes of her brother. A sorrow burst forth from her quaking soul, and set her wailing loudly.

8

Hearing the noise, Hou Rui went in. Angrily he thrust himself between Hou Yong and Hou Ying, saying to Hou Yong, "Why do you keep playing the tyrant? How can you expect Xiao Ying to go on night shift if she doesn't get to sleep during the day! What did you rouse her for?" Hou Yong stood up straight, and answered imperturbably, "She's a big girl now, it's not right for her to be sprawled out there in the daytime! I want her to move down there to sleep."

The mother had followed Hou Rui into the room. Her emotions were complex. In her heart she knew that it was wrong of Hou Yong to treat his sister so. Yet the ever growing sense of despair she felt about her daughter made her not all that sympathetic to Hou Ying, weeping into her hands. Seeing the confrontation between the brothers, which was in danger of erupting into a fight, she felt both worried and helpless. Shakily she walked over to them and said in a spirit of reproach to all, "What is all this? Lao Er:* You're too rough! If you want to wake her, can't you do it more gently? And Xiao Ying:

---

* *Lao*, or "old," is a term of respect, and is always used by a younger person addressing an older person. *Er* means "second," in this case, second son.

don't be such a sissy—stop howling. If you want to sleep some more, move down there and sleep. Lao Da:* I don't know why you keep looking for trouble with your brother. Can't you both cool off a bit?"

But this confrontation was not going to end here. Hou Rui said to Hou Yong sternly: "Of late you've become more and more unfeeling. Why is it you treat us and Xiao Ying as if were thorns in your side?"

Hou Yong countered loudly, "Who do you say is unfeeling? Look what I've done for you! And what have you done for me? When I get back to such a home, I feel fed up! Look at the way you live! It's a pigsty!

Hou Rui turned pale with anger. "If this is a pigsty, why stay here? Just get the hell out!"

"You want me to get out?" Hou Yong suddenly felt he had been wronged as he had never been wronged before. Clenching his fist, the veins in his neck standing out, he said with righteous indignation, "It's *you* who should get the hell out! Everyone knows you work in the suburbs, yet you hang on like grim death to your household register here. What is it you want? Why, these two rooms, of course! Then you go around playing the humane one. As though you really cared for Xiao Ying. Who knows what plots you have in mind! Let me tell you—I've seen right through you! Before, I was too young. I thought you were really learned and had great ambitions. But now I know you're just a jerk! A jerk! You keep your register here, but you can't even get half a room. So you stick your wardrobe here, and imagine you've staked your claim to the house! Fat chance! You're the one who should get the hell out! Just clear out!"

In his anger, Hou Rui had grabbed hold of Hou Yong's collar. Hou Yong broke free and grabbed Hou Rui by *his* collar. Hou Rui gave him a shove, tearing his own collar. Hou Yong was forced to let go, and fell back against the sewing machine. A bottle of ink was knocked off the machine, fell on the floor, and shattered, splashing blue ink all over the floor. Drops of ink also splashed onto the bedding and the partially drawn curtain next to it.

The mother was just about to dash in to separate the two brothers when Hou Ying, who had been deeply shaken, emitted a piercing scream, leaped off the bed, and ran off in bare feet. This made the brothers and the mother all pause instinctively. Then they followed her to the front room. When they saw the state Hou Ying was in, they froze.

Hou Ying had not rushed out into the yard, nor lain down on the bed in the front room; instead, she was sitting underneath the table.

* Eldest.

When the three of them emerged from the inside room, Hou Ying was startled and looked askance at them. Then she shuffled backwards as though to get away, covered her face with her hands, and began weeping.

The sight of this was like a thunderbolt to Hou Yong. In a flash he remembered how all those years ago, he and his sister had played games under this same square table. Once, he had placed a square stool under the table, and on the stool a few cups of water. One had sugar water in it, another had salt water, another had tea in it, and yet another one had plain water; the last one was a pink drink of water with a few drops of Mercurochrome in it. He had sat on a tiny low stool selling drinks; his sister, her hair gathered into two short, slender ponytails, sat on a low folding stool on the other side, buying drinks. She used candy wrappers as money: each wrapper bought a mouthful of drink. She had bought mouthful after mouthful of the "pink drink". . . . Oh, how lovable his sister had seemed then! Then they had not felt in the least that the room was small, still less did they have any desire to fight over this space. One square table— two meters square at most—was enough for them to live together lovingly. Hou Yong shut his eyes. In the space of a few seconds, the clouds that had accumulated in his heart had been blown away by a strong wind. He was suddenly seized by a feeling of repentance. Oh, little sister, he thought, my own dear sister! I shouldn't treat her so!

In Hou Rui, however, the sight of this odd behavior on the part of Hou Ying inspired a strange feeling of disgust. Every time he came home, his mother would tell him privately, "Your sister may not be quite normal. . . ." He had always thought it was merely a certain melancholy springing from repeated failures in courtship—a distorted manifestation of a young woman's longing for love that had been forcibly repressed. But the scene before his eyes could only lead one to the conclusion that Hou Ying's nerves were indeed abnormal. Please, he thought, may she not become schizophrenic!

When the mother perceived that her daughter had indeed gone mad, she felt as though a thousand arrows had pierced her heart. She immediately felt that she had made Lao Er too much of a favorite, and had been too unfeeling toward her young daughter. After all, Xiao Ying was efficient and dutiful. Every day she would come home from work, wash and clean, do the shopping, cook—she never slacked off. Every month she brought back her pay and handed all of it over to her mother. When she needed money, she would come to her mother coyly and ask for some. And afterwards, if there was any left over—anything over a yuan—she would give it back. . . . Such a good daughter, she thought. Heaven must be blind not to have her matched with a good mate! Such a good daughter should not end up crawling under the table to cry!

In the course of seconds, very complex struggles had taken place in the minds of the three, yet they all emerged with the idea of going over to Hou Ying to help her up. But the first one to do so was neither Hou Rui not their mother, but Hou Yong—much to his own surprise when he thought about it later.

When Hou Yong went over to help her up, Hou Ying instinctively shrank back, but Hou Yong was strong, and also, when Hou Ying peeped out, she saw unexpectedly a kindly face and a startling pair of eyes. For these were eyes that she had seen some twenty-odd years before—also under this table. So she stood up and, helped along gently by Hou Yong, went to the back room. Hou Yong helped her to the double bed, on which she sat down. He then said, ashamed, "You just go back to sleep, Xiao Ying. I was too rough just now. It was wrong of me."

Old Mrs. Hou and Hou Rui were both quite astonished by this. In such a short time, such a tremendous change had taken place in Hou Yong's attitudes. They could not get over it; it left them in a bit of a daze. Hou Ying was even more dazed. Her extreme fright turned to total numbness. She obediently lay down, shut her eyes, and stopped weeping, except for an occasional twitch in her throat.

9

A little after 7:30, Cai Bodu arrived at the Hou compound.

10

Once inside the gate, he turned and went to the second door on the left. The door was half open; half a curtain hung across it. Cai Bodu knocked on the glass in the door, and heard Hou Rui from within say, "Come in!"

"It's been long since we've had the pleasure of your company," Hou Rui complained.

"Oh, I'm kept so busy!" Cai Bodu explained. "One day it's some forum or other; the next day it's a presentation meeting; then there's foreign affairs—it drives you up the wall."

"Foreign affairs—isn't that fun? Hou Yong asked enviously. "Isn't it all banquets?"

"Oh, no! One time out of ten, at most! You imagine foreign affairs to be interesting. Actually it's quite boring."

"You should let me go! I wouldn't find it boring," Hou Yong said loudly. "You can't imagine how boring life is in Shanxi!"

"That's true, I can understand that. I've found that in your kind of factory, the way the boys and girls dress is even more risqué than the way they do in Guangzhou* or Shanghai. Even the young people strutting along on Beijing's Wangfujing Street seem tame in comparison. . . ."

"You really know everything," said Hou Yong. I suppose it's no surprise, seeing that you're a playwright. Whenever you decide to come and stay in our factory to learn about the life there, I'll be your secretary!"

"*You* be a secretary?" Hou Rui said to Hou Yong, "Why, your writing looks like a bunch of sticks dropped by a monkey! You would teach my old chum all about the back door, more like!"

Not only was Hou Yong not angry at this, he admitted it with a smile. He felt that his brother had a right to speak this way before Cai Bodu.

How had Cai Bodu become famous? Was it really as Hou Rui had said, without recourse to any back door? Just simply by coming out with a brilliant play and suddenly becoming famous? Well, that was credible. But having once become famous, how was it that he still did not have it as good as Ge Youhan? This, to Hou Yong, was a complete mystery.

"Bodu," Hou Yong remarked, "You have a very shrewd notion of what goes on in society. You're wise to all the con tricks people use. Yet how is it that when it comes to *action*, you are such a chicken, so feeble?"

Cai Bodu and Hou Rui looked at one another. Cai Bodu smiled and said, "One must live honorably! Now someone like Ge Youhan— though he's not an actual *criminal,* he spends all his time plotting and scheming, searching for loopholes and opportunities, sometimes completely sacrificing his self-respect. Even if he does gain some actual advantages, what purpose is there in his life?"

Hou Yong found himself nodding in agreement. Every time he talked with Cai Bodu, he felt as though his base thoughts faded away, and in his soul he felt pure and at peace. He thought to himself: If only all people in society were like Cai Bodu, how wonderful it would be! If only half the people in his Shanxi factory were the Cai Bodu type, he wouldn't be holding out like grim death to get into Beijing!"

* Canton.

11

Hou Yong set there musing, and then suddenly realized that Cai Bodu and Hou Rui were now talking about something else. They were discussing Hou Ying.

"How about it? Hasn't it been solved?" Cai Bodu was saying.

"Afraid not! Next year she'll be twenty-seven. It really shouldn't wait any longer," Hou Rui said with a sigh.

"Brother Cai, you're a man of the world. Why don't you make her a match?" Hou Yong struck in. "Find her someone from your artistic circles!"

"That's precisely the business that brought me here today!" At this, Hou Rui and Hou Yong both leaned forward with eyes fixed on him, eagerly waiting for him to continue.

Just at this moment, the mother came in from the kitchen with a dish of freshly fried peanuts. Cai Bodu immediately greeted her, addressing her as "Auntie." The mother, finding it to be Cai Bodu, was immediately wreathed in smiles, and welcomed him saying, "Do you know, you're so famous now! When I went to my son's in-laws, all those people wearing uniforms and medals spoke of you as they used to speak of Mei Lanfang* in the old days! Please join us for supper. The brothers will join you for a drink.

"No, Auntie! I've *had* supper, honest!"

"Now, now! Just do as I say. You don't have to eat much—a couple of chopstickfuls and we'd be honored."

"Mother!" Hou Yong was eager to report. "Do you know, Brother Cai has come today especially to fix Xiao Ying up with someone."

"Really?" Mother was filled with exceptional joy. She immediately felt that the room was filled with light. She thought to herself: Truly Providence takes care of the virtuous. Why, only a moment ago the whole family was squabbling and fighting over this matter of Xiao Ying's getting married. Who would have thought that good destiny would show itself this very day?

She could barely contain herself and sat down on the cane chair, still clutching the dish of fried peanuts. Impatiently she asked, "Well, Bodu, what sort of a person is he?"

Cai Bodu answered, "An editor from a publishing house."

Mother felt frustrated. She did not understand. "And what line of business is that?"

"Oh, they're men of culture, like lecturers and professors in universities," Hou Rui explained. "They put books together."

* One of the most famous Chinese operatic actors in his day.

Cai Bodu continued, "He's getting on a bit—he's now forty-four. In '57 he was wrongly labeled a rightist and suffered quite a bit. After he was made a rightist, his old fiancée was afraid to have anything more to do with him, so they broke off. He never got married after that. Now he's been rehabilitated, restored to Administrative Level 18 status.* He's been reassigned to the publishing house to edit art books. This last year I've gotten to know him quite well. I, and other friends, have all been at him to get married without further delay. He's made up his mind."

"But, surely, isn't someone like that going to have pretty stiff requirements?" Hou Rui asked. "Our Xiao Ying knows nothing of art and literature. Will she suit him?"

"He said it didn't have to be someone in culture. His old fiancée had been an artist. At first it was great. While one was playing the violin, the other would write poetry. But then came the anti-rightist movement, and the girl was scared out of her wits. Couldn't do a thing. It left a deep scar in his heart. What he's after now is someone who would make a good wife and a good mother. Anyone with pleasant looks and a gentle temperament would do."

"Then Xiao Ying fits the bill exactly!" Hou Yong said excitedly. "Why, you could search by torchlight and not hope to find such a good wife and mother."

But the mother felt that all this talk had been rather beside the point. She asked, "How much does he earn? If he gets married, will he get housing?"

Cai Bodu told her, "At Level 18, you get eighty-seven fifty a month. And since his case is one in which the new policy applies, he has just been assigned a one-room apartment. Even though it's only one room, the hallway is quite large—plenty big enough to serve as living room/dining room.

Hearing this, the mother was all agog. No time should be lost in getting Xiao Ying together with this man. Why, as they sat there talking, some other family might already have sent their daughter over for him to look over. Still clutching the dish of peanuts, she kept up a string of questions. "When can a meeting be fixed up for the two of them? It's not easy for you to get out here. Could we settle on a date right now?"

Cai Bodu answered, "Recently I've really been too busy. I was afraid if I left it, I might not be able to get through to you in time. As I see it, it would be best to have a preliminary meeting this very evening. Just a little chat—to check out impressions. This comrade

* State cadres are graded on a 27-grade scale (1 is highest, 8 is minister, and so forth).

lives in the big new building at Chong Wen Men—very close to here. Every evening he goes for a walk in Dongdan Park. I've just come from his place. Before coming, I told him something about Xiao Ying. He said, if convenient for her, they could meet in Dongdan Park this evening and have a little chat."

The Hou brothers and mother, on hearing this, all started exclaiming with joy, "You think of *everything*!" "Xiao Ying doesn't go on night shift till ten. There should be plenty of time." "How could it not be convenient for Xiao Ying, with Dongdan Park so close by!"

The gratitude they felt for Cai Bodu reached a zenith. Years back, when Hou Rui despaired of finding a suitable partner, it was Cai Bodu who had introduced him to Bai Shufen. . . . Now, at this critical juncture, he had suddenly turned up, and once again come to the rescue with a solution to this problem that had been plaguing them for so long.

The mother went into the back room with the dish of peanuts. Several of them rolled off, so she laid the dish down on the sewing machine nearby. Only then did she discover that Hou Ying was already sitting up. Obviously she had heard them talking about her in the front room. From the bright look in Hou Ying's eyes, she judged that, like herself, she was looking forward to meeting that editor in Dongdan Park.

Indeed, Hou Ying had been wakened by the voices in the front room, and when she realized it was Cai Bodu talking about her matrimonial affairs, a new, happy feeling of anticipation was born in her heart. The dark shadows left on her heart by the squabble that had taken place scarcely an hour before were quickly dispelled by this unexpected news. My! An editor! That was a man of culture such as Er Zhuang could not begin to compare with. Forty-four years old—a full seventeen years older than herself. But she preferred to marry an older, more dependable, mature person.

The mother only had to give her one pep talk before she agreed to go for the meeting. Hou Yong mixed warm water for her to wash her face; Hou Rui picked out some simple, elegant clothes for her; and the mother put aside her housework to do her daughter's hair. When Hou Ying was done dressing, and stood gracefully there before them, everyone was quite struck. Was this the same Hou Ying who usually looked so plain and unexceptional?

The mother forced her and Cai Bodu each to have a bowl of egg noodles before allowing them to set off. For once, Hou Rui and Hou Yong were in accord. They both urged her kindly: "Be more open. Take the initiative in making conversation. Above all, don't act dumb."

When Hou Rui walked out of the compound gate with Hou Ying, Er Zhuang was still standing there under the street light outside, with his arms still folded across his chest. The gaze he fixed upon Hou Ying as she emerged from the compound was a complex mixture of astonishment, sullenness, longing, and contempt. Hou Ying lowered her eyes to avoid looking at him, but was clearly aware of his presence. An image from her dream flitted across her mind. She felt the evening breeze blow upon her face, and it felt like ants were crawling all over it. Cai Bodu smiled at Er Zhuang by way of a parting. Er Zhuang answered with an unmistakably blank stare.

15*

When Hou Yong had finished on the phone, and had brushed aside the door curtain to come in, he could not help but find it oppressive. The room was completely filled with people. A few dishes of food had been laid upon the square table, and the father, Hou Qinfeng, was back from work, sitting at the table drinking with Hou Rui. Hou Yong's niece, little Linlang, was leaning against the bed, playing with an old plastic doll with a broken head and eating a lollipop at the same time. The mother and Bai Shufen—one seated on the cane chair, the other standing in front of the wash stand—were talking animatedly about something. A smell of sweet and sour ribbon fish pervaded the room. The smell made him feel in his bones just how lowly and vulgar the room was. This plus the recent phone call made him feel agitated—he felt like having a tantrum, to dispel some of the frustration he felt.

"Ah, Lao Er, come and join us for a drink or two!" When the father saw Hou Yong come in, it was as if he'd acquired some great treasure. He actually made as though to get up, and made a gesture as though he were inviting a guest. Seeing this, Hou Yong suppressed his pent-up frustration. It seemed to him that his father's every gesture and expression revealed in concentrated form his kindness, virtue, vulgarity, shallowness, feebleness, and honesty. Hou Yong forced a smile and said "No, you go ahead, Dad. I feel a bit tired. I'll go in the back room and lie down for a bit." So saying, he strode into the back room, completely ignoring his sister-in-law, who was beckoning to him.

Hou Qinfen differed from his wife in that he was filled with equal pride and confidence in all three of his children. He could never forget the time Hou Rui had had a poem published in the *Beijing Daily*. Whenever, in the post office, he sold a magazine that carried works

* Ch. 12, 13, 14 omitted.

by Cai Bodu, he would immediately think of his eldest son. He always felt that with his eldest's talent, he would surely, one day, be selling magazines carrying great works by *him*. As for Hou Yong, his contentment with him went without saying. Only he had more self-respect than his wife, and he limited his visits to the in-laws to twice a year: once on October 1st* and once over Spring Festival.† Furthermore, he would never stay the night, nor even take a bath there. He always felt that there were certain privileges to which the mother-in-law was entitled, and that there was no need for him, the father-in-law, to try to cash in on them. As for Hou Ying, he was confident that a pretty good man could be found for her. Having just heard that Cai Bodu was working on an editor, he was in raptures. Merry from this and the wine, he murmured laughingly, "Wonderful! My eldest can write poems, the son-in-law will edit them, and I'll sell them—the whole family will be in the same line of business!"

In the back room, Hou Yong sat down on the bed in which Hou Ying had just slept. He had not been paying any attention to the conversation going on in the front room, when some words, spoken in his sister-in-law's penetrating voice, broke in on his consciousness: "The overpass at Dongdan—I've heard work could start on it next spring! Wouldn't that mean we'd all be relocated by the end of this autumn or winter?"

Oh, overpass! In his mind's eyes, Hou Yong immediately saw a bird's eye view such as he had seen in films—the overpass delineating beautiful lines and curves on Mother Earth, cars gliding freely to and fro. . . .

True, true! With the completion of the overpass—why, it need not even be completed—with work begun on it, and all the ancient hutong in the vicinity dismantled, what a very great effect it would have on the lives of all those families, including the Hous!

Upon relocation, the Hous would get at the very least a three-room apartment—that would be enough. Hou Rui and his wife and little Linlang could occupy one room, Father and Mother could occupy another, and when Hou Yong was home, Hou Ying could temporarily move in with Mother, while Father shared a room with Hou Yong. Wouldn't that be heaven? And when Hou Rui and his wife as well as Hou Yong were away, how spacious home would be! In all that space Hou Ying's nerves would surely recover, making it that much easier for her to get married. And what if Hou Yong and wife got their transfer back to Beijing? What then? Why, when Hou

* National Day.
† Lunar New Year.

Ying married, that would leave an extra room—perfect for them! And once the relocation was over, Hou Rui could switch his family's register away temporarily to facilitate Hou Yong's and his wife's transferral back. For in any event, they'd have gotten their beautiful apartment; no point in clinging to the old folks' register.

Oh, overpass! Hurry up and build the overpass! Or, if that could not be done for a while, at least hurry up and relocate! For the government and those who already lived in roomy dwellings and enjoyed plenty of space, this should not be too difficult.

With the overpass there would be no need for him to seek out Ge Youhan and engage in those shady dealings nor need he suffer from the stark contrast between his home and that of his in-laws. He would not be so brutal to his brother and sister. Even toward Er Zhuang there would be no natural barrier and hate. His soul would not feel so cramped, so withered and oppressed, so disgruntled and frustrated. . . .

Hou Yong just leaned there, dreaming. Theories, propaganda, sermons on virtue, enculturation, conferences, slogans, government circulars, spirit, democracy, bonuses . . . all these meant nothing to him. All I want is an overpass, he thought. Just give me an overpass!

The overpass signified the expansion of limited space to wide, open spaces; it signified the channeling of the crowded human stream into wider flows. It would mean more space for people, providing human relationships with more opportunities for seclusion, which was necessary. It therefore also meant solace for the countless anguished, stifled souls.

This evening, the Hous once again brought up this matter of the overpass. Yet they never realized that everytime they gathered, this theme would naturally crop up and override all other themes, becoming the chief topic of conversation for a long time.

This time it was Bai Shufen who brought up the overpass. She had heard it from an old college friend of hers who had later been transferred to the Municipal Construction Company. It therefore seemed to be on good authority. But in actual fact, it was still merely a rumor.

17*

All the talk about relocation and overpass construction drew Hou Yong out of the back room. Hou Yong's return to the front room delighted his father, and even elicited in him a certain feeling of gratitude toward his son for "bestowing the grace of his presence."

* Chapter 16 omitted.

Seeing her brother-in-law come out, Bai Shufen greeted him saying, "You three go ahead, eat and drink, and I and Mother and little Linlang will wait until you're done." Hou Yong muttered a vague "okay," but thought: So you think saying that proves you're a pious sister-in-law. You know very well it's only because the room is small and there's no space. Why, if this room were larger, and we could move the table away from the wall, I bet you'd join us.

Thinking in this vein, Hou Yong sat down facing the wall and started drinking with his father and brother.

Normally, this subject of the overpass was the one best able to make everyone forget their gripes. But as soon as he started to drink, Hou Yong remembered the telephone conversation he had just had. Ge Youhan was still waiting for him to go over. What for? To try and figure out a way to get back to Beijing. And what was the prerequisite? That his brother and his family transfer their register away, and that Hou Ying be married off! Overpass? Relocation? Just a dream! Reality was *here* and *now!* Having got this far, Hou Yong set his face, and answered in monosyllable to his father's questions.

"Come on, Lao Er, help yourself," the father said, as he would to some rare guest. Wreathed in smiles, he urged him, "Have some ribbon fish! Since she retired, the old woman has become quite a cook!" He picked up a piece of fish to serve into Hou Yong's bowl. Hou Yong picked up his bowl and jerked it away. The shock to his father made his chopsticks slip and a big central section of braised ribbon fish fell on the floor.

This scene angered Hou Rui intensely. His face burning red, he shouted at Hou Yong, "What's the matter with you? How can you be so ungracious?"

Happening on this scene, the mother hurried over to intervene, first saying to her husband, "That Lao Er is above eating such "scaleless" fish these days!" Turning to Hou Rui, she said, "Come on! It's not often the whole family gets together like this! Go easy on him!"

It was indeed very embarrassing for the father. He suddenly remembered the time when he had been an object of the dictatorship* at his unit. He was locked up in a cellar and asked to write a confession of his past crimes. Every day he would fill several pages of stationery with neat handwriting. After the writing, he would naturally think about something else. What he often thought about was the braised ribbon fish, as his wife used to make it. He thought of this

* The Chinese refer to their government as a dictatorship of the proletariat, which in Communist theory is a transitional state of socialism that creates the conditions for communism. An object of the dictatorship is an enemy of the working class who must constantly be watched and struggled against.

especially when the person on guard duty brought him his steamed corn bread and cabbage soup. He would recall most vividly the color, aroma, and taste—and even the shiny, crackling little bubbles that appeared on the fish sections when they were fresh out of the wok. Later, when his became a case of "policy realization," he was allowed to go home. As he came in the door, the first request he made to his wife was, "How about some ribbon fish for me?" The old woman went off with her basket and traipsed all the way from Dongdan to outside Hademen in her search, and finally succeeded in getting two catties.* When she got home she went straight to work preparing the fish for cooking. At that time, Hou Rui was not home, and Hou Ying was still not back from the construction brigade. Only Hou Yong was back on leave from the countryside, where he had been sent to join a rural team. He had literally leaped on the fish! Of that big dish, he had gobbled down two-thirds—he could see it still, clear as the day it happened! But now Hou Yong had married into the "high and mighty," and would not deign to touch such "scaleless" fish! The father could hardly bear it. His eyes turned red and his nose throbbed. He sighed, raised his head, and drained the best part of his glass of ergu.†

His father's reaction made Hou Yong feel some qualms, which he covered up by saying, "On the plane I felt a bit sick. I seem to feel even worse now. I just want something bland." He picked up a mouthful of cucumber salad with his chopsticks and then had another drink.

Seeing Hou Yong back down of his own accord, Hou Rui merely glared at him, but said nothing, and kept drinking. By now, the room had turned extremely quiet.

Hou Yong drank a little more, then rose and announced, "I have to go out—got some business. I won't eat at home—you all go ahead without me."

The parents could only look at him, and ask with their eyes, "Where are you going?" They dared not say it. Naturally, Hou Rui was not one to be silent. He craned his neck and asked, "Where are you going at this time of night?"

Hou Yong glanced at his watch: it was already 8:05. He had no time for an argument; he was afraid if he was late, he would miss Ge Youhan. You never knew when he'd be in. So he just said to Hou Rui quite amicably, "I have to go down to Bei Xin Quiao on business.

* A catty is a unit of weight varying around 1⅓ pounds or 600 grams.
† An extremely powerful spirit made from grain.

The person's at home evenings—it's easier to talk to him when he's at home than when he's at work." He set about to leave.

Unexpectedly, it was Bai Shufen, his sister-in-law, who kept him with a question.

19*

"Xiao Yong, when will you be back?"

She had reason to ask, for this concerned the night's sleeping arrangements for the whole family. This night was not the most populous—as Hou Ying would be going on night shift, there were just three males and three females. But among these six people, there were two types of relationship that should properly be kept apart—*i.e.*, father-in-law and daughter-in-law on the one hand, brother-in-law and sister-in-law on the other—and the one person caught in both relationships was Bai Shufen. When Bai Shufen had returned home with her daughter and heard that Hou Yong was back, she had immediately begun to consider the night's sleeping arrangements. Of course, all there was left to do was to go by "common denominators." As the back room had more bed space, it seemed natural that the men should sleep there, leaving her, her mother-in-law, and her daughter to sleep on the big bed in the front room. After the men had gone in, the door in between had to be locked before the women could undress and go to sleep. This arrangement was practical. But then Hou Yong announced he was going out when it was past 8 o'clock; and when he went out, he customarily stayed at least two or three hours. So it was qiute likely he would not be back until 11 o'clock or so. Thus, either the women had to stay up till he got back, or they would have to decide to let the women take the back room and the men, the front room. In the front room there was only the one big bed. The father and sons would have to sleep across it and rest their feet on chairs placed against the bed—that, of course, was not comfortable. When Bai Shufen called Hou Yong back, it was in the hope that he would announce either that he would not be back too late or that he would say, "You women can take the back room!"

Who would have known her words would be like a spark landing on dry firewood? For Hou Yong was feeling extremely irritable, with nowhere to vent his rage. Her words set him blazing.

Hou Yong had not been at all aware that behind her question was

* Chapter 18 omitted.

the question "What about tonight's sleeping arrangements?" He only saw it as a challenge to his dignity. In this household, his parents always showed him deference; his brother Hou Rui might display anger against him, but that in itself was a sign of impotence; as for Hou Ying, she hardly dared breathe before him. Only this sister-in-law of his did not wrangle with him or argue—in fact she was always quite courteous toward him. Yet from the expression in her eyes, and the faint smile about her lips (the smile he interpreted as derisive laughter), Hou Yong was deeply conscious of the contempt in which she held him. This university graduate knew of his ignorance, and was also aware that in actual fact such sons-in-law of "high-and-mighty families" were in an extremely awkward situation. Furthermore, she was not in the least afraid of his high-handedness.

Hou Yong turned toward Bai Shufen and answered viciously, "What business is it of yours when I'll be back?"

Bai Shufen would not back down an inch. With the sweetest expression, and without raising her voice one whit, she had him speechless. "If you're going to your in-laws, then of course it's none of my business. But if you're coming back here, then we need to discuss the night's sleeping arrangements."

Bai Shufen had stated the problem clearly, and this made Hou Yong all the more angry, it hurt his pride. What she had said implied that, though he had married into the high-cadredom, he had not been able to gain a rightful place in the space that the family occupied; it also implied that in this tiny space, he was not an absolute monarch—he still had to discuss things with others.

Hou Yong shook with anger and started shouting, "You sleep where you please, it's none of my business. And I come back whenever I please and sleep wherever I please, that's none of your business!"

The other four people in the room were immediately thrown into disarray. Little Linlang started to wail from fright: Hou Rui literally leaped from his chair. Glaring at his brother, he wanted to shout at him, but was temporarily at a loss as to what to shout. Hou Qinfeng gazed in helpless terror at brother- and sister-in-law poised for battle. The mother kept muttering, "How can you talk like that? How can you talk so?"

But Bai Shufen was quite unruffled. She was not even angry. She continued quite amiably, "As we're one family, living under the same roof, everyone's business is everyone else's business—it wouldn't do not to talk things over."

The cooler Bai Shufen was, the more barbarous Hou Yong became.

The muscles on his face twitching, he said recklessly, "*One* family indeed! This isn't *your* family! Get out of here!"

Before his words had faded from his lips, Hou Rui had rushed over to him, and, emboldened by the liquor he had drunk, gave Hou Yong a slap on the face. Hou Yong would not, of course, leave it at that. He immediately seized Hou Rui by the collar. The father dashed over to part the two brothers, and broke into an anxious sweat. In her heart, the mother blamed her daughter-in-law for provoking it all. She glared at Bai Shufen, stamping her foot, then looked at the father and sons—the three all in a bunch together—and sighed. Little Linlang was so frightened she grabbed her mother around the waist and started bawling even more loudly. Seeing things had come to such a pass, Bai Shufen felt that there was no need to hold back. She raised her voice slightly and said clearly but with no trace of rancor, "I've no reason to get out. Let me tell you: I married into this family, all right and proper. My register is here; this is my home, and I conduct myself properly. No one's going to kick me out!"

As they were arguing, Old Man Qian came in the door. As soon as he entered, he began to mediate loudly, "Here! What's this? Can't a family talk properly? Calm down!" Before entering he had heard them arguing inside. Hearing others in discord aroused in him an eagerness to interfere. At this moment, when he observed the faces full of anger, fear, discomfort, embarrassment, and harshness, his eagerness reached a zenith. First he half-shepherded, half-dragged Hou Qinfen over to a seat; then he dragged Hou Rui over to the bed and made him sit down; then he entreated the mother to sit down on the cane chair and calm down—all the while muttering something nobody could hear, or cared to hear. But when he came around to pacify Hou Yong and Bai Shufen, Hou Yong had already said venomously "You haven't heard the end of this!" With a stamp of his foot, he brushed aside the door curtain and left. Bai Shufen responded very quickly by raising her voice to carry beyond the door and saying with exaggerated courtesy, "I have nothing more to say to anyone so unreasonable!"

Hou Yong stomping off like that made Hou Qinfen feel most uncomfortable—all the liquor and fish rose from his stomach to his throat. He felt anxious, angry, embarrassed, and afraid. His aim in life was always to maintain a modest prosperity, with all the family together, living together cozily and peacefully. He hated airing dirty linen in public and more especially he hated airing it before the likes of Old Man Qian, whom he considered lowlier than himself. He was afraid Hou Yong, having gone out in a fury, would go and make trouble. He was even more afraid that he would return very late and seek to continue the argument. But he could not for the moment decide who was in the wrong. The daughter-in-law seemed not to have done anything wrong; one could not fault her for asking a question of her brother-in-law so that the family could sleep well. And it was natural enough for Hou Yong to be unhappy at being called back when he was in a rush to leave. Under the circumstances, there was nothing remarkable in his speaking a few angry words. And for Hou Rui to have struck his brother once, after seeing him speak so irreverently to his wife (and he did not strike him hard), and this having been done after he had been drinking—it seemed he could be forgiven. . . . No one had done anything terribly awful—they were all good people. So how was it they had gotten into such a predicament? He just sat there for a few seconds. Then, suddenly he stood up as though by instinct. And before Old Man Qian could say a word, he had rushed out the door after Hou Yong. In desperation, he had come up with a scheme. He wanted to catch up with Hou Yong and say to him, "I'll go and sleep in the post office—I'll do Old Zhang's night shift for him and let him go home. I'll tell him it's not an exchange, and when it's my turn again I'll do it. He's sure to agree! I'll tell them at home: Your brother and his wife and child can sleep with your mother in the back room. You can have the front room all to yourself! Only please don't be angry, please don't make a fuss!"

To sacrifice himself in exchange for peace in the family—that was Hou Qinfeng's tried-and-true method. Now he wanted to try it again.

But he ran all the way to the end of the alley and still caught no sign of Hou Yong. A breath of evening breeze blew on him, and his drunken eyes went bleary.

20

The two symmetrical clocks struck 9 o'clock. On the square before the station people were standing, sitting, reclining, or lying anywhere and everywhere. Other people stepped on either side or in between to avoid them. Among the crowd was Hou Rui. He had been wandering about there for over half an hour.

When the family battle adjourned temporarily with Hou Yong's retreat, Hou Rui had come here. At first, feeling the gentle evening breeze on his face, the cool fresh air in his nostrils, he felt relieved. Like a beetle that had been shut in a paper box and was allowed to fly out, he stretched his torso in relief. By the entrance to the subway he bought a bottle of the new "Shanghai Cola." Drinking it slowly through a straw, he thought back over the two clashes he had had with Hou Yong since he had gotten home that evening. He felt the disgrace was chiefly not his brother's but his own. He seemed to be sitting in front of a screen, forced to watch a video recording of himself over the past two hours. He—who had read a fair amount of the writings of the ancients and the moderns, Chinese and foreign, who prided himself on his appreciation of both Western symphonic music as well as the various styles of Chinese opera, who was forever harping on virtue and cultivation before his students—when faced with his brother's barbarity and incivility, could think of nothing better to do than bang the table and shout, glare, and hit. . . . Did this not show a shallowness and vulgarity?

A human being should at all times be mindful of his dignity. Yet how is it that to be so in this world is so very difficult? Hou Rui, smoking a cigarette, deliberately strolled over to the most crowded part of the square to pace out his quandary. There were two people with necks outstretched, bawling at each other as a crowd of people looked on. Why did it not occur to them that on this planet they all belonged to the same species, and in this land they were fellow countrymen. Furthermore, they were both on the road, and if they didn't get along, they could go their separate ways. So why did they have to keep squabbling over such trifling business? Why not maintain some vestige of manners? He did not squeeze in to look, but headed for where it was not quite so noisy. But where it was quieter it was even more crowded. He saw men and women who obviously came from remote little places. They just found any old nook, spread out their bedding roll and lay down. Why had they come to Beijing? Were they planning to catch the next train back? One was a woman who had obviously come a long way and was preparing to go back. She sat there, beside many pieces of luggage of all shapes and sizes. One was a stack of wooden washboards; there must have been at least ten of them. Why was it that this most primitive and easily made article could not be made where she came from, making it necessary to shop for them in Beijing and why had she to resort to so strenuous a means of transporting them? What has gone wrong with this country, that even wooden wash boards become valuable merchandise? Hou Rui saw a man who had for some reason decided not to stay at an inn for the night. Instead, he had rolled a large plastic sheet into a tube, tied up one end, then crawled inside to sleep, right under the eaves of the subway exit. He reminded Hou Rui of a snail. Hou Rui stood some ten paces away from him, and studied him for several minutes. So! The space an individual required could be reduced to that of his physical volume! Might it be that if every individual reduced his desire for living space to this degree, the society would turn correspondingly pure, and human relations would improve accordingly?

The chimes announcing that it was 9 o'clock brought Hou Rui back from his musings on mankind. He had to come back to his own family. Consequently his spirits dropped. He did not, after all, have the courage of those people at the station, who could simply sleep on the ground. No, he still had to go back and sleep in that confined, cramped home. Well, how should they sleep? Bai Shufen and his brother had had a row, but it had not solved this problem. Hou Yong was still a time bomb: if he came home late to discover sleeping arrangements of which he did not approve, he was quite capable of rousing everyone from their beds!

How had Hou Yong turned into such a brute? Just as Bai Shufen had turned so cold and aloof, and Hou Ying so petty, himself so vulgar and irascible. One very important factor was the lack of sufficient living space. But when people had sufficient living space—say, in the next century—when the country's economy was built up, other problems might arise in homes in which each member had his own room: people might become insincere, cold, and alienated from each other. Even so, it would be better than the present situation. We should not refuse to treat present ills and suffering simply because the next stage of development is not without blemish.

Hou Rui trudged home. When he turned into the ill-lit alleyway, he found himself thinking: You pathetic creature! When it comes to thinking about all mankind, you're a high-minded philosopher, but when faced with problems in the family, you turn into a totally ineffectual person! How can I shake off this petty, vulgar state of mind and be filled with confidence in life? Perhaps I should, after all, sink roots in the countryside and work untiringly for enlightenment.

22*

. . . Er Zhuang poked his head in the door and spoke to Hou Rui, but his eyes were fixed on Hou Ying, "Brother Hou, phone call for you! It's from Brother Cai!"

All four Hous present felt their hearts start pounding. Hou Rui rushed to answer.

* Chapter 21 omitted.

23

"Hello, Bodu! Where are you?"

"I'm downstairs, at their place—it's a public phone box."

"Well? Is he willing?"

"How shall I put it? Well, not exactly. . . ."

"Wh-what's this? What's wrong with our Xiao Ying?"

"I know, I know! I was saying to him myself, such a simple, kind girl as Xiao Ying—there are not many of them to be found these days."

"Wasn't he after a good wife and mother? Among girls of Xiao Ying's age, there are not many of that sort around Beijing these days!"

"He said Xiao Ying may make a good wife and mother, but he thought she was too ignorant, too lacking in the most rudimentary knowledge. . . ."

"How could he know that, after only half an hour or so?"

"Don't rush me! That's what I said. But he said she didn't even know where Hong Kong was. He said she'd seen a Hong Kong film, and liked it, but thought that Hong Kong was a city on Taiwan, ruled by the Nationalists. . . ."

"Is that what she said? Well, he should know that when Xiao Ying was at school, they didn't get taught geography. Same with Xiao Yong—he never had geography. . . ."

"But he felt that Xiao Ying was a little too ignorant, that they simply had no common interests. After all, he did not simply want a *maid*, who could do the washing and cooking. . . ."

"How could he say such a thing!"

"Don't be angry at him! Or, if you will, blame me! It's all my fault. I should have thought about it more carefully before getting her involved. What did Xiao Ying say? Was she willing?"

"Why ask that now?"

"I know. I'm sorry. I find that really I'm useless at this sort of thing. Please forgive me."

"All you can do is write plays! You're completely out of touch with reality!"

"True! Life is far more complex, far more subtle. I can't grasp it all! But don't be angry with me. I had planned to write to you at the school tomorrow to tell you. But that would have meant an extra couple of days of false hopes for Xiao Ying. She shouldn't be tortured that way. So, even though it's late, I decided to call you. It's a good thing you have a phone so close at hand! And Er Zhuang's no stranger. . . ."

"You should never have got her entangled so rashly!"

"I know! I *am* sorry! You must break it to her gently—don't get her too upset."

"What can I say? You break it to her! It's your doing!"

"One of these days I'll go over and visit you, I promise. And I'll have a good talk with Xiao Ying. Just tell her it's nothing to worry about. Brother Cai will look around for a younger one for her."

"But I couldn't say that. You know that our Xiao Ying has acted strangely a couple of times over these matters."

"So you must put it nicely to her. Don't tell her that he thinks her ignorant."

"But what should I say then? That he's pleased but just doesn't want to marry her?"

"Well, just say that on meeting her, the other party thought himself too much older—didn't want to ruin her youth, so. . . ."

"But supposing Xiao Ying says she doesn't care if he's old and doesn't care about ruining her youth—what do I say then?"

"Well, well—just blame it on me. Say that Brother Cai was a bit careless, and hadn't got it straight—that the man wanted someone over thirty."

"That won't do! If a younger one is willing, why would he refuse?"

"Well, you tell me then. What can one say?"

"I can only tell her the truth. It's good for her to know that she's ignorant. Maybe she'll force herself to do some reading."

"Well . . . I guess . . . okay. But put it nicely—don't hurt her pride."

"You're the one who's made her lose her pride. . . ."

Cai Bodu didn't respond.

"Oh, I'm just saying that out of frustration. Don't take it to heart!"

"I feel terrible. I had hoped to do you all a good turn, then what should happen but. . . ."

"That's all right. We should still be grateful. Don't stop trying."

"I haven't given up. After all this, I feel a special responsibility toward Xiao Ying."

"Aim lower in the future. Just find her a common sort of person—one who wouldn't require her to be so up on Hong Kong, just someone who'll live happily with her!"

"You're right. That would seem to be the right approach."

"I must thank you again. Thank you for the timely phone call!"

"This cursed call!"

"The later such phone calls are made, the worse it is."

"And apologize to your mother. Your father doesn't know yet, does he?"

"Of course he does! He was home a while ago. Now he's gone back to his workplace to do night shift. When he heard he was very happy. My parents are both crazy about you. They think you're our family's lucky charm."

"You must say a few words to them to redeem me. I'm no lucky charm, but I want to be of service to all these good, kind people of your family."

"Bodu, you've touched me! Before I was blaming you. Now I've really forgiven you."

"But I haven't forgiven myself. I now feel a certain emptiness inside. I feel my plays, my fame, my intuition, are all worthless."

"Why? Don't think such a thing!"

"I can't help it. I feel that when I come up against real life itself, I'm ignorant, powerless, impotent!"

"Don't say that!"

"Well, let's leave it at that."

"Now, don't you be miserable! I'm not miserable, so why should you be?"

"Of course. We must brace ourselves and overcome misery. We must fight on bravely along the path to happiness."

25*

When Hou Rui got back after the phone call, Hou Ying was sitting in front of the mirror combing her hair. Because she knew it was time to set off for work, she was feeling flustered. She combed her hair hard. It kept her mind from running wild, so she kept combing.

When Hou Rui came in, the three people all looked at him. Hou Ying saw Hou Rui in the mirror. She only saw his profile, but she knew intuitively that she had blown it again. Her hands shook. The comb fell on the floor, but she just sat there, not bending down to pick it up.

The mother was still wrapped in her dreams of red brocades.† Eagerly she asked, "Well? Where will they meet next? When?"

Bai Shufen had already guessed what had happened from Hou Rui's look. She stood behind her brother-in-law, making signals at Hou Rui with her eyes, but she did not succeed in preventing him

---

* Chapter 24 omitted.
† What women marry in.

from coming out with the truth. Hou Rui felt that the sooner he dispelled his mother's and sister's illusions, the better. That way they could all calm down, think about it, and look realistically for a solution. He walked over to the table and sat down, saying in cruel tones, "There will be no more meetings! The man says Xiao Ying's too ignorant—doesn't even know what kind of a place Hong Kong is! Hong Kong is joined to Guangdong province. They still have a governor sent there from Britain; but Xiao Ying thought it was in Taiwan, ruled by the Nationalists. Just this, for one, he couldn't take. The fellow's a literary editor at a publishing house—he wanted someone he could talk to. How could he have someone who doesn't even know a simple geographical fact?"

The mother could not follow Hou Rui's logic. All she knew was that Xiao Ying had once again not been chosen. In her utter despair, she dropped down on the big bed, and started to mutter—one couldn't be sure whether it was against some editor or Xiao Ying—"Courting is courting! What has it got to do with Hong Kong? There's no connection! What's he going on about?"

Bai Shufen was on the point of comforting her mother-in-law when, suddenly, Hou Ying went into the back room. She followed her in. Inside, the television was still on, but little Linlang had dropped off to sleep. Bai Shufen switched it off and turned on the light. There was Hou Ying sitting perfectly still on the small bed, not a ghost of an expression on her face.

Bai Shufen sat down beside her and reached out for her hand. She found that her hands were icy cold. Rubbing them in her own, she comforted her: "Never mind, Xiao Ying, it's nothing. The man's too old, anyway. Even if he had agreed, we would have had to think twice. You're not old yet—there will be plenty of chances in the future."

While she was saying this, the mother came in. Seeing the dumb look on Hou Ying's face—with her mouth half agape and a glazed look in her eyes—her mother felt a surge of resentment in her breast. She immediately started muttering, "Just look at you! It's no wonder he didn't want you. As for that stuff about Hong Kong, I don't believe it had anything to do with it! It's that dead-fish look of yours! Can't you be lively? How many times have I told you, and you still look like a washboard! Who would go for such a girl?

Bai Shufen, with her arms around Hou Ying's shoulder, begged her mother-in-law, "Please, Mother, don't say that. Xiao Ying is feeling bad enough as it is. Don't let's make it any worse."

The mother sighed a long sigh. Then she suddenly remembered: it was time Hou Ying set off for the night shift. If she did not get going, she would be sure to be late. So she nagged her, "Come on, I won't keep after you. Just hurry along and don't be late, or they will take away your bonus. We've suffered quite enough as it is. Can't lose the bonus as well!"

Hou Ying had been sitting vacuously. When she heard this, suddenly the tears rolled down. But she did not cry—did not even snivel. She just let the big tear drops roll down her cheeks, and did not wipe them away. Seeing her like this, Bai Shufen, through some complex association, felt a funny feeling in her nose, and tears welled up in her eyes.

Seeing the pair of them like this made the mother even more annoyed. She also had a vague, superstitious feeling that this scene was a sign of an ill omen. How come today had turned out so miserable? Was nothing going right? Not a single thing happened in this room that was happy! Out of her feeling of frustration, she raised her voice and started to shout, "Xiao Ying! Go off to work! First you can't catch yourself a husband, then you want to throw away the bonus! Shufen, you too! What are you up to, making trouble? Do you see what time it is? Hurry up and help your sister-in-law hurry off to work!"

Hou Rui walked into the back room. He was regretting a bit what he had done a little while back. He urged his mother, saying, "Look, Mother, Xiao Ying is feeling pretty bad. Let her off work for once. It may be that Er Zhuang is still up. I'll go and call her factory."

Bai Shufen chimed in too, "I agree. Don't make her go to work. She can sleep on the lower bunk with me, and I can make her come around."

The mother suddenly became obstinate and angry. She complained loudly, "It's all very fine for you. If you don't want to work, you don't go to work. I'm the mother, but, for all the notice you take of what I say, I could be farting. No wonder you're always going on about me behind my back! Why do I carry on, if it's not for your good? I run around all day long for you for nothing!" The words made her sad; she wiped her tears on the front of her jacket.

Seeing all the other occupants of the room so tearful made Hou Rui feel bad. Oh, dear! Why, in this crowded room, was so much misery crammed in?

Hou Rui was just about to say something to pacify all three at once, when suddenly, before anyone could say a word, Hou Ying leaped up. Bai Shufen could not hold her back; Hou Rui did not block her. She flew to the front room and dove under the table.

When Hou Rui, Bai Shufen, and the mother rushed to the front room and saw this, they were all struck dumb.

Hou Ying had gone mad! It hit them like a bullet in the heart, and they felt a confusing mixture of emotions.

27*

"Xiao Ying! Come out of there! Come on!"

Hou Rui just had to go over and tug at Hou Ying—she could hardly be left under the table! But as soon as he had dragged her out, she started howling. And as she howled, she kept pounding her brother on the chest. If he tried to hold her, she would struggle like mad. This scene scared the mother out of her wits. She was filled with vain regret. She should not have been after her so ruthlessly to go to work.

Seeing Hou Ying go crazy made Bai Shufen become cool and collected. Sorrowful thoughts about her own sad fate, which had resonated in her heart, vanished utterly. She clasped Hou Ying tightly and tried to drag her to the bed, thinking to calm her down there. But when she was only half way, Hou Ying suddenly broke loose, and, wailing loudly, started pounding her shoulders with her fists. Her fists were like rocks; Bai Shufen kept crying out from the pain. All this furor in the front room made little Linlang wake up from fright. She immediately started to cry.

In the midst of this confusion, Er Zhuang dashed in. After a glance, he unhesitatingly walked up, and with his two big strong hands grasped Hou Ying by her wrists and stopped her pounding. At first, Hou Ying still struggled, but Er Zhuang was so strong he eventually held her fists still. After that, she suddenly stopped wailing, and gazed fixedly at Er Zhuang. Er Zhuang, in turn, gazed fixedly at her. She held her gaze for a few seconds, then suddenly her eyes rolled, a string of pearl-like teardrops rolled down, and her body turned limp and started to sway. When Er Zhuang let go of her wrists; she collapsed against his body.

From the time Er Zhuang rushed in, the whole scene lasted only a few seconds. The mother's initial reaction was one of extreme aversion. She was on the point of screaming, "Get out! We don't need you!" But when Er Zhuang had calmed Hou Ying down, and she had stopped wailing, the mother could only be thankful for this turn of events, and from her heart she had uttered, "It's a good thing he's

---

* Chapter 26 omitted.

strong!" Then when Hou Ying collapsed onto Er Zhuang, the mother got anxious again, and wanted Er Zhuang to get out of the way.

But Er Zhuang had not taken any notice of the reaction of the people around him. When he had held fast Hou Ying's wrists and gazed intently into her face, boundless love was born in his heart. Hou Ying's face was a mess—matted down by cold sweat to her parchmentlike brows and face. Hou Ying's eyes were glazed, but from her pupils he thought it was possible to detect a piteous expression. When she had collapsed onto his body, he felt as though he had been electrified, dealt a shock both agonizing and sweet. He felt he was going to swoon himself. At the same time, he felt this was a most precious, happy moment.

Er Zhuang very quickly recovered his wits, and before the others had time to react, he grabbed Hou Ying around the waist, carried her over to the big bed, and set her down. He then grabbed a pillow, which he put under her head, leaned over, and tried to revive her.* Hou Ying moaned. She rolled her head a few times on the pillow and opened and shut her eyes while the tears flowed incessantly.

"Good. She's out of danger." These words were the first that Er Zhuang uttered.

"Thank you, Er Zhuang!" Hou Rui declared.

"Won't you sit down, Er Zhuang?" Bai Shufen offered.

The mother said nothing. She sat down on the edge of the bed, took one of Hou Ying's hands in her own, and, overcome by sadness, started weeping softly.

"Please, Ma'am, don't go on so. If you do, you might set Xiao Yingzi† off again," Er Zhuang cautioned her.

At this, the mother held back her tears, and nodded at him to show her appreciation of his good intentions. . . .

28

Late summer and early autumn nights in Beijing are most unpredictable. It may be oppressive, yet the next morning may be damp and chilly. Or it may be quite cool, only to be followed by the return of summer heat and an unpleasantly hot day.

Hou Yong's emotions were just like such Beijing nights. When he came out of Ge Youhan's and felt the evening breeze on his face, he felt sick. The physical sick feeling brought on a mental and emotional sick feeling.

---

* By pressing the acupuncture point between the nostrils and the upper lip.
† Er Zhuang uses a different—more vulgar, country-sounding—diminutive.

What had Ge Youhan taught him? Regaling himself with liquor from Luzhou and jellyfish salad, Ge Youhan, with his gleaming, oily face, had counseled him, "Well, if Yingzi can't be married off right away, that's okay too. Look, you could take her along to Anding Hospital to get some medicine. . . . Go a few times, and all the neighbors will know about it, and everyone will agree she's got that sickness. That settled, it would be possible to get a certificate proving that she cannot look after the old folk, and you have to come back to look after them. When you're back, you can work on her, get her some good medicine, and she'll be cured. Then she can carry on with this business of getting married. All you can think of is marrying her off. Now suppose she marries someone in your hutong? Or someone in Dongdan? Even supposing she got married off to that guy Cai Bodu introduced, and settled down in Chongwenmen—that's only one bus stop away, after all. They'll say that she doesn't live too far away, and can take care of the old folk. Then you won't get your certificate. I tell you, if you want to succeed, you must first of all be shameless, and secondly be hard-hearted. If you can't harden your heart, you won't get anywhere. If you don't like what I'm saying, just pretend I never said it!"

True, he did not like what he said. When Hou Yong, walking along the pavement leading from Chongwenmen to Dongdan, recalled what Ge Youhan had said, he felt nauseous. But he had said it, and he had heard it, and it was as though it had been burned into his brain. How could he pretend he had not said it?

Perhaps these words of Ge Youhan's were not all that vicious. After all, the way Xiao Ying carried on—wasn't that hysteria? Well, that was a mental illness. So she ought to go to Anding Hospital and have it seen to. And if she had this hysteria, she would indeed be unable to take care of the folks!

But why did they not embark on a large housing project? Hou Yong wondered. No money? Where had all the money gone? No workers? Which hutong did not shelter hundreds of unemployed youth! No materials? If homes were what you wanted, there were no materials you couldn't get! You don't build, and people are not satisfied being crammed together any old way. So they have to try, by hook or by crook, to squeeze others aside, and expand their own living quarters.

Well, there was the Dongdan intersection before him. It was 10 o'clock, and at last there were no more traffic jams. But it still needed traffic lights to regulate the flow of vehicles; the vehicles still had to stop and start. It seemed so awkward, so pathetic. He thought, Oh, overpass! When will you appear there? Oh, overpass! You've seduced my soul! I long for you madly. Maybe I've been smitten with "overpass-osis," and should go along to Anding Hospital too!

In such a frame of mind, Hou Yong reached home.

As soon as he entered, he saw Hou Ying on the big bed in her clothes for dating, lying half asleep, his mother and brother sitting glumly by the table, and Shufen sitting beside her on the bed, sticking a thermometer under her arm.

"What's happened?" Hou Yong asked, feeling surprised and delighted, plotting confusedly in his mind. He had never imagined that an opportunity would arise so soon—that it would be so easy, so natural, to put Ge Youhan's plan into effect. Before he had even heard out his mother's sad, rambling account, he had knit his brows, struck an imposing, serious pose, and begun to reproach his mother, brother, and sister-in-law: "What's come over you? You just sit there, doing useless things. . . . Hurry up and get Xiao Ying off to an emergency clinic!"

"But look at the time . . . go now?" The mother felt spasms in her breast. What she really wanted to say was: "What kind of illness do you call this? Madness? We can't take her to a hospital clinic for that! If it got about, not only would Xiao Ying have trouble meeting people, it wouldn't look good for me, as her mother. . . ."

"It's merely that Xiao Ying has had a bit of a shock. It's her nerves," Hou Rui added. "I just called her factory and asked for sick leave for her. I said she had a headache. All she needs is a good sleep and plenty of rest—she'll recover."

"This is no mere trifling complaint. If she's ill, she should be treated. It doesn't make sense to avoid the doctor just because you don't like the illness," Hou Yong said, all proper and benign. "If you leave it, it could get worse. Then what will you do?"

"Xiao Ying hasn't got a temperature." Bai Shufen had taken out the thermometer from under Hou Ying's arm and was studying it under the fluorescent lamp. "Thirty-six point eight degrees centigrade—normal."

"What she's got doesn't necessarily involve temperatures." Hou Yong did not look at Bai Shufen. He still remembered their argument of two hours before. He spoke only to Hou Rui. "Sometimes an illness without a temperature can be worse than one *with* a temperature."

"But with no temperature they won't take her in the emergency clinic," Hou Rui said. "Let her sleep tonight. We'll take her to Tongren Hospital tomorrow."

"Tongren's no good for her kind of illness!" Hou Yong insisted. "Nor are Beijing Hospital and Xiehe Hospital any good." Tongren, Beijing, and Xiehe hospitals were all quite close to their home. Mother, Hou Rui, and Bai Shufen had all thought he was suggesting they take Hou Ying to these hospitals.

"No, for this kind of illness, only Anding will do." Hou Yong at last came out with the crucial words. "At Anding Hospital there's always an emergency clinic, and they don't ask whether you have a temperature or not."

"Anding Hospital!" To the mother, the sound of the words was like a hammerblow to the head. It was common knowledge that Anding Hospital was a mental hospital! A young woman who had once entered the portals of Anding, even if she were a beauty, and had come out without the slightest taint, would find it next to impossible to find a marriage partner. Who would ever want to go near the place!

"Anding Hospital?" Hou Rui was also startled. Except for a fleeting moment when it had occurred to him, after seeing Hou Yong dive under the table, that his sister had really gone mad, when he was calm he consistently believed that it had merely been a case of "nerves." But then wasn't "nerves" simply an early stage of mental illness?

"No need to go to Anding Hospital," Bai Shufen pronounced with clarity. Looking straight at Hou Yong, she said, "We cannot send her there so lightly."

"You're not a Hou—we don't need you to interfere." Hou Yong stared back at Bai Shufen, holding her gaze. He felt that just now his heart was about as hard as a stone.

These words destroyed Bai Shufen's self-esteem. Quite true. Why should she bother to get so deeply involved in the Hou family's affairs? Hou Ying was indeed acting a bit abnormal. So why should she stop the Hous from taking her to a mental hospital? In anger, she went to the back room. Little Linlang was there fast asleep. She nestled close to her, hugging her. In a fit of sadness, tears welled up in her eyes. Well, little Linlang took the surname Bai after her. At least she could concern herself with the life of this Bai, could she not?

Just then, Hou Ying woke up with a start. She sat up, her eyes half open, looking before her. She muttered incoherently, "Don't go! No, don't go! I . . . I'm frightened. . . ."

At this, both Hou Yong and his mother lost their heads. They felt that Hou Yong's suggestion was quite right after all. Besides, Hou

Yong was so serious, so conscientious, so firm. After all, he was her brother. Would he do anything to hurt her?

So it was decided—they would take her to Anding Hospital right away. Hou Yong would go and knock on Er Zhuang's door to use the phone to call a taxi.

As Hou Yong walked out the door and headed for Er Zhuang's dark room, his heart suddenly softened. Hou Ying had indeed gone mad—that was painfully clear. It was not at all what he really wished for. He thought of what used to go on under the square table. He gazed at the starry sky, the sky that was confined by so many roofs crowding around: it was merely the underside of a somewhat larger table. What drinks should he sell under this starry table top? And who would buy his drinks for candy wrappers? Why was it that one's childhood invariably flashed by? And why was it that, once grown up, one had to hustle for food, clothing, housing, and travel? Why was it that practically no one wanted to stay where things were hard, and all wanted to transfer to where it was nice? Why was it that even if one *wanted* to stay where things were hard, in order to build up the country, one could so easily be deprived of one's high, pure, and beautiful ideals by people like Ge Youhan, and the injustice they represented? And, having lost their ideals, why was it such people would often go and rely precisely on the Ge Youhan types for petty, personal gains? And when one realized that one was after petty, personal gains, why was it that one was nonetheless unable to refrain? Or, if one could, why was it that one was laughed at not by a few, but by many? How long had this been going on? And why was it that, though this state of affairs was well known to all, from talking and writing about it in public, no one wanted to, or dared to, acknowledge it? Even in the works of sincere writers like Cai Bodu, the matter was merely touched on lightly, or skirted altogether.

It was only some twenty or thirty steps from the Hous to the Qians, but for Hou Yong, every step was a battle—so painful, so difficult.

At last he was there. He knocked just once and the light came on inside. By the second knock, the door was open. Er Zhuang did not look as if he had just got out of bed. He looked at Hou Yong with bright eyes.

"We've got to get Xiao Ying to the hospital. I've come to call for a taxi."

"Why go by car? Not to mention the expense. There's no saying whether they have a car in; it could be some time before they get here."

"Then . . ."

"I'll ride her there in the pedicart.* Our house repair team's warehouse is just down the hutong. There's someone on duty. I'll be around at the gate in ten minutes. You go and get the bedding ready."

Hou Yong nodded. He turned away. At this moment, though his heart was encrusted in a shell, inside it was soft as egg white and egg yoke. Fresh egg white and egg yoke, when it is inside the shell and has not been damaged, stands a chance of hatching into a new life.

Epilogue

At 10:47 that night, the telephone rang at a certain post office in town. Hou Qinfeng, who was sitting up on a bed reading "Travel/ Tourism" magazine, jumped up and answered the phone. It was Hou Rui. He told his father Hou Ying was ill—and not with any common illness—she had to be taken to Anding Hospital. The magazine fell out of Hou Qinfen's hands. His heart was broken, yet he could not leave the post office, as he was the only one on duty. What could he say? He could only reply shakily, "As soon as someone comes in the morning, I'll go home—no, I'll go straight to the hospital. . . ." He put down the phone and went into a daze. He was not aware that he had stepped on the magazine. Sitting on the bed, he took out his handkerchief to rub his eyes. Later, he started to weep softly. On a late summer's night in Beijing, who was there to comfort this old man? Who would be kind to him?

At 10:48, a flat-back tricycle was tearing down the street away from Dongdan Crossroads. Qian Er Zhuang, the cyclist, swung his wide, strong shoulders back and forth as he rode. The tricycle carrier was lined with a cotton quilt. On it lay Hou Ying, her head resting on a pillow, her body covered with a quilt pulled right up to her nose. Her eyes open, she gazed at the dancing stars in the heavens, and, beneath this starry sky, the trolley bus cables crisscrossing overhead from time to time. On one side of the tricycle sat her mother. She reached one hand in under the quilt to grasp one of her daughter's. Her daughter's hand was soft and warm. Her daughter's eyes made her surprised and slightly suspicious. They now seemed so clear and bright. Was she ill or not? The mother sighed, feeling suspicious and worried; she did not want to think about tomorrow.

Behind the tricycle, Hou Rui and Hou Yong cycled abreast. They both looked ahead and neither spoke.

* Not a pedicab. This tricycle is designed to carry freight, not passengers. It has a large, flat platform behind the cyclist's seat.

As they rode away from Dongdan, Hou Rui started thinking wildly. First he thought of Bai Shufen and little Linlang who had stayed at home. How strange that tonight, for the first time, they should have sole enjoyment of all their family's space—averaging more than seven and a half square meters each. In this sprawling capital city, how many people enjoyed more than seven and a half square meters of living space? And for how many families were there only three square meters, or even two square meters, for each member? It would seem that too much space or too little space both lead to distortion of the spirit. Then how much space was just right for a person? People could not live their whole lives indoors—they had to go out into the street and move around. The streets were the city dwellers' common space. Changan Boulevard was an expression of the spirit of the People's Republic when it first arose. It seemed to announce with its straight and wide expanse: if you want to know our society's future, only look at my proud form! Yet thirty years had gone by, and the streets running north and south off Changan Boulevard, especially the street running north of Dongdan, had for the most part retained their dilapidated appearance. Compared with the traffic flow along this street thirty years ago, the flow of bicycle traffic had increased by many orders of magnitude. So was it any wonder that people were often jammed along this narrow thoroughfare and that they should become angry and rough, develop frictions and clash? Oh, overpass, Hou Rui thought, when will you appear? The overpass at Jianguomen two bus stops away had been under construction for five or six years now, and it was still not completely finished to this very day! My beloved Beijing—why is it so very hard for you to transform your decrepitude? And while *you* remain unchanged, how can one prevent the dwellers in your thousands of ancient *hutong*—the blood coursing through your ancient body—from becoming mean, shallow, and selfish?

The group cycled past "Dahua"* Cinema. This theater looked basically the same as it had decades ago, when it had been called "Guanglu."† All the faces on the posters posted around the theater entrance seemed to look askance at the caravan cycling past. And Hou Rui, gazing at the faces on the posters, began to think all the more. They came to the east end of Dengshikou, where they had to turn. Ah! There on either side of the road, building was going on. Though it was close to 11 at night, the arms of the giant crane still

* "Great China" Cinema.
† "Bright Land" Cinema.

moved to the directions of the whistle, and the cement mixers rumbled on. This scene sent a warm feeling through Hou Rui's troubled heart. Though such scenes were still not common around the city and though these buildings might not be destined for the use of common citizens such as themselves, housing construction *was* going on. Oh, hurry up! Tear down the old houses in Beijing City and put up new buildings! Remodel the streets! Build a whole series of overpasses, with parks and fountains at the intersections. In this silent night, the public servants who could plan, direct, and realize all these—were they sleeping without a care in the world? Or were they caring and toiling for the common city dweller? When a new morning was about to dawn, would they keep on arguing back and forth over trifles, or would they work wisely and diligently? If they only knew all the joys and woes of this little family! It was a common drop of water, and seemed perfectly ordinary to the naked eye. Yet studied under the microscope and analyzed, it might yield important discoveries!

At this moment, Hou Yong—quite unlike his brother—was feeling quite empty inside, as though something was missing that he could not replace. He did not know whether to be glad or worried. He suddenly felt he was quite comical. Why could he not settle down in Shanxi? And why had he not gone to his father-in-law's for the night, or even phoned them? It would obviously be forever before the overpass appeared. So how survive the morrow? What was the next step? Oh, Hou Yong! He had still not realized that to become pure and free he must first build an overpass in his heart.

It was 11 o'clock. The tricycle drove past Capital Theater, and Qian Er Zhuang, peddling with all his might, was filled with an unusual feeling of joy and happiness. He could see how scared Auntie Hou and the others were of Anding Hospital. They were sure to think that once Hou Ying had been there, she'd be even less desirable. Those stuffy, rotten people—it was they who had done her in. If they didn't want her, all the better. Er Zhuang was more confident than ever. He rode the tricycle as though it had wings. As it whizzed past the art gallery, he turned his head around and said to the mother loudly, "Don't worry, Auntie! You've still got me!"

Hearing this, the mother felt a sudden warmth. She could not help looking up at Er Zhuang's smooth, strong back, and in her heart there burgeoned forth a little sprout that hitherto had been unable to break through the pod.

Hou Ying, as she lay there, heard Er Zhuang's words perfectly. She was now wide awake, feeling very good and very healthy. She had no temperature, no headache, no nausea or discomfort. She knew where they were taking her. She knew it was completely unnecessary, yet she had no fear and no regrets. She now felt it was silly to be for-ever thinking of Li Wei. Why should she want Li Wei to wait for her? Why should she fear the living? It was so nice to be alive, to be breathing this pure cool air, to gaze at this beautiful starry sky, and to feel that near her was a strong, dependable back, and a perfectly ordinary, yet very dear heart pounding away. For the first time she realized that happiness was not far away; it had long lain hidden nearby, and it had long lain hidden in her heart.

Hou Ying smiled contentedly.

Abridged from *Shiyue* (*October*)
February, 1981
Translated by Michael Crook

III. Love

Indulging in feelings of romantic love has been considered an improper, or at least suspect, use of one's time in socialist China: one's energies are better spent contributing to the collective goal. The fact that many of the New Realism writers have chosen to write about romantic love is in itself a protest. Ever since the Yanan Forum on Literature and Art in 1942, at which Mao issued guidelines on the proper themes for literature in a revolutionary society, writing about romantic love has been taboo.

Zhang Jie's "Love Cannot Be Forgotten," condemned as "immoral" and "maudlin" by official critics in China, describes a chaste romantic relationship between two cadres who are married to others. In this story, true love is in conflict not only with prevailing social mores, but with political obligation: the man who is loved by the "heroine" has married his wife out of a sense of political duty and "class concern." "Love Cannot Be Forgotten" seems to be asking the question: in China's socialist society, are individual emotions incompatible with political duty?

On another level, however, some Chinese readers interpret the story's remarks about love and marriage metaphorically as comments on the nature of political commitment. When, for example, the narrator worries that law and moral obligation may be all that will bind her to her husband once she marries her handsome but not too intelligent boyfriend, these readers claim that the author is warning that infatuation with beautiful political ideals may lead to a loveless marriage to a political system.

In Zhang Xian's "The Corner Forsaken by Love," which has been made into a movie in China, physical love between two unmarried young people is cruelly punished by the commune members, whose traditional views on morality are reinforced by a political system that sees such blatant self-gratification as immoral in a society committed to the collective goal.

Although its theme is love, the story is primarily a comment on the material and spiritual impoverishment of rural life—an indictment of a revolution that, in the eyes of the author, has not only not substantially improved the lives of China's peasant masses, but has often added to their burden. Far from sweeping aside feudal morality, the revolutionary society depicted in "The Corner Forsaken By Love" has fused it with a new, state-enforced socialist puritanism; instead of eradicating poverty, it has enacted policies that have sometimes resulted in even more hardship in the rural areas.

The love poem that ends the chapter, Shu Ting's "Longing," may seem rather tame to Western readers, who are used to much stronger expressions of private emotion in their literature. In socialist China, however, where the expression of inner emotion is viewed as a form of bourgois individualism, which undermines the collective spirit, the poem is quite daring in its validation of the existence and worth of inner feeling. Critics in China have attacked Shu Ting's writings for being "self-centered," "individualistic," and "too melancholy."

Love Cannot Be Forgotten
ZHANG JIE

The Republic and I are the same age. For a republic, thirty years old is too young. But for a woman, it may be too late to get married.

Nevertheless, I do have a serious suitor. Have you seen the statue "The Discus Thrower" by the great Greek sculptor Myron? Qiao Lin's body is almost an exact replica of that sculpture. Even in winter, his bulky quilted jacket cannot hide the beautiful lines of his body. His face is dark. The lines of his nose and mouth are rugged. He has long, narrow eyes under a broad forehead. By just looking at his face and body, most women would like him.

Yet, it is I who cannot make up my mind whether to marry him or not. Is it because I am not certain what I love him for, or what he loves me for?

I know there are already people who gossip behind my back: "Given her own qualifications, what does she expect?"

In their eyes, I am nothing but a poor sort of creature, trying every trick to lure the "foe" into offering favorable terms. This makes them angry, as if I have done something really immoral and offensive.

Of course, I can't ask too much of them. In a society where commodity production still exists, marriage, like many other problems, cannot avoid being branded as a type of commodity exchange.

Qiao Lin and I have been together almost two years, but I still haven't figured out his habit of silence. Is it that he doesn't like to talk, or does he just have nothing to say? Every time I plan to test him on his intelligence by insisting that he give me his opinion on some issue, he can only use kindergarten words: "good" or "not good"—just these two categories. He never seems to change his pattern.

When I ask him, "Qiao Lin, why do you love me?" he thinks seriously for a long while. Judging from the rare appearance of wrinkles on his broad forehead, I know that the network of cells in his beautiful skull must be carrying on nervous thinking activity. I can't help feeling pity and sympathy for him, for it is as if I have posed this question to make it deliberately difficult for him.

Then he lifts up that pair of clear, childlike eyes and says to me, "Because you are nice!"

A deep loneliness fills my heart. "Thank you, Qiao Lin!"

I can't help wondering: when he becomes my husband, and I his wife, will we be able to shoulder the responsibilities and duties of wife and husband? Maybe we will be able to because the law and moral obligation will already have bound us tightly together. Yet how sad, if all we are doing is complying with the law and moral obligation. Is there nothing more solid or firm than this tying us together?

Whenever I have such thoughts, I get a strange feeling, as if I am not a woman who plans to get married, but an old scholar of sociology.

Maybe I don't have to think about it so much. We can go and live like most families: bear children, be together, be absolutely faithful and sincere as prescribed by law. . . . Though society has entered the seventies of the twentieth century on this point, it does no harm to do what human beings have done for several thousand years—consider marriage an instrument for continuing families and generations, a kind of exchange, a buying and selling. Marriage and love can be separated. Since so many people have lived through the experience, why on earth is it that I alone can't?

No, I still can't make up my mind. I remember when I was young, I always cried for no reason, disturbing not only my own sleep but waking up the whole family as well. My old nurse, who did not have much education, but who did have strong opinions, used to say that "ill winds" had "entered my ears." I feel this prophetic observation probably had a grain of scientific truth to it. I am still the same; I always manage to take issue with some nonissue, disturbing not only my own peace but others' as well. I suppose this is what is called "an unchangeable disposition!"

I also think of my mother. If she were still alive, what would she have said about these views of mine, about Qiao Lin, about my accepting this proposal or not?

Though I constantly think of my mother, it is certainly not because she was a strict mother who even after having left this world would still use her spirit to dictate my destiny. No, she was not even a mother, but a very close friend. Maybe that is why—because I loved her so much—whenever I think of her having left me, I feel so sad.

She never lectured me. She only talked to me in her low, unfeminine voice, gently telling me about her experiences, letting me find what I needed from her mistakes and successes. However, her successes seemed few and far between; her whole life was marked by failures.

During her last days, she always followed me around with those fine, quick eyes of hers, as if she were measuring whether I had the ability to live on independently and, at the same time, as if there were something important she had to tell me, but couldn't. I bet it was my casual mood that made her anxious. She would suddenly break out with this sentence: "Shanshan, if you don't know exactly what you want, I think you are much better off staying single than getting married with no idea why."

In other people's eyes, such words from a mother to her daughter might seem heartless and unreasonable. Yet from my point of view, her words embodied the very painful experience of her past. I do not feel that her advising me thus was because she had slighted or underestimated my experience with life. She loved me, and hoped that my life would be free of troubles, that's all.

"Mother, I don't wish to marry!" I did not say this out of shyness or pretense. To tell the truth, I really don't know when a woman should show shyness or pretense. Everything people generally consider inappropriate to expose to children, Mother had already deliberately exposed me to.

"If you do meet the right person, you should marry. But only if he's the right person!"

"I'm afraid there is no 'Mr. Right!' "

"There is, but it's a bit difficult. The world is so large, I am worried you won't meet him!" She was not worried about whether I would get married or not. What she worried about was the real substance of the marriage.

"As a matter of fact, haven't you done well by yourself?"

"Who said that I've done well?"

"I feel you did."

"I cannot help being so. . . ." She stopped and fell into a reverie. A faint worried expression came over her. Her anxious, wrinkled face made me think of those dried flowers that I put between the pages of books.

"Why do you have to be like this?"

"You ask too many 'whys.'" She was avoiding me. Her heart must have been hiding feelings she didn't want to reveal. I know she didn't tell me, not because she was ashamed of revealing them to me, but most likely because she was afraid that I would have distorted them by not being able to estimate their depth accurately; it might also have been because there is always something we cherish inside and take with us to our graves. When I came to this thought, I felt uneasy. The uneasiness forced me to pursue the subject crudely: "Is it because you still love Father?"

"No, I never loved him!"

"Did he love you?"

"No, he didn't love me either!"

"Then why did you marry each other in the first place?"

She hesitated for a moment, obviously searching for more precise words to clarify this perplexing, contrary phenomenon. Then, with immense remorse, she said to me: "When one is young, one does not always understand what one is pursuing or what one needs. A marriage can be made just by other people's clamor. When you grow older and more mature, then you understand what you truly want. But by that time, you have already done many foolish things that make your heart ache with regret. You would pay any price in order to live your life over again. Then you would be smarter. People say, 'The contented are always happy,' yet I have never enjoyed this happiness." As she said this, she gave a slight, self-mocking smile. "I can only be a miserable idealist."

Haven't I inherited the problem of an "ill wind entering the ears" from her? Probably in our cells there is a special gene that is responsible for this inherited problem.

"Why didn't you remarry?"

Reluctantly, she said, "I'm afraid I still don't know what I really want." Clearly, she didn't want to tell me the truth.

I don't remember my father. My mother and he split up when I was very young. All I remember is that once Mother told me shyly that he was a very handsome, stylish fellow. I understand; she must have felt ashamed for having pursued such superficial, meaningless things. She once said to me: "When I can't sleep at night, I often force myself to think back on the foolish, mistaken things I did in my youth with the intention of making myself conscious of them. Of course, it's not at all pleasant. Often, full of shame, I cover my face with the sheets, as if, even in the dark, there were people staring at me. Still, there is somehow a kind of pleasure in this unpleasant feeling, as if one's crime has been redeemed."

I feel sorry that she never remarried. She was an interesting person. If she had married someone she loved, she would no doubt have had a very interesting family. Though she was not very pretty, she was graceful and spare, like a landscape painting in light ink. She also wrote beautifully. A writer who knew her well used to kid her, "People have fallen in love with you simply from reading your works!"

Mother would say, "If they knew that the person they loved was nothing but a white-haired, wrinkled old granny, they would be scared off."

At that age, she could not possibly not have known what she really wanted. This was obviously an evasion. The reason I say this is because she had strange idiosyncrasies that aroused my suspicion.

For example, no matter where she went on an assignment, she had to carry with her one of the twenty-seven volumes of Chekhov's selected works published between 1950 and 1955. She would say over and over to me: "Do not ever touch these volumes of mine. If you want to read, read the ones I bought you." It was obviously unnecessary for her to say this. I had my own, why would I wish to touch hers? Moreover, she repeated the same instructions countless times. Yet she was always afraid of that one chance in a million. She loved those volumes as if she was possessed.

Our house had two sets of the selected works of Chekhov. Perhaps this showed that it was our family tradition to like Chekhov, but perhaps it had more to do with having to take care of me and other Chekhov lovers. Every time someone wanted to borrow the books to read, she would always give them the set from my room. One time, when she was not at home, a very close friend took one from her set. When she found out, she was extremely upset, and instantly took one of mine to exchange for her volume.

Ever since I can remember, that set has been kept in her bookcase. Though I admired the great Chekhov very much, I couldn't understand how it was that after over twenty years, he could still be so interesting that she felt the need to read a little from the set every day.

At times, when she was tired of writing, she would hold a cup of strong tea in her hands and sit opposite the bookcase gazing at the set, lost in thought. If I entered her room at that moment, she would appear startled and anxious and would either carelessly spill the tea all over herself or blush like a girl in love who had been discovered with her sweetheart on their first date.

Then I would think: Is she in love with Chekhov? If Chekhov were still alive, who can say whether such a thing could really happen?

When she was semi-conscious and just about to die, her last words to me were: "That set of books—" She did not have the strength to say the whole phrase, "That set of Chekhov's selected works." But I understood that that was what she meant. "And that notebook . . . the one on which is written, 'Love Cannot Be Forgotten' . . . have it cremated with me."

Some of her last instructions—the ones that had to do with that set of books—I have carried out. Some, like the one about the notebook entitled "Love Cannot Be Forgotten," I haven't. I cannot make myself get rid of it. I often think that if it could be published, it would be the most moving of all the pieces she has written. But, of course, it cannot be published.

At first, I thought that it was nothing but raw, scattered material she had gathered for her writing, because it is not like a novel, or sketches, or letters, or a diary. It was only after I had read through it from beginning to end that gradually, by knitting those scattered sentences together with the fragments of my memories, the indistinct shape of something emerged. After thinking for a long time, I finally understood. What I held in my hands were not lifeless words without flesh and blood, but a burning heart full of love and pain. I can also see how that heart struggled and seethed. For more than twenty years, one person possessed all her emotions, yet she could not have him. She could only substitute the notebook for him and pour her heart out to him in it—every hour, every day, every month, every year.

No wonder she had never been moved by any of her serious suitors. No wonder she had always treated lightly the indistinguishable mass of honest hopefuls and gossips with bad intentions. It was because her heart was already so full, there was no room for anyone else. I thing of the lines, "Having been the vast sea it is hard to be only water / Without Mount Wu it is not a cloud."* When I think that most of us will never love to this degree, and that nobody will love me this way, I feel unspeakably depressed.

I know that at the end of the 1930s, when this man was doing underground political work in Shanghai, an old worker trying to cover for him was arrested and killed, leaving behind a helpless wife and daughter. Out of moral principles, a sense of responsibility, class concern, and gratitude to the victim, he unhesitatingly married the woman.

* Mount Wu is a beautiful mountain in eastern Sichuan, whose peak is always ringed by clouds. The poet is saying that a cloud is not really a cloud, or hasn't really achieved the highest state of a cloud's existence, until it has been a cloud at Mount Wu. The lines are taken from a quatrain written by the Teng Dynasty poet Yuan Zhen (779–831).

Every time he saw couples who had married for "love" and were having endless worries over "love," he would feel: Thank heavens, even though I did not marry for love, our life somehow has been harmonious and we have been compatible, like a person's left and right arms. Having weathered the storms of several decades, they could be said to be a couple who had faced many hardships together.

He must have been a comrade in her office. Had I ever met him? Looking back on the visitors to our home, I had detected nothing. Who was he?

Around the spring of 1962, my mother and I went to a concert. The theater was not far from our house, so we did not take the bus.

A small black car quietly stopped at the side of the road. Out came a white-haired, elderly looking man in a black wool Zhongshan suit.* His white hair gave him a grand, dignified air. He gave people the impression of being solemn, meticulous, refined, crystal clear. His eyes, especially, twinkled coldly with a chilling glow. When he quickly shifted his glance, he reminded one of lightning or of the flashing of swords. It would take a tremendous love to cause this icy pair of eyes to fill with tenderness; it would take a woman who was really worthy of being loved.

He came over and said to Mother: "How are you, Comrade Zhong Yu? I haven't seen you for a long time."

"How are you?" Mother's hand, which was holding mine, suddenly became ice cold and trembled.

They stood facing each other, their faces wearing melancholy, solemn expressions. Neither looked at the other. Mother stared at the bushes that had not even sprouted leaves yet by the side of the road. But he was looking at me: "She's already grown to be a young girl. How nice—too nice—just like her mother."

He did not shake hands with Mother, but he did shake hands with me. And that hand was like Mother's—also ice cold and trembling. As if I had become a conductor of electric current, I immediately felt a tingling and the suppression of it. I quickly withdrew my hand from his, and said, "No, not nice at all!"

Shocked, he asked, "Why is it not nice?" Or perhaps I thought he deliberately appeared surprised. Whenever children say something so lovably honest, adults always wear such an expression.

I looked at Mother's face. Yes, I looked like her. This disappointed me a bit: "Because she is not pretty!"

He started to laugh and said humorously: "What a pity, how can there be a child who feels that her mother is not pretty enough? Do

---

* The national uniform for officials in China: the "Mao" suit.

you remember in 1953, when your mother was first transferred to Beijing, the day she reported to the office with you? She left you—you naughty little thing—outside in the corridor. You went from one stairway to another, prying at the door cracks, and you hurt your little finger at my door. You cried and cried, and I carried you to look for your mother."

"No, I do not remember." I was not very pleased. How could he mention events that had taken place when I was still wearing split-bottom pants?*

"Oh, it is the adults who cannot easily forget." He suddenly turned to my mother and said, "I read the novel you wrote recently. I have to be honest and say there is one point you did not write about very accurately. You should not have made it so difficult, in your work, for the woman character. . . . You know, there is nothing wrong with one person's feeling strong emotions for another. She did not harm the other person's life. . . . As a matter of fact, the male character may also have had tender feelings for her. But for the happiness of another, they had no choice but to give up their own love. . . ."

At that moment, a traffic policeman came over to the curb where the car was, loudly lecturing the driver that it was not a place to park. The driver explained with embarrassment. The man stopped talking, turned his head to look over, hurriedly said "good-bye," and with big strides walked toward the side of the car, saying to the policeman: "I am sorry. Don't blame the driver, it was I. . . ."

I watched this man of advanced years listening to the policeman's lecture with lowered head, and I felt amused. When I turned to Mother with my mischievous face, I realized that she was embarrassed! She was like a young girl in first grade timidly standing in front of the serious headmaster, as if the person being scolded by the policeman were she and not he.

The car drove away, leaving a trace of smoke. Very quickly, even this trace disappeared with the wind, and it was as if nothing had happened. I do not know why I didn't forget all about it right away.

Analyzing it now, I think it must have been his tremendous spiritual strength that moved Mother's heart. That tremendous strength came from his mature, steadfast, political mind; the risky experiences he had had in the turbulent revolutionary era; his dynamic thinking; his energy for work; and his literary and artistic cultivation. . . . Moreover, strangely enough, he and Mother both liked the oboe. Yes, she must have worshipped him. She said once, if she had not worshipped the person she loved, her love could not have lasted a day.

* Instead of diapers, toddlers in China wear pants that are deliberately split in the back.

As to whether he loved my mother or not, I couldn't have guessed. If he didn't love her, why is there this passage in the notebook?

"This present is too much. But how did you know that I like Chekhov?"
"You said so once!"
"I don't remember."
"I remember. I overheard you one time when you were casually chatting with someone else."

So, that set of Chekhov's selected works had been given to Mother by him. To her, it was practically a gift of love.

Who can know for sure? This man who did not believe in love didn't realize until his hair was all white that there was something in his heart that could be called love. Just as he reached the point when he had no power to love, there emerged a love to which he could have given his entire life. It was tragic, really. Perhaps it was not only tragic, perhaps it went even deeper than that.

All I can remember about him are these kinds of small details.

It must have been so frustrating; she was so infatuated with him, and yet she couldn't have him. In order to catch a glimpse of his little car and the back of his head from the rear window, she painstakingly calculated which road he would take and what time he might pass by from work. Whenever he gave a report on stage, she sat below the platform, separated from him by distance, clouds of smoke, dim lights, moving heads. Watching that blurred face, she would feel as if something had soldified in her heart, and she was unable to check the tears that filled her eyes. To avoid being discovered, with great effort she swallowed her tears. Whenever he coughed so much that he could not continue, she would wonder fretfully why nobody stopped him from smoking and worry that he had bronchitis again. She could not understand why he seemed so close and yet so far from her.

And he, in order to catch a glihpse of her, every day from the window of the little car anxiously watched the stream of bicycles along the bicycle path until he was dizzy. He worried whether the brakes of her bicycle were in order, whether she would have an accident. Whenever there happened to be an evening without a meeting, he would leave his car and go out of his way to come over to our neighborhood for nothing more than to take a quick walk past the entrance to our compound. Even when he had a hundred things to keep him busy, he would not forget to look at every sort of publication, just to see if any of them contained Mother's work.

In his life, everything was so clear, so unequivocal, even in the most difficult moments. Yet faced with this love, he became weak, helpless. From the standpoint of his age, it was actually ridiculous. He could not understand it: why had life deliberately arranged it this way?

However, when they did have a rare chance to meet in the office compound, they tried hard to avoid each other, hastily nodding and then hurrying on. This alone was enough to cause Mother to become totally distracted and lose her hearing, sight, and capacity to think. The world instantly became a void. . . . Sometimes she ran into a comrade named Lao Wang and would undoubtedly address him as Lao Guo, and converse in a way that was unintelligible even to herself.

She must have struggled desperately, because she wrote:

> Once we vowed, let us both forget. Yet I deceived you, I did not forget. I think you have not forgotten either. We have just been deceiving each other, hiding our pain deep inside. But I have not deliberately tried to deceive you. I have tried so hard to make it work. So many times I intentionally had myself detained in places far from Beijing, placing my hopes in time and space. I even felt that I had almost forgotten. But when I returned from my assignments, and the train was approaching Beijing, I simply could not stand my pounding, dizzying heartbeats. Eagerly, I stood on the platform looking around as if there were someone waiting for me. But, of course, there wasn't. I understood then that I had not forgotten anything; everything was in the same old place. Year after year, like a big tree, the roots had penetrated deeper and deeper. It was too difficult to try to pull out this rooted thing. I was powerless.
>
> With each day that passed, I felt as if I had forgotten something important, or I would suddenly wake up with a start in the night: what had happened? No, nothing had happened. I clearly sensed that you were not there! So everything seemed flawed, incomplete, and nothing could make up for the lack. We have already reached the stage when our lives will soon be over. Why must we still lose ourselves in our emotions like children? Why is it that life always makes us go through difficult journeys and only then unveils before our eyes the dream we have pursued for a lifetime? And because we closed our eyes earlier while walking, the dream was missed at forks in the road; then, too, there were so many unbridgeable ravines.

I see now that every time Mother returned from one of her assignments, she would never let me meet her at the station. No doubt she wanted to stand alone on the platform, enjoying the illusion that he was coming to meet her. Her hair was already white; poor Mother, she was simply like an infatuated young girl.

Those words do not describe very much of their love. Mostly they record trivial things in her life: why her essay was a failure; her anxiety and doubts about her talent; why was Shanshan (that's me) mischievous and should she be punished; distracted, she had read the time of the show wrong and so had missed a brilliant play; she had gone out for a walk, forgetting her umbrella, and had gotten thoroughly soaked. . . . Her spirit was so clearly with him day and night, it was as if they were a loving couple. Actually, if you calculate the total amount of time the two of them spent together in their lifetimes, it would not have added up to more than twenty-four hours. Yet these twenty-four hours were probably richer and more deeply felt than the time others may have enjoyed in a whole lifetime. Juliet, under Shakespeare's pen, once said: "I cannot sum up sum of half my wealth."* Probably, she could not sum up half her wealth, either.

It seems that he died of unnatural causes during the Cultural Revolution. Maybe because of the particular historical conditions at that time, her diary in this period is very vague. I wonder how my mother, who was so fiercely attacked because of her writings, persisted in her habit of keeping a diary. From the veiled words, I can still guess that he probably raised doubts about the theories of that prominent, powerful "theoretical authority,"† and had somehow said to someone, "This is simply rightist talk." From mother's tear-stained pages, he must have been terribly persecuted. But the old man was very tough; never did he bow his head to this powerful personality. When he was dying, the last words he uttered were: "Even if we have to go to Marx, this dispute must be fought to the end!"

This incident must have happened in the winter of 1969, because that winter Mother, who was approaching fifty, suddenly turned white-haired. Also, she began to wear a black armband. At that time, her situation was also quite difficult. Because of this black band, she was severely struggled against;‡ they said that she had insisted on the "four olds," and they tried to force her to reveal who the armband was for.

"Mother, who is this for?" I asked her anxiously.

"For a relative!" Then, fearing that I would be upset, she explained, "A relative you are not familiar with."

"Should I wear one?" She made a gesture that she had not made for a long time and patted my face lightly, as she used to when I was small. She hadn't shown such tenderness in a long time. I often felt that with her increasing age and experiences in life, particularly those

---

* "But my true love is grown to such excess
  I cannot sum up sum of half my wealth."
                        Act II, Scene 6,
                        Romeo and Juliet

† Probably Mao.

‡ A person who is "struggled against" is subjected to struggle sessions in which he or she is criticized and cross-examined by a group of peers. This is a form of party discipline employed to correct the ideological thinking of those who are considered to have deviated from the party line.

several years of trials and hardships, that kind of tenderness seemed to become more and more removed from her. Or maybe she hid it deeper and deeper, which often led me to feel that she was like a man.

She smiled a little in a distracted, melancholy way and said, "No, you don't need to."

Her dry, tired eyes held not a single drop of moisture, as if there were no more tears left to be cried. I wanted so much to comfort her, or to do something to amuse her. But she said to me, "Do go!"

I do not know why at that moment there arose in me a feeling of horror; I felt as if half of my dear mother had left me and was following something else. Involuntarily, I called out, "Mother!"

My sensitive mother must have clearly detected my mood. Gently she said to me: "Don't be afraid, do go! Let me be by myself for a while."

I was not mistaken, because she wrote this:

You are gone. It is as if part of my spirit has gone with you.

I could not even find out where you were, let alone take a last look at you. I do not have the right to confront them either, because I was neither a family member nor a close friend when you were alive. . . . So we parted like this. I hate the fact that I could not shoulder that inhuman affliction for you, and let you live on! For the day of your exoneration, for working for this society again, for those who love you, you should have lived on! I will never believe that you are what is called a "three-anti element."* You were the most brilliant among those who were killed. If you had not been, how could I have loved you? I am no longer afraid of saying these three words.

Heavy snow falls without letup. Even God is hypocritical. He uses a stretch of white to cover up your blood and this murderous evil.

I have never taken my own existence seriously. But now I never stop wondering whether any of my words or acts would make you wrinkle your brow. I have come to feel that, just like you, I will deliberately keep alive, deliberately live, in order truly to work for the sake of our society. It won't always be like this; the sharp sword of punishment is already hanging over the heads of that villainous gang.

Alone, I walked along that paved path that we had only once walked along together, listening to my lonely steps echoing in the silent dusk. . . . Time after time I have wandered along this little path; no other time was as heartbreaking as this. Before, even though you were not by my side, I knew you were still in the world, and I felt that you were accompanying me. Yet now, you are definitely gone; I really cannot believe it!

I walked to the end of the path, turned back, and began again to walk it once more.

---

* A political slogan referring to someone who is "anti-party, anti-Mao, and anti-socialist."

I leaned over the fence and turned my head back, out of habit, as if you were still standing there, waving good-bye to me. That day we smiled weakly, distractedly, like two who had no deep friendship, in order to make an effort to hide our deeply engraved love. That was an evening in early spring that was not a bit poetic; a chill wind was still blowing. We were walking silently, quite far apart from each other. Since you had chronic bronchitis, you were panting slightly. I was concerned about you, and wished to walk a little more slowly. But I did not know why I couldn't. We walked quickly, as if there were important matters we had to attend to so that we had to hurry and finish walking this part of the path. How we cherished this one and only "walk" in our lives. Yet we were clearly afraid, afraid that we could not control ourselves, that we would reveal those three horrible words that had afflicted us for many years: "I love you." Except for ourselves, probably there isn't a person alive in this world who would believe that we did not even once hold hands! Not to mention anything else!

No, Mother, I believe it. Nobody else but I could have seen the ways in which you revealed your soul.

Oh, that paved path. I truly did not know that it was a path so full of bitter memories. I think we must never ignore any common little corner in the world. Who knows how much hidden pain and joy those unexpected little corners might silently be hiding?

No wonder whenever she was tired from writing, she would slowly pace up and down that paved path. Sometimes it was in the early morning after a sleepless night, sometimes even on a dark and windy night; it did not matter if it was winter, or if the fierce wind was howling like an animal gone mad, swirling up gravel so that it noisily hit against the window lattice. I thought that it was nothing but a strange habit of hers; I never knew that she went to meet his soul.

She also liked to stand lost in thought in front of the window, gazing at the paved path outside. Once, the special expression on her face led me to think that our most familiar, most welcome guest was coming down the path. I hurried to the window; in the dusk of deep autumn there was only the cold wind sweeping withered yellow leaves across the deserted path.

As if he were still alive, her habit of having heart-to-heart talks with him through writing was not broken by his death. It lasted until the day she herself could no longer pick up a pen. On the last page, she said her last words to him:

I am a person who believes in materialism. Yet now I am eagerly awaiting Heaven. If there is truly a so-called Heaven, I know you must be waiting there for me. I am going there soon to meet you; we shall be together forever; we shall never be apart. Never again will we have to fear affecting another person's life and so separate ourselves. Dear, wait for me, I am coming—

I really had no idea that Mother, on her dying day, could still have loved so deeply. Just as she said, it was engraved on her bones and her heart. I feel that this is hardly love, but a kind of suffering, or a kind of strength greater than death. If there is truly something called everlasting love in the world, this might be its limit. She clearly felt happy until her death; she had truly loved. She did not have any regrets.

And now, their wrinkles and white hair have long since changed from carbohydrates to some other elements. Yet I know that no matter what they have become, they are still in love with each other. Even though there was no worldly law or moral obligation to tie them together, and though they had not held hands even once, they possessed each other totally; this nothing can separate. What is there to fear if hundreds of thousands of years pass, as long as there is one white cloud chasing another, one blade of green grass leaning against another, one wave beating against another, one light breeze pursuing another . . . Believe me, these must be they.

Every time I read the notebook entitled "Love Cannot Be Forgotten," I cannot hold back my tears. I cry and weep, and not just once, as if I am the one experiencing this miserable, sorrowful love. If this is not great tragedy, it is great comedy. No matter how beautiful it is, how moving, I would not like to repeat it!

The famous English author Thomas Hardy once said: "The call seldom produces the comer, the man to love rarely coincides with the hour for loving."* I can no longer use common moral standards to condemn them for having or not having loved. What I wish to condemn is this: Why didn't they wait for each other?

If we could all wait for one another, and not unthinkingly get married, how many tragedies of this kind could be avoided!

When we have arrived at communism, will there still be this kind of separation between marriage and love? Since the world is so wide, there will always be times when those calling one another will not be able to respond to each other. Then will this sort of thing still happen? Yet, that is so tragic! But maybe by that time there will be ways to solve such tragedies!

Why should I let myself pursue a dead end?

Ultimately, maybe we ourselves are responsible for this sorrow. Who knows? Maybe we should hold responsible the old consciousness left by past experiences. Because if a person never wants to get

* From *Tess of the d'Urbervilles.*

married, it will become a challenge to this kind of consciousness. Some people will say that you have a psychological problem, or that you have some shameful private matters you want to hide, or that you have some political problems, or that you are sly and capricious, contemptuous of common people. Since you do not respect social customs that have been passed down for thousands of years, you must be an evil person who deviates from the classic norms and rebels against tradition. . . . Anyhow, they would think up all kinds of vulgar tricks to ruin you. Therefore, you would reluctantly comply with the pressure of this kind of consciousness, casually marry, and harness your own neck to that unbearable chain that separates marriage and love. Then, in days to come, you would suffer for the rest of your life from this unbreakable chain.

I really want to shout: "Don't worry about the pettiness of others! Let us patiently wait—wait for the person who calls us. Even if we never get one, we should not unthinkingly marry! Don't worry about this single life turning into a horrible disaster. One should realize this may just be a sign that society is advancing in the realms of culture, cultivation, taste. . . ."

from *Beijing Wenyi* (*Beijing Literary Arts*)
November, 1979

The Corner Forsaken by Love
ZHANG XIAN

I

Even though it was the last year of the seventies in the twentieth century, love—in the eyes of the young people of Tiantang Commune— was a strange and mysterious word, embarrassing to mention. That was why, when the new Youth League secretary pronounced the word during a meeting in the commune hall to oppose the "buying and selling of marriages," the entire audience was startled. The young fellows winked mischievously at each other and broke into loud laughter, while the girls, hastily lowering their heads, blushed, giggled, and exchanged bashful glances.

But the delicate young woman, Shen Huangmei, sitting in the corner by the window—the party Youth League group leader of the Ninth Team, Tiantang Brigade—did not smile. Her face was pale. Her large, melancholy eyes gazed aimlessly out the window. She acted as if she heard nothing, as if nothing concerned her. Suddenly, however, her eyelashes quivered, exerting themselves to shake off the crystal-like things that wet them. "Love"—the word she could not understand—was at that moment strongly stirring the heart of this nine-teen-year-old girl. She felt humiliated, sad, inexplicably fearful. She thought of her elder sister Cunni, whom she missed terribly, yet would always blame. Ah, if only there had been no Xiao Baozi; if that incident hadn't happened, everything would have been fine! Her sister would have sat beside her, laughing heartily like a boy. After the meeting, her sister would have pulled her along with her strong arms, and together they would have picked out two bundles of orange thread in the commune cooperative and returned home to embroider their pillows. . . .

Of the five sisters, Cunni was the most fortunate. She had come into the world immediately after the bumper harvest of 1955. When she was a month old, her family could easily afford a banquet table.* The young father, Shen Shanwang, held up the precious little bundle wrapped in a patterned quilt and said in high spirits:

". . . I took Linghua to the midwives' station and then went off for a moment to deposit some money in the credit cooperative. When I came back, the baby had been born! Nobody could believe that the delivery had been so smooth the first time! Some said that we should name her Shunni [Smooth Girl]. I thought, 'For poor farmers like us, it was a miracle that we had money to deposit in a bank!' Having had her at this time, we thought we should call her Cunni [Deposit Girl]. Wait till she grows up; we'll have even better days!"

The happiness that flowed from his heart was infectious; it spread to everyone who came to congratulate the new parents. At the time, he was the deputy leader of Kaoshanzhuang Cooperative.† Optimistic, competent, he radiated courage and strength. The pear trees he had grafted in the orchard over the hill had produced a bumper harvest the first year they bore fruit. And, as for wheat and corn, they had more than enough, even after taxes. In the little village of twenty-odd households, everyone was as happy as he. Just like him, they confidently looked forward to a bright future.

When Huangmei was born five years later, conditions were very different. Kaoshanzhuang Cooperative had been incorporated into Tiantang Commune as the Ninth Team of Tiantang Brigade. The fine name Tiantang [paradise] had been given to the brigade personally by the party secretary at the county level, who had reasoned, "Communism is paradise, and the people's commune is the bridge." At the time, all the commune members, including team leader Shen

---

* In China, when a child is one month old, parents who can afford to throw a banquet, the size of which is measured by the number of tables of guests. Very few farmers are able to afford even one table. The fact that this banquet was given for a girl baby shows that her father is very progressive.
† Literally, the Cooperative at the Side of the Mountain.

Shanwang, firmly believed that paradise was only a few feet away. All they had to do was wholeheartedly cut down all the collectively owned pear trees together with all the gingko nut and chestnut trees around the houses,* and with the greatest haste deliver the wood to the backyard furnace operated by the commune†—as if, as soon as that marvelous puffing stove ejected bright, beautiful flowers of steel, they would easily stroll across the "bridge" and enter communism. But aside from a pile of iron that occupied cultivated fields and turned tons of trees into ashes, there was no other effect. Moreover, due to a drought, they couldn't even collect seedlings for the wheat and corn.

The taro roots that replaced the pear trees were as thin as the tips of Cunni's fingers. When Linghua, who was big with child, returned after begging for food at a nearby village, Shen Shanwang had already been dismissed from his post because he had "attacked the great effort to process steel." When his second daughter was born—a weak little baby—Shen Shanwang gazed at her with a bitter smile on his swollen face and sighed, "Who told her to arrive in this lean year? What a Huangmeizi [Lean Little Sister]!"

Perhaps because her mother had been well-nourished when she was born and nursed, Cunni grew and thrived. She could grow just by eating leaves, and generate energy just by drinking cold water! Before her sixteenth birthday, she had already developed into a healthy, robust young woman. With a wooden pole,‡ she replaced her sickly mother who had given birth to three more sisters, and helped her father shoulder the responsibility of the family. In the most strenuous activity of the year—carrying lumber down the mountain to the state lumber farm—she ranked third highest in work points among the women workers. She left for the fields before dawn, and returned under the starlit sky. After gulping down a large bowl of taro or corn-meal, she would fall off to sleep without a thought. Even when, at the annual distribution of income, the figure for the family's overspend-

* The nut trees around the houses would have been privately owned.

† This refers to the attempt to make steel in backyard furnaces during the Great Leap Forward, the campaign begun by Mao in 1958 to catapult China into communism and the position of a major industrial power. Central features of this campaign were the formation of people's communes from agricultural cooperatives that had been established in the early years of the Republic and an emphasis on economic development through "self-reliance" as well as greater collectivization. During the Great Leap Forward, communes were told to produce steel in backyard furnaces, and massive construction and land reclamation projects requiring the labor of vast numbers of peasants were undertaken. For a variety of reasons—among them severe droughts and poor central planning based on inflated reports by local officials—the program was not a success. Today the official view of the Great Leap Forward is that it was overly ambitious.

‡ For carrying baskets of things, or lumber.

ing was greater than ever and they could not get a cent of cash, she was still just as optimistic as ever, not knowing what worry was. On the spur of the moment, she would put her arm around Huangmei, pressing her full breast tightly against her sister's frail body and lightly hum an old folk song that had been popular in her mother's day.

There are often strange things in life that happen only once in a great while and yet have obvious origins. They take people by surprise, yet they are not really anything extraordinary. Take deformities, for example. Whatever strange forms they take, there is always a physiological reason for them. People are surprised by them just because their occurrence is so rare. What happened between Cunni and Xiao Biaozi was just that.

Xiao Baozi was the only son of Uncle Jiagui at the east end of the village. His real name was Xiao Bao, and he was the same age as Cunni. This strong young man worked with fearful energy. One time, when he was carrying lumber, a cold rain began. Aunt Jiagui slipped and fell in front of him and broke her pole. Xiao Bao helped his mother to her feet. Then he tied the two piles of wood together over his bare shoulder, and—gritting his teeth and panting and puffing—carried the wood all the way down the mountain. The wood weighed in at three hundred and five catties. People were amazed. They said, "That Xiao Bao is really something—just like a little leopard! So that is how Xiao Baozi [Little Leopard] became his nickname.

In the early spring of 1974, the team cadres went off to the commune early one morning to criticize Confucius* while the strong labor power† went to work at the reservoir. Caretaker Grandpa Xianger kept Cunni behind to help him put the storage room in order. The old man directed the young woman's work, nagging and complaining all the while.

"The cadres come around once and point their fingers: 'There!' We busy ourselves the whole year cutting through mountains and chipping away at rocks and then a flash flood comes along and whoosh! Everything is washed away! Next year, the cadres come again and point their fingers: 'There!' They have no regard for the harmony of wind, water, and earth."

"Isn't that like 'the foolish old man who moved the mountain?' "‡ Cunni asked, disinterestedly continuing the conversation.

"As if moving a mountain will fill bellies! . . . Come, first sieve this pile—slowly—don't spill it! . . . Look at this corn grown over

---

* This took place during the height of the anti-Lin Biao, anti-Confucius campaign.
† All strong, able-bodied adults.
‡ A story that was often quoted by Mao to illustrate that with the right motivation and effort, anything can be accomplished.

the roots of the pear. It is so lean, who knows whether it will sprout?"
The old man complained about the corn seedlings.

"Isn't that 'taking grain as the basis?' "* the young woman answered, still distracted. Her heart wandered. Though putting the storage room in order was light work, it was a great deal more fun to
carry soil with the young men at the reservoir.

At that moment, a sturdy figure appeared in front of the storage
room. "Let me do some work, Grandpa Xianger."

"Xiao Baozi!" Cunni cried out happily, "Didn't you sprain your leg
carrying stones yesterday?"

Grandpa Xianger said, "Go back home and rest!"

"I can't stand lying around," Xiao Baozi smiled earnestly. "So long
as I don't carry heavy loads, a little light work won't hurt!" While he
spoke, he picked up the winnowing spade to help Cunni with the
sieving.

Grandpa Xianger happily squatted on the side and smoked a cigarette. Then, remembering that he needed to ask the carpenter to come
and repair the plow, he gave a few orders and left. Activities like
cleaning out the storage room and sieving seedlings were really no
tasks at all in the hands of two such quick and diligent nineteen-
year-olds. In a very short while, the seedlings had been packed, and
the taro spread out to dry. Xiao Baozi said, "Let's rest awhile!" He
spread his cotton jacket out on top of a full sack, and lay down on
top of it.

Cunni wiped her sweat and sat down on a sack facing him. She
had taken off her cotton jacket a long time ago, and was wearing a
dark green sweater that had been part of her mother's dowry. Though
it had been taken apart and washed many times and patched with
several different colors of yarn, and though it was getting too short
and too tight for her body, in the eyes of the young women in the
Ninth Team, the sweater was still an enviable luxury.

Xiao Baozi stared at her healthy face reddened by the sun; he
stared at her full bosom. A strange, itching feeling that he had never
experienced before arose in his heart. It excited him, but made him
apprehensive. So, distractedly, he tried to make conversation.

"The day before yesterday Wuzhuang showed a movie. Didn't
you go?"

"Of course I didn't go. It was too far away!" Trying to avoid his
burning stare, she lowered her head and began pulling at the loose
ends on her sweater sleeves.

Wuzhuang is a brigade in Linxian County. To get there, you have
to go over two big hills. Even young fellows like Xiao Baozi had to

---

* A party line, meaning that self-sufficiency in grain should be given priority.

walk more than an hour to reach it. It was not regarded as a rich team; the value of ten work points the previous year had been only thirty-eight fen. But this was enough for the members of Tiantang Commune to cluck their tongues in envy. What attracted the young men most was the train station thirty kilometers west of Wuzhuang. Last spring festival, Xiao Baozi had gotten together with a few fellow workers to go there to see the train. The round trip had taken half a day, and they had waited at the station for two hours. When they had finally seen the dark green passenger train zoom past the station, they were satisfied. Members of the Ninth Team rarely had such an opportunity. As to actually boarding the train, only the commune accountant, "Xu the Blind,"* would have had that enviable experience.

"I didn't want to go anyway," said Cunni. "*Tunnel Warfare, Mine Warfare, The Battle from North to South*—I've seen them eight hundred times! I can recite every word in the scripts. . . ."

Xiao Baozi stretched and sighed, "If you don't go, what else is there to do? The playing cards are already in shreds. I tried asking a friend to go through the back door at the commune supply cooperative, but he still hasn't been able to get more."

Apart from going to the movies and playing cards, the young people had nothing to do after work. The team subscribed to a provincial paper, but it only came into service when Xu the Blind held a meeting.† And even he would always mispronounce "Confucius says" as "Confucius days." Of course, nobody would correct the only intellectual in the team. In the past, it had been popular to sing folk songs about love, but now these were considered "immoral" and forbidden.

Suddenly, Xiao Baozi excitedly sat up, "Hey, Xu the Blind says that in foreign movies he has seen . . . Huh! That was really something!" He clucked his tongue and snickered. "There are. . . ."

"What?" Cunni could not help asking, seeing the amused look on his face.

"Hee, hee, hee . . . I can't say it." Blushing, Xiao Paozi kept laughing to himself.

"What is it? Come on!"

"Okay, I'll tell, but don't you scold me!"

"Come on! Say it!"

"There are—" He stifled his laughter until he was doubled over.

Cunni already anticipated the terrible thing he was going to tell. She picked up a clod of soil.

Sure enough, Xiao Baozi gathered up his courage and proclaimed: "There are men and women hugging and kissing! Hee, hee, hee. . . ."

---

* A nickname—he wasn't really blind.
† Because most of the team members were illiterate.

"Yich, disgusting!" Cunni blushed and quickly threw the clod of soil at him.

"It's true! Xu the Blind said so himself!" Xiao Baozi dodged the attack.

"Shameless!" Another clod of soil. The earth, mixed with particles of corn, fell on his shoulders and down his neck. He retaliated. A handful of soil dropped down Cunni's open collar. The young woman pretended she was cross. "Damn you!"

Xiao Baozi smiled, embarrassed. He took off his shirt and wiped his muscular chest with it. Cunni stiffened her mouth to show her annoyance, and began to take off her sweater, intending to shake off the particles of soil sticking to her chest. . . . That instant, Xiao Baozi froze as if electrified. He stared blankly, his breath stopped, and a gush of warm blood rushed to his head. It was because when the young woman took off her sweater, her shirt was pulled up, exposing half of a pale, full, and bouncing breast.

Like a leopard springing from its cave, Xiao Baozi leaped forward. He embraced her tightly as if he had completely lost his senses. Startled, the young woman tried to lift her arm to block him. But when his burning, quivering lips touched her own moist lips, she was overcome with a mysterious dizziness. Her eyes closed and her outstretched arms were paralyzed. All her intentions to resist disappeared instantly. A kind of primitive reflex burned like a fierce flame in the blood of this pair of materially poor, spiritually barren, but physically robust young people. Traditional morality, rational dignity, the danger of breaking the law, the shame in a young woman's heart—all of these, everything, in a moment were burnt to ashes.

II

The lean-looking corn sprouted few shoots. After the first hoeing, fourteen-year-old Huangmei began to notice that her sister had changed. She no longer laughed with the same carelessness, and she always sat by herself on the edge of the bed, lost in thought. When you talked to her, it was as if she hadn't heard a sentence. At times she saw her with pale face and lowered head, wiping away tears, but at other times she would be blushing and laughing to herself. . . . The strangest thing of all was the night Huangmei suddenly woke up to discover that, beside her, her sister's bed was empty. The next morning, when Huangmei asked her about it, Cunni became so anxious; her face turned red, then white; she even insisted that Huangmei had been dreaming.

Just around that time, Mother came down with a kidney disease. Father was busy going to their uncle's place at Wuzhuang to borrow money in order to get a doctor. The house was in a state of confusion. Nobody had the time to pay attention to the changes in Cunni. Only Huangmei, in her sensitive young heart, had a subtle premonition that some horrible trouble was about to descend on her sister.

When indeed the trouble inevitably came, it was far more horrible than anything Huangmei could have imagined.

That was the season when the corn grew to about half a person's height. After working a whole day, the commune members gathered after dinner at the team's headquarters to listen to Xu the Blind recite "Confucius days" in front of the oil lamp. Huangmei did not wait for the meeting to finish; she slipped back home, and after putting her three younger sisters to bed, went to bed herself. But after only a little while she was awakened with a start by a blast of noise and commotion; yelling, bursts of laughter, hitting and scolding, crying and swearing, were mixed up with the barking of almost all the village dogs and echoes from the hills. She had never heard such a clamor. Frightened, Huangmei lit the lamp. The horrible noise came closer and closer, until it was right outside the door. Suddenly, her sister rushed headlong through the doorway, and, clothes disheveled and hair all over her face, fell heavily on the bed wailing. And then, with his back bared and both hands tied behind him, Xiao Baozi was ushered into the house by the captain of the local militia. Under the light of several torches, Huangmei saw that his body bore bloody marks where he had been beaten with branches. He knelt down stiffly, intense shame and remorse on his face, and let Huangmei's pale-faced father slap him across the mouth. Mother was already paralyzed in a chair, covering her face and whimpering. Outside the door, crowded around in a solid mass, were nearly all the adults and children of the entire village, each contributing to the chatter, scolding, ridicule, insults, and stirred-up feelings. Huangmei, terrified, finally understood: her older sister had committed the most shameful thing in the world! Suddenly she broke down and cried. She felt utter shame, disgrace, hate, and anger. Her dearest sister had brought disaster to the whole family and had brought upon herself misfortune that could not be washed away. The beginnings of womanly self-respect had not yet formed in her young heart, and therefore she was particularly sensitive and easily hurt. Huangmei cried and cried tears of sorrow that gushed forth like a river bursting its dike. At the same time, she was muttering in a muffled voice even she could not hear clearly, "Shame! Disgraced the whole family! . . . Shame! Disgraced the whole team! . . . Shame! Shame! . . ."

The commotion lasted till midnight.

Afterwards, in a faint, she fell asleep. Half asleep, she heard the sound of the team leader driving away the crowd, the sound of Uncle and Aunty Jiagui sincerely apologizing to her parents, the sound of Grandpa Xianger consoling and reminding them, "Don't make it difficult for the child. Be careful! She may not be able to take it!" Mother's scolding gradually subsided into a low, consoling murmur. Huangmei finally fell asleep on the tear-soaked pillow, only to be continually frightened out of her sleep by nightmares. During the last nightmare, she suddenly heard shouts in the distance: "Help, someone! Help, someone! . . ."

Huangmei sat up sharply. The east was already bright. Sister Cunni was not in bed, and her mother had also gone. She quickly scrambled up and ran outside with bare feet, following the shadowy figures in front of her running to San Mu Pond at the edge of the village. Her sister had already been clumsily dragged out of the water and was stiffly lying there. So quickly, so easily had she died!

Mother, holding her daughter in her arms, was sobbing hoarsely, crying out as if she were mad. Time after time, she was dragged to her feet by her fellow villagers and relatives, only to fall paralyzed to the ground again. Father sat motionless at the edge of the pond, distractedly staring at the calm surface of the water, totally motionless, as if he were part of a withered tree stump.

The rosy morning light was reflected on Cunni's wet face, restoring color to her pale cheeks. Her expression was very calm, very peaceful, and showed not the slightest bit of pain, protest, complaint or sense of having been wronged. She had paid the highest price for her own blind burst of energy. Now she had already washed clean her shame and her crime. Of course, her death was a waste. But for her, was there anything in life worth cherishing anymore? Before she leaped into the abyss of death, she had even had time to think of another matter: that was, to take off the torn, palm-green sweater she wore and hang it on a tree. The only property that had been given to her by the human world she left to her sister; it still carried her the warmth of her body and the fragrance of youth. . . .

The matter did not end there. After about two weeks had passed, the sounds of weeping could be heard at the house of Uncle Jiagui: two public security officers had taken away Xiao Baozi. Again the whole village became the scene of a commotion. The villagers ran from the fields and stood, frightened, along the road, silently staring at the pair of shining things on Xiao Baozi's wrists. Only the Jiaguis, tearful and sniffling, followed behind their only son.

"Comrade, Comrade!" Shen Shanwang put down his hoe and ran forward. This team leader of the fifties had seen a bit of the world. Though the death of his daughter had added ten years to his age, and he had cooled toward life, at this moment his sense of responsibility

kept him from remaining silent. He said to the public security officer:
"Comrade, we have not made any accusations against him!"

The public security officer gave him a fierce stare, and said contemptuously: "Go, get out of here! What is this nonsense about accusations or no accusations! A rapist and a criminal who caused a
death! What is this nonsense about no accusation!"

Xiao Baozi remained very calm. He lifted his head, and his eyes
stared aimlessly around. Suddenly, he slowed his pace a bit, and
then, with a burst of energy, started running toward the deserted hill
opposite.

"Stop! Where are you going!" the public security officers yelled,
immediately taking off after him.

But Xiao Baozi ran recklessly on, stumbling as he trod on the wild
grass and scrub. At last, he threw himself, sobbing, on Cunni's new
grave, his hands frantically scratching, his fingers digging deeply into
the wet yellow earth. Not until the public security officers ran over
and shouted at him did he stop his tears. And then, stiffly kneeling
before the grave, he respectfully kowtowed three times.

III

After the meeting, Huangmei went out of the commune hall with a
heavy heart. Tientang Commune occupies a corner of the county, and
Tientang's Ninth Team occupies a corner of this corner. She took a
look at the setting sun hanging low in the pine woods to the west,
worrying that she wouldn't make it home before dark. Abruptly, she
gave up her plan to take a look at the supply and marketing cooperative, and from the back street went right through the wheat fields,
climbing the hilly path with quick steps.

"Shen Huangmei, wait! Let's go together!" the voice of the Youth
branch secretary, Xu Rongshu, called out from behind her. He lived
with the Eighth Team, which was separated from the Ninth Team
only by San Mu Pond. Huangmei had hoped very much to have
someone to walk with on this part of the long mountain path. In the
winter dusk, the flat areas between the hills were very desolate. But
she did not wish her fellow traveler to be a young man, and she particularly did not wish him to be Xu Rongshu. Therefore, after hesitating a little, she quickened her steps. At the end of the wheat fields,
when Xu Rongshu caught up with her, she cautiously moved away,
making sure that there remained more than four paces between them.

The death of her sister Cunni had not only left her the palm-green
sweater, it had left in her heart an unshakable shame and fear as well.
She had taken over her sister's wood pole prematurely; her frail

body was weighed down with having taken on the responsibility for her family, and her frail young heart was weighed down with a heaviness of spirit. She was afraid of, and hated, all young men. When she saw them, she would never strike up a conversation, and she avoided them by keeping her distance. She even despised her girl friends who did not fear or hate young men. She had become an unapproachable, eccentric girl.

But somehow, irresistibly, adolescence arrived. The yellowish cast of her face had faded, revealing a rosy, tender blush; her eyebrows had grown thick; her eyes had become clear black and white, moist and shiny. She felt her breasts swell, her shoulders and back gradually fill out. When she wore her sister's palm-green sweater, it already felt tight. In the depths of her heart there often arose a fresh, subtle kind of pleasure. When she saw flowers in bloom, she felt that the flowers were so beautiful, she could not help picking one to put in her hair. When she heard birds sing, she felt that the birds' song was so pleasing to the ear that she could not help standing still to listen for awhile. Everything had become so beautiful—leaves, fields, wild grass, drops of water on the grass. . . . Everything around her stirred her. Often, in front of her mother's broken mirror, she secretly checked herself over, and, even when she was getting water at the edge of the pond, she could not help casting a satisfied smile on the slender shadow of her figure. She began to go around with her girl friends. During festivals, she let them hold her hands for a look around the commune's supply and marketing cooperative. Even though she remained cautious with young men, gradually she came to feel that they were not really that disgusting. . . . At this moment, Xu Rongshu appeared in her life.

She had met Xu Rongshu when she was still very young. It had happened when she was attending first grade at the primary school established by the Eighth Team. The boys were bullying her. A classmate from a higher grade who was about the same age as her sister Cunni, came over to defend her, and even used his sleeves to wipe away her tears. Afterwards, because her mother had given birth to her youngest sister, she left school, not even finishing the second grade. Whenever Rongshu saw her carrying her younger sister on her back, cutting grass for the pigs near San Mu Pond, he would secretly leave his friends, snatch the sickle from her hands, and quickly cut a huge pile of grass. After throwing this in her basket, he would leave hurriedly. Not long after, the sounds of gongs and drums could be heard coming from the Eighth Team. Huangmei took her sister over to watch, only to see Rongshu along the path at the edge of San Mu Pond wearing a red flower and a new military uniform that was too big for him. He was going off to be a soldier.

She didn't see him again until last year during a meeting of the local branch of the Communist Youth League. He had just returned from service a few days previous. Entering through the doorway of the brigade's meeting room, he shyly glanced around and, just as Huangmei and the others who had newly joined the Youth League had done, quietly sat down in a corner. At that moment, several of the more active members who knew him came over, and insisted that he talk about military life. He blushed furiously with embarrassment and shyly declined, saying: "I was a peacetime soldier. I never saw any action, so what is there to talk about! . . ." He was entirely without the kind of majesty and pomp that went with a young person's image of a revolutionary soldier. She didn't understand why, but this aroused in Huangmei a good feeling toward him. When a vote was taken for committee members of the local Youth League and Xu Rongshu's name was read, she bravely raised her hand straight up in the air, expressing her genuine desire.

During the next Youth League activity, the newly elected branch secretary, Xu Rongshu, made an unusual suggestion that displeased the branch deputy secretary, who had been the captain of the militia. In the past, except for meetings, there had been only one content to the activities of Tiantang Commune's Youth League: labor. They would organize heavy labor such as gathering manure and moving stones beforehand. First they would have a meeting; then they would work. This type of unpaid labor was often conducted until very late, and was called "the model example of members of the Communist Party Youth League." But Rongshu broke this rule, saying: "Young people have their own special characteristics. I suggest that tonight we see a movie!"

When they heard this, everyone was dumbfounded. And then, laughing loudly, they began to clap. He had been so considerate and efficient, he had already booked the tickets beforehand in a factory near the commune. He had a friend there, a fellow soldier who, after the service, had gone to work at that factory. After a short meeting, he led everyone out. Young men and women walked happily in threes and fives amid much laughter—some boldly humming mountain love songs. It was just like a festival. This was the first time in her life that Huangmei had sat in a chair with a back and handrest and comfortably watched a movie. And that evening, also for the first time in her life, a young man entered her dreams. He looked like the male character in the movie who had led the young people in repairing the reservoir, and even more like her party Youth League secretary. Laughing in a goodnatured way, he said something very close to her. When she woke up, the moonlight shone on the edge of the bed, soft, bright, and clean. For the first time in her life, her heart overflowed with a range of sweet, tender emotions. But then she immediately became fearful. "What is going on?" Vexed, she thought: Oh, Oh! Thank goodness, it was just a dream! . . .

Nevertheless, after she became Youth League group leader,* Rongshu came around often, looking for her. As usual, Huangmei's attitude was solemn and cold. She never invited him into the house; one stayed outside the door, one inside, maintaining a distance of more than four feet. They talked about nothing but matters like announcements of meetings, one asking, the other answering—strictly official business. After the conversations Rongshu would leave. Huangmei always pretended she was busy with something, and then would go outside secretly to watch him go. How she longed for him to stay and chat a bit more, to come in and sit for awhile and talk about something else; yet she was afraid for him to do this. When their contact with each other increased, the contradictory feelings grew.

One day, she returned home later than usual, and her eleven-year-old sister said to her, "Brother Rongshu dropped by!"

Her mother had also returned, and now she quickly asked, "What was he coming here for?"

Father said, "He came to see me to ask me about transplanting mountain pear trees: How many years would they bear fruit? About how much money does a mu† of hilly ground cost? I said, 'Is that not a capitalist road?' He said, 'This is not called capitalism, it said so in the papers!' That boy!"‡

Father shook his head disapprovingly, but Huangmei observed that he liked this young man, and secretly she was delighted. But her mother was not pleased. She knit her brows, saying: "He is acting out of place!"

Huangmei had long heard that Rongshu, because of a matter about limiting the commune members' raising of ducks, had quarreled with the leader of the Eighth Team (his uncle). Some people said that he was wild, that he wouldn't obey the leaders, et cetera, et cetera, but she never paid any attention to these remarks. Now, when her mother said this, she became annoyed. She wanted to argue and say a few words in his defense, but observing her mother's suspicious glance focused on herself, she could only remain silent, lower her head to

* The party group corresponds to the team level of the commune. The party branch corresponds to the brigade level.

† A *mu* is one-sixth of an acre.

‡ Under the rule of the Gang of Four, each commune was to be as self-sufficient as possible; the growing of fruit as a cash crop was considered capitalist and was therefore taboo. After the fall of the Gang of Four, the government policy on cash crops changed.

eat, and pretend unconcern. After dinner, her mother began mumbling in the next room. Through the crack in the door, she heard: "There's already been gossip! We must be careful that she doesn't follow in Cunni's footsteps!"

Huangmei felt as if her heart had been pierced with a knife; she threw herself onto her bed crying. She resented her sister for having done such a shameful, unforgivable thing and resented her mother, who did not understand her daughter's heart. And she hated herself. How could she really like a young men? It was unthinkable, shameful! Shameless! Liking a man! . . . Shameless! Reluctantly, she scolded herself, burying her face deep inside the blankets, not letting her sad cries be heard.

She made up her mind, from that day on, not to take any more notice of him. If there was any matter to be discussed, let him look for the deputy group leader! Would he feel strange to be treated so unjustly? Let him do what he wanted! Who had asked him to be a man!

After a while, she truly began to hate Rongshu. That was because she had accidently heard Xu the Blind at the team's headquarters saying, "This boy Rongshu does not really know what's what. Again he has quarreled with the deputy secretary of the brigade!" Someone asked, "What about?" Xu the Blind said; "Ha! He wanted to seek justice for Xiao Baozi!"

"What?" Startled, Huangmei nearly cried out. Xiao Baozi's sentence was due to his own deeds; he deserved what he had gotten for his crime. It had not been any kind of misjudgment or false case. It could not be reversed. This seemed to be the view most people held. Huangmei could not have held any different view. Because of her sister's death, she only felt toward Xiao Baozi more of a share of hate. But how could Rongshu, a Communist Party member, a Youth League branch secretary whom she respected, speak up for the kind of bad person Xiao Baozi was? Was he sympathetic to Xiao Baozi? Or had he received some favors from the Jiaguis? . . . She was shaking with anger, and wanted to confront Rongshu. But when, at the edge of San Mu Pond, she saw Rongshu smiling and goodnaturedly walking toward her, her gust of courage disappeared. How could she mention that matter? Really, how could she say it to him? So she hurriedly turned around, pretending that she was heading elsewhere. She took the long way around to go home. Then she began to regret that she had. . . .

So it was like this: she was angry with him; she hated him; she wouldn't acknowledge him; she feared him; yet she couldn't stop thinking about him. . . . She kept going back and forth, contradicting herself. Such was the heart of this nineteen-year-old country girl.

If we call this love, then, for those young men and women living in other places, it may be difficult to understand. But Huangmei is in Tiantang's Ninth Team, this corner of the county's corner. Of the young women here who are Huangmei's age, more than half have also had Rongshu and Huangmei's kind of subtle, secretive love, contradictions, and pain. But usually, before too long, the problem disappears, and all is calm. A relative or somebody comes with a palm-green or rosy red wool sweater as a gift, proceeds with what looks like haggling over prices, and reaches an agreement. Then, one day, accompanied by this relative or someone else, the young fellow comes. This pair, who had not even dared to look at each other, then go together to Wuzhuang or somewhere and take a picture together. By the agreed upon date, she leaves her parents and departs from this corner. . . .

This is a road that people here are used to and often consider publicly proper, but in today's meeting the person giving the report was talking about it as "the buying and selling of marriages." She even said something like "love!" Sister and Xiao Baozi, that was called "love?" No, no! That was shameful, illegal! But then, was there really another way? Huangmei felt confused, and could not help thinking of Rongshu. At this moment, he was right behind her, her silent companion. Her girl friends who had come to the meeting had all gone to the supply and marketing cooperative. On the quiet mountain path, there were only the two of them. She heard her own pounding heartbeats. . . .

Suddenly, Rongshu stopped, looked all around, and in a smooth, deep voice began to sing: "I love this blue sea, Our mother country's ocean frontiers are so vast! . . ."

Huangmei was startled. But as she listened, the warm, passionate song affected her. Unconsciously she turned her head, revealing an approving smile.

"Looking at this spread of pine forest on the hill, I think of the ocean! The days on the ship! . . ." As if talking to himself, he said smilingly, "Your heart swells when you see the sea. If only our fellow villagers and relatives could have a look at the ocean."

Huangmei listened smiling. Her caution was quietly disappearing.

"Huangmei, have you been to the main street? In the market, people are selling eggs and vegetables and nobody is driving them away!* Did you know? Rural policy is to be changed! Hilly land must be taken out of grain production and planted with pear trees. The

---

* Under the Gang of Four, private marketing was branded as capitalism and suppressed. Around 1977, the policy began to change, and private trading activities were allowed.

good cadre Uncle Shanwang will again be useful! First you must grow young trees on your family's private plot!" He was making his points in a jumbled way, he was so excited. "Aunty Shanwang's health is not good, so she can cut some weeds to weave baskets at home, to exchange for some petty cash. Your next oldest sister can start working next year, right? The two younger ones can take care of a few lambs! I have an army friend who is a cadre in the commune, and he told me that the central government will issue a document in the very near future to let the peasants get rich. Really! You don't believe it?"

His eyes twinkled with optimism; his voice sounded like the water in a stream, sincere and moving. Huangmei did not believe this talk. As to getting rich, she had never hoped for it; she had never even thought of it. Ever since she was old enough to understand things, any talk of getting rich and prosperous had always been linked with capitalism as something to be criticized and struggled against. What shook her was that Rongshu knew so clearly the conditions of her family, and was so caring. He was using this way to answer her coldness, her caution, and reluctance. She was ashamed and felt her face burning.

"Yes, if you can't get rich and prosperous, if you live poorly all your life, then there is nothing to be proud of!" Shaking his head as if he had a lot in his heart, he said, "Take the case of Xiao Baozi. Can you blame him? Poor, backward, ignorant, foolish! Put those together with the old feudalism and an honest young man is dragged off to jail! Your sister was treated even more unjustly! . . ."

On hearing him mention this, the young girl instantly felt humiliated. Angrily, she gave him a severe look and shouted: "I will not allow you to mention that subject! I will not allow you to speak of my sister! . . ."

Desperately, she tried to hold back the tears in her eyes; then she abruptly rushed up the hill, and with long steps ran downhill, leaving Rongshu bewildered.

IV

By the time she reached the door of the house, it had already become completely dark, and she had calmed down. Her little sister called to her from inside and came rushing to meet her. Right behind her, Mother, her face wreathed in a happy smile, also came running. This made Huangmei feel strange. Her poor, hardworking, sickly mother had aged prematurely. Particularly after the death of her sister, her face wore a blank expression when it wasn't showing sadness. What had happened that had made her so happy?

"Quick, quick, go have a look at your bed!" Mother nearly broke into a laugh.

On the bed lay a brand-new, sky-blue sweater. Under the faint oil lamp, it radiated a gentle, tempting glow.

Huangmei took it in her hands, but before she had even felt its softness and warmth, she instantly, as if having received an electric shock, threw it away. Startled she asked, "Who is that for?"

"It's yours!" Mother was just pouring out steaming hot corn soup from the pot. Excited, she gave her a meaningful glance, "Your Second Aunty* brought it over. . . ."

"Second Aunty?" Huangmei shivered. Her legs felt weak, and she collapsed onto the edge of the bed, stunned. Second Aunty had come over a short while ago, and had spent half a day muttering with her mother, all the time looking her over from head to toe. At the time she had been very aware of that stare; there had been something very secretive about it. And now here she had presented her with the sweater! . . .

Mother sat down beside her, and in an unusually gentle voice said: "He is in Second Uncle's Third Team in Wuzhuang, and he is three years older than you. His brother is a worker at the Beiguan train station, getting more than fifty a month! . . ."

Huangmei felt ice-cold sweat crawl slowly down her back. She was shaking all over, her ears were ringing, and she could no longer hear anything clearly.

"I don't want it!" she cried, struggling. "No, I don't want it!"

She threw the sweater at her mother, but her mother still held onto her, smiling: "No one is demanding that you be married off immediately! During the Dragon Boat Festival, he will come to meet you and give you clothes. Sixteen suits! . . . Then when you get engaged he will give five hundred yuan in cash!"

"No, no, no!" A feeling of humiliation rose up in Huangmei's heart. She felt a choking horror. She did not know what to do; tears at having been wronged quickly flowed. She could only angrily throw aside her mother's comforting arm and run outside.

At the doorstep stood her father, weighed down with a heavy heart, and three young sisters who blankly stared at her. She covered her face, rushed out the door and stood in the yard, crying loudly and resting against the half a wall that remained around the crumbling pigsty. "What is the matter? What is the matter?" Her mother hurriedly followed her outside, taking her hand, "Huangmei, you are a mature child. What do we have in the family? Your mother is sick, your three young sisters only know how to open their mouths when

---

* The wife of the mother's second oldest brother.

they want to eat. There is no feed for the pigs. After we fed them for over half a year, we can't even get our costs back! Somehow I manage to gather a few eggs to sell in the streets, but I am driven back and forth by people and am as fearful as if I were a thief. Last year at distribution time we overspent again and were left without a bit of cash in our hands. I'd like to buy a pair of socks for you, but. . . ."

Mother was also sobbing as she calculated: "Your older sister did not live up to our expectations, so who can this family rely on? We must repair the roof on the house. We are in debt. Where will we find the money? Second Aunty said as soon as they can lay hands on the five hundred yuan, then. . . ."

"Money, money!" the young woman cried, shaking. "You use your daughter as if she were something to sell!"

Mother instantly began to choke. Feeling weak all over, she held onto the mud wall and slowly collapsed to the ground. "Use your daughter as if she were something to sell!" How this statement stabbed her, how familiar it sounded! Who, at about her daughter's age, with the same anger, had cried out the same thing? Oh, no one but she herself!

That was the winter after the land reform team had come to Wuzhuang. Linghua had gone to see the musical play *The White-Haired Girl* that evening, where she met an honest, handsome young farm worker named Shun Shanwang. From that moment on, she understood the meaning of the word "lover" in the mountain love songs they used to sing. Nineteen-year-old Linghua was not only bravely participating in the mass meeting to struggle against the landlords, she was also bravely meeting her lover at night in the corn fields. However, she was already engaged, by the decision of her parents, to the young owner of a general store in Beiguan Market Town. The man's family heard the gossip and presented her family with fifty silver coins, insisting that the wedding take place within the year. Linghua cried and made a scene, which was contrary to her usual manners, and publicly admitted that she had set her heart on a poor fellow in the village near the hills. She announced that she would follow him to the hills to face a harsh life, and would never return to the "old feudal" home of her birth. This shocked her parents; they shut her up inside and scolded and beat her. She cried, making a row, rolling back and forth on the ground, scattering the silver coins all over the floor. Angrily she screamed, "You are trying to use your daughter as something to sell!"

That was the time of the antifeudal flame, the era that had already burnt "parents' orders and words of go-betweens" along with landlords' contracts and debtor's i.o.u.'s. A poster publicizing the Marriage Law hung on the wall at the doorway of the rural adminis-

trative office. Liu Qiaoer* on the stage and the village's child daugh-
ter-in-law† served as models for Linghua. Honest, handsome Shen
Shanwang—holding out a beautiful, happy future—awaited her.
What Linghua had was the courage to break out of the prison of
feudalism!

"They want to sell their daughter as if she were a thing!" The following day, in the newly painted rural administrative office, not need-
ing anything else but this statement from Ninghua, the land reform
work team, with encouraging smiles, issued both her and Shanwang
a marriage certificate with Mao's picture on it.

Never had she expected that today, after a lapse of thirty years,
her daughter would actually use the same words to scold her!

What is it all about? How have those days come back? Shocked
and fearful, she slowly lifted her head, looking at the late winter evening sky. Several cold stars emitted a sad, plain, dim light, mocking
her with their blinking. She shivered as if she had suddenly received
a revelation, and broke into loud cries, all the while muttering to
herself: "Retribution! Retribution! This is called retribution!"

Out of her shriveled eyes flowed thick tears. Inside, in the depths
of her heart, she was filled with sorrowful hatred. She hated Huangmei; she hated Cunni; she hated their father. She hated that her life
had been fated to be harsh, hated this piece of land to which she had
brought her youth and happy visions of the future, this land to which
she had given more than half a life of hard labor, for which she had
received nothing in return except sorrow and worry!

In contrast, Huangmei had become calm, and was trying to console
her mother, saying: "Mother, on the main street of the commune,
those who sell eggs and vegetables are no longer driven away. You
can cut some weeds to weave into baskets to sell. Younger sister can
herd sheep. The fields on the hill will be converted to fruit orchards,
and Father is the one who knows the best methods! . . . They'll let
us peasants become rich and prosperous! Rongshu said so, the central
government has issued a document! . . ."

"Documents, documents! Today this, tomorrow that! I've seen
many! I've seen enough! Aren't we still poor! Huangmei, your mother
does not want you to live the life she has had to live" Mother was
sobbing, but she had also gradually become calm, "Child, you are a
mature young girl. Mother can see that Rongshu loves you, and you

---

* In a story based on a true incident, this was the name of a child bride who
defied tradition and claimed for herself the right to marry whom she chose. The
story was circulated among Communist-occupied areas before the Revolution and
was also performed as a play.

† Child daughters-in-law, married into a family at a very early age, were seen as
the most oppressed victims of the traditional Chinese marriage system.

him. But think, without a full stomach, all of this is empty! Your mother should not have done what she did." She sighed. "Now she's reaping her reward!"

The wind stopped. Her mother's weak body lay against Huangmei. Mother and daughter silently sat without stirring, each immersed in her own thoughts.

"Mother, you go back in!" Huangmei said in a low voice. Her eyes swept the village houses of the Eighth Team, looking for one of them. "I still have some business to do!"

Then, she stubbornly walked in the direction of San Mu Pond. What had just happened had suddenly made her wise, experienced. All the things she had been against, including the matter of seeking justice for Xiao Baozi that had so upset her, now seemed reasonable. She believed that Rongshu could give his reasons. Then, too, he knew a great deal; he even knew about the sea! Why should Huangmei doubt the document about letting the peasants get rich that he firmly believed in? He would certainly be able to give her the best suggestion, to tell her what to do!

Across the surface of San Mu Pond, a gentle, warm breeze blew, the very first sign of spring returning. Silently it caressed the withered grasses at the side of the pond; quietly it dried the tears of the young girl rushing by. Had spring really come, come to this corner forsaken by love?

from *Shanghai Wenxue* (*Shanghai Literature*)
January, 1980

Longing
SHU TING

A hanging scroll in a swirl of colors, lacking line
An algebraic formula, simple but unsolvable
A one-stringed lute, strumming a rosary of raindrops from the eaves
A pair of oars that never reach the opposite shore

Silently waiting, like a swelling bud
Distantly gazing, like the setting sun
Somewhere, perhaps, a vast ocean lurks
But only two tears trickle out

O in the vistas of the heart
In the depths of the soul

from *Wenhui Yuebao* (*Wenhui Monthly*)
February, 1981

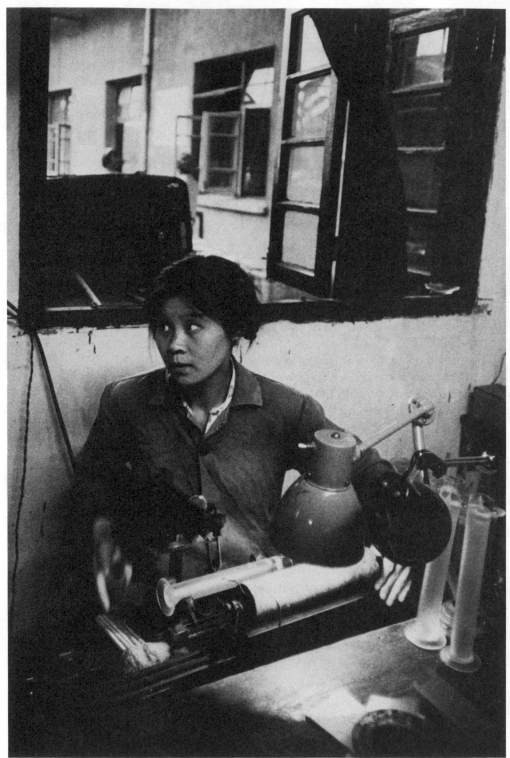

IV. Work

Unlike romantic love, "production," as the Chinese always refer to work, is considered the proper channel for the individual's energies in a socialist society, for production contributes directly to the collective goal of material well-being for all. Yet, according to the New Realism writers, the reality of socialist production has fallen far short of the ideal, and politics has often interfered.

"The Foundation" by Jiang Zilong, focuses on the problem of corrupt leadership in the workplace. The young workers at the forging shop seem more interested in overtime pay and bonuses than in working for the collective good. Their ideological education has taught them that such self-seeking behavior does not reflect the proper motivation in their revolutionary society, but when they look around them, they see their leaders—the various shop directors and department heads—using their talents and energies to further their own ends rather than to arouse enthusiasm for socialist construction. The inefficiency, stalling, and shoddy workmanship that result from these attitudes further frustrate the efforts of the truly dedicated, properly motivated cadres like the story's hero, the old shop director Lu Yongcun.

The obstacle to production in "Trust," by Chen Zhongshi, is mistrust—the legacy of past political campaigns that have set different groups of people against each other at different points in time. The complicated web of hostility and suspicion that remains prevents people from working together and extends even into the next generation. Like "The Foundation," "Trust" places the responsibility for solving the problem on those in leadership positions. In both stories, it is the old, committed cadres who finally arouse the idealism of the younger workers, allowing everyone to forgive, forget, and get on with production.

The Foundation
JIANG ZILONG

1

National Day* was approaching. Many workers in the forging shop crowded around the shop director, Lu Yongcun, clamoring for extra shifts during the holidays. Since overtime paid double, three days of overtime work meant that a level-three worker could make seven or eight yuan, a level-four worker more than ten. And what a level-five worker and above could get need not even be mentioned! The question was: What could the overtime workers do? After all, there was no urgent task at hand. Everybody suggested that since the shop's major piece of equipment—the foundation for the five-hundred-ton speed forging press—had already been poured, the machine could be installed ahead of schedule during the holidays. Lu Yongcun would not agree to this at all. His reason was that this foundation would be the basis for long-term development, and so was extremely important. It was therefore necessary to insist on absolute quality, and to follow through with the scheduled maintenance before installing the machine. Those who wanted extra shifts looked at one another, groaning inside, but were unwilling to disperse.

Lao Lu was tall, thin, and hunched over, with a head of bushy white hair. It was difficult to tell his age. Probably he was somewhere between fifty and sixty. His face, rough but friendly, had half a century of important events written on it. He was stubborn as a mule. People said he was so inflexible that he would let an opportunity slip by rather than change his course. Actually, it wasn't that he did not understand others' feelings; it was just that he was dead serious when it came to matters of principle.

The workers all tried to get a word in. Some said that they could not see how installing the machine ahead of schedule would affect the quality; others suggested finding odd jobs to do. Some even bad-mouthed Lao Lu. Lu Yongcun was neither anxious nor angry. He could hold his own, and was not one to let go of a principle easily. Just as he was getting hopelessly entangled in the hubbub, someone came to his rescue. It was the shop's clerk, Kang Tongyan.

Although Kang Tongyan was also over fifty, his hair was still shiny black. His face, soft and smooth, radiated a youthful glow. He was not tall, but he had a huge belly. It bulged so much his back was

---

* National Day, October 1, commemorates the founding of the People's Republic of China.

bent. His clumsy appearance was misleading. In fact, he was extremely agile. He pushed his way through to the front of the crowd and addressed everyone in a very solemn tone: "Fellow workers, don't waste time arguing here. Get on with your business. I have something urgent to discuss with Director Lu." His small, shrewd eyes swept the crowd, and, just in case his words might be doubted, he added: "Starting this month, the factory office wants to suspend the bonus for the entire shop. It is urgent that the director and I come up with a plan so that we can fight the issue out at the accounting department."

Not only had they not won overtime pay, but on top of everything there was this rumor that bonuses would be suspended. The workers felt that the situation was really getting sticky, and so, not very happily, they left the office.

There was laughter in Kang Tongyan's eyes. He was at his usual best. Every time Lu Yongcun was confronted with a dilemma or besieged by pestering people, Kang Tongyan would be sure to show up at his side like a guard, bluffing and making up excuses. Either there was an urgent call from the factory manager for Lu Yongcun or a problem had arisen elsewhere that needed the immediate attention of Director Lu. His performance was perfect, and he always managed to break the siege for Lu Yongcun. Oftentimes even Lao Lu himself was taken in. On occasion, this honest fellow Lao Lu took what Kang Tongyan made up on the spur of the moment so seriously that Kang sometimes had to follow through with the charade.

After the workers left, Lu Yongcun asked with serious concern: "Who wanted the suspension of our workshop's bonus?"

Kang Tongyan gave a mysterious smile: "Rumors."

Lu Yongcun was not pleased: 'Huh, 'rumors' again! If it was only rumor, why did you announce it right in front of everyone? And so convincingly? As if it were a fact. That's not a good thing to do."

"My 'rumor' is over ninety-five percent accurate. As soon as I hear of anything I keep you informed. Otherwise, when the time comes and the factory office really suspends bonuses, how could you, the shop director, face all the workers?" Rebuked, Kang Tongyan was not too pleased. But still he kept a smile on his face as he answered. He and Lu Yongcun had a long-standing relationship of over thirty years. Before Liberation, Kang Tongyan had been the boss's son at "Kang's Iron Works" and Lu Yongcun, the factory's craftsman. Today, the craftsman was a shop director, and the boss's son a clerk who did odd jobs.

Kang paused a moment and then advised Lao Lu further: "Director, don't ignore the workers' requests. I have asked around and I found out that other shops are all giving overtime. Whether there is work or not depends entirely on how one manages the shop. Forget about the foundation. If you could somehow dredge up some odd jobs for the men, wouldn't there be overtime? Why must you lay yourself open to their curses? Why ask for trouble?"

"What else can I do! Give out two hundred percent overtime pay for trivial work, and let the country suffer for it? Ai, being a cadre, one way or another you're bound to be cursed!"

"A cadre is bound to be criticized?" Kang Tongyan shook his fleshy head, unconvinced. If this factory were your own, he thought, it might still be worth your while to tolerate the insults. But to perform this thankless task of being shop director for the state, earning a measly seventy or eighty bucks a month, is it really worth it to take shit from people? If the workers get overtime, it doesn't mean that you, Lu Yongcun, will lose money, so is it worth the trouble to resist them? Moreover, if the workers have their overtime, you as director can do the same. What's wrong with making a few extra bucks? You really are stubborn as a mule! Well, what's the use. Lu Yongcun is just too damn honest. No wonder he has been a cadre for years, and still holds the same position. I am afraid that he will never be promoted. He would miss an opportunity if it hit him over the head.

Lu Yongcun suddenly remembered something: "Lao Kang, the political office just called and asked you to stop by."

Kang Tongyan eyes instantly lit up; his heart pounded. Immediately he turned to leave, but was stopped by a thought. In an admonishing tone, he said: "Director, don't forget to go to the accounting department to inquire about the bonus matter."

"I'll go in a little while. On your way, please ask Xiaoqing to stop by here," said Lao Lu, already pondering another matter.

2

Xi Xiaoqing hung up the phone, feeling as agitated inside as a pot of boiling water.

Her boyfriend—Lu Yongcun's son Lu Jie—had just called to invite her home for the holidays. This was known as "getting to know the household"—formally meeting his parents. In particular, it was a chance for his friends to look her over. Lu Jie also told her on the phone that he had brought her several very fashionable outfits and some fine material from the south. Xiaoqing was uncomfortable. Never had she imagined that only a few months after they met, Lu Jie would already be preparing a solid material foundation for marriage. The problem was that after a few times, she felt that Lu Jie was really not her type. They hardly had anything in common. As a person, he had a long way to go to catch up with his father. Just now, Lu Jie had invited her to his house for the holidays. If she went, wouldn't it mean that she had committed herself to the relationship? She had neither accepted nor refused over the phone. She told Lu Jie that before leaving work for the day, she would give him a definite answer.

At that moment, the one who had introduced them, Kang Tongyan, came to tell her that Director Lu wanted to see her. Furthermore, with obvious merriment, Kang whispered to her: "I still have some good news to tell you. Lu Jie said your new home lacks a television set. Leave it to me!"

After saying this, he gave her a mysterious smile, and his fat body glided away like a chubby fish.

Xi Xiaoqing's looks were not outstanding, but she had a plain, healthy, natural beauty. With a quiet, gentle air and a solid, down-to-earth manner of speech, she was a woman with depth of character. It might have been precisely this quality that had won Lu Yongcun's appreciation. She was the shop's party Youth League secretary.

The girl's heart was pounding when she walked into Lu Yongcun's office. After letting her sit down, Lu Yongcun asked: "Xiao Xi, these days the men are not very motivated. They slight their normal work, yet they want overtime during the holidays. Your Youth League branch should concentrate more on its members' political thinking."

Thank goodness Lao Lu hadn't brought up the subject of his son's wedding plans. The girl nodded slightly, relieved inside.

"Is there any problem? Has the Youth League branch held elections yet?"

Xiaoqing said: "The elections were held, but the work assignments haven't been made. Nobody wants to be League cadre. Those chosen could not very well refuse, but they were only willing to participate as ordinary committee members, not as propaganda committee members."

"How come?"

"Propaganda committee members have to write public reports, print material, and drum up enthusiasm. These are thankless tasks. Organizational committee members only have to collect dues, which is quite an easy job."

"Hm? This attitude still prevails?" Lu Yongcun was surprised.

The League secretary smiled, "Director Lu, I myself am not sure why. Nowadays the prestige of the League branch is not high. Nothing seems to motivate people. The feeling of pride and responsibility among League members is not strong. Our shop has only ten or so members. The number dropping out exceeds the number joining. There are too few young people around. Even those few apprentices would not even have applied to the League if we had not sought them out."

Xi Xiaoqing's words alarmed Lu Yongcun. He was concerned about the issue that the League secretary had presented him. He stood up, paced a little, and stopped in front of Xiaoqing. He looked at this young woman, and he was greatly disturbed. In her work and character, Xi Xiaoqing was head and shoulders above the other young people in the shop. But Lao Lu always felt that she was hiding something in her heart. So he asked at this point: "We should be straightforward with each other. Is there something else on your mind?" The girl blushed and lowered her head. After thinking for a while she raised her head and looked straight at him, saying: "Director Lu, may I ask you a few questions?"

"What are they? Go ahead."

This thoughtful girl, trying hard to suppress her own agitation, said: "When *The Communist Manifesto* was published, communism was nothing but a spectre, but that was enough for the capitalist world. They were scared to death. Now that there are many socialist countries in the world, capitalism is no longer afraid; it is even contemptuous of socialism. Why? If socialist institutions are superior, why haven't our productive powers developed as quickly as those of capitalism's? Why is our economic construction and technological development lagging behind capitalism's? On the basis of faith, I believe that communism will be realized; it will win over capitalism. On the other hand, when I listen to technical reports and read magazines on technology, it is clear that capitalism is more advanced than socialism. How can this be explained?"

Lu Yongcun was really shocked. He was a practical man—not one for much theorizing. Although the questions posed were not too difficult to answer, clarifying the complicated web all at once would not be easy. Never had he imagined that Xi Xiaoqing would raise these issues.

It was obvious that XI Xiaoqing had been pondering these things for some time, tossing and turning these questions around in her head. She became more excited as she spoke. Noticing that the shop director's eyes, which had been scrutinizing her, were becoming wider and wider, she brought the discussion around to Lao Lu himself: "Director Lu, you joined the union and participated in strikes before Liberation. Has your faith in communism changed since then? In the past many revolutionary martyrs would have died proudly for communism, firmly believing that the revolution would win. But today, how many people are there left with this kind of faith? Even among the remaining old cadres—in their minds, how much weight do they give communist ideals? In their lives, how much does the future count?"

Lu was dumbfounded. He just could not connect these strange, sharp questions with the ordinarily progressive party Youth League secretary. His first reaction was not to think how he would answer the girl's questions, but to feel sorry for her, to be concerned about her. How complicated her thoughts were. Perhaps she would be better off if she acted like other frivolous young girls who cared only about eating and dressing well. With a solemn face, he said severely: "Don't think about nonsense!"

The girl kept silent, only staring at Lao Lu stubbornly, as if to say: Aren't you troubled by similar questions yourself?

3

Lu Yongcun met with a flat refusal when he went to the bonus evaluation group to negotiate the shop's share. On his way back to the shop, he was still debating with the group leader in his mind: "Your shop ruined all the facilities and halted production for months. Every month it incurs losses, and you still have the nerve to ask for a bonus? What an absurd idea. . . ."

After he had heard this, Lao Lu had been struck dumb with anger, but now he had finally come up with the reasons he should have given in defense: "Right. Logically, bonuses should not be given if the unit halts production and incurs losses. But why did our shop halt production? Who should be blamed for the losses? Ask anywhere, has there ever been a case where a speed forging press has collapsed with its foundation in three to four years? In February, when the speed press broke down, we made an emergency report to the factory office. From the very beginning, nobody gave the matter any attention; no one was anxious about it. When we got the cement, the reinforcing bars weren't available. When those were finally obtained, we ran out of stone. When, with difficulty, the material was assembled, we lacked workers. Before we knew it, half a year had passed. It takes less than half a year to build and install a new press from scratch, but our factory waited for eight months just to replace a foundation. How could we prevent a deficit? Should I, Lu Yongcun, be blamed? Should the workshop be held responsible? Why must our workers' bonuses be withheld? All the other workshops are given bonuses. How can I stay on as the workshop director? How can I explain it to the workers?"

He was in the right, but the moment he became anxious, he developed a mental block. After he calmed down, he would think of the arguments, one after another. Lao Lu was filled with regret. Actually, he was not stupid. If allowed to make his points slowly and calmly, he could be quite articulate. He would not interrupt others' arguments, but neither could he be interrupted. However, in a confrontation, when arguments became heated and people got worked up and cut him short, he would be at a loss for words. All his reasons stayed cooped up inside. Therefore, he was often frustrated during the middle-level cadre conferences in the factory. Factory managers often took out their frustrations and anger with other workshops on him, seeking Lu Yongcun out to let him have it. It was because they knew that Lao Lu would not kick up a fuss and put them on the spot. Though everyone bullied him, there was unanimous agreement that Lao Lu was a good man, a diligent and solid old ox.

The workers in the forging shop were all waiting anxiously for the good news to be brought back by Director Lu. But when they saw Lu Yongcun's dejected and distracted manner, their enthusiasm cooled. Deducting six or seven bucks was no small matter for these men. Some immediately started gossiping, deliberately raising their voices to make sure that Lao Lu heard them:

"It is always the honest people who get the short end of the stick. Our Lao Lu is really useless! An army without a shrewd leader is bound to be defeated. The whole workshop has to suffer because of him."

"A good horse has strong legs, a good fellow has a sharp tongue. Our Director Lu is incompetent!"

Originally, honesty had been a virtue, the manifestation of high party commitment. Now it was equated with stupidity, incompetence, boorishness.

At first, Lao Lu pretended not to have heard. For causing such disorder in the workshop he felt he should blame himself for not having handled things properly instead of blaming the workers for complaining. But the more he ignored their talk, the more excited the complaints became. Some of the workers actually stopped work altogether. Finally he blew up: "Stopping work for the loss of a mere few bucks? Only working for money? Don't you have a conscience?"

Seeing that the director was angry, the men dared not grumble anymore. It was clear to everyone that the director was upset too, and that his hands were tied. However, one unconvinced young fellow stubbornly retorted: "Conscience! My conscience tells me to work and earn a wage, to eat and dress myself."

"If everyone behaved like you, how can we ever achieve modernization?"

"I am a worker. I can't be bothered with these issues."

Lu shook with anger as the other workers persuaded the hotheaded fellow to back off. When he returned to his office he was very troubled. Sandwiched between pressures from above and below, how could he function as workshop director? If this situation dragged on, the forging workshop was going to fall apart. But he also felt that no matter how the workers complained, he should grin and bear it, in order to arrange properly the work after the holidays. He suddenly thought of Lu Jie, who should have returned home quite some time ago. Wondering about this, he picked up the phone.

In order to install the five-hundred-ton press, they needed a shock absorber. Twenty days before, the Supplies Department had sent Lu Jie to the south to buy one. Before he left, Lu Yongcun urged his son a thousand times to make sure that he got the shock absorber and to return as soon as possible. Lao Lu got through to the Capital Construction Department, and it was Lu Jie who answered the phone. Detecting enthusiasm in his son's voice, Lao Lu felt relieved for a moment, thinking that the shock absorber had been obtained. But Lu Jie lightheartedly told him that the factory no longer stocked this product, and so he had not been able to get it. Lu Yongcun's ear hummed. If at this instant Lu Jie had stood right in front of him, he would surely have slapped him on the face. His son had ruined the matter! Oblivious to his father's troubles, Lu Jie excitedly told him that he had acquired a shipment of lumber from the south. He urged his father to take off from work a bit earlier to help him transport the lumber home from the train station. When confronted with a negative answer, Lu Jie changed his tone immediately and started complaining that Lao Lu was not concerned with his affairs. He also gave his list of reasons loud and clear. What kind of father would not plan for his children's marriage! Off the top of his head, he reeled off examples: so and so's father had bought his son some furniture, so and so's father had arranged for new living quarters for his son. Lao Lu, according to this reasoning, was the only father who did not seem to care a bit.

Not waiting for his son to finish, Lao Lu angrily hung up the phone. Plans, plans, he had only met the girl a few times, and already he had made all the plans for the marriage. But how about the plans for the workshop? The plans for the factory?

Lu Yongcun was extremely troubled. He could not sit still, yet he could not come up with any solution. He stormed out of the office, and without knowing where he was heading, found himself at the foundation of the speed press. He suddenly realized that the workshop was unusually quiet. Why were there no hammering noises in the forge? Why couldn't he hear the rumbling tracks of the overhead crane? Even the furnace, usually roaring with activity, was lying still, in dead silence. At this moment, how he longed to hear that familiar deafening sound of the hammering iron! A quiet forging shop was a bad sign. This was a deadly, oppressive calm.

Lao Lu had spent more than half his life in the forging business. Technically speaking, the facilities were now much better, but the business seemed to be getting more and more difficult and was losing more and more money. When he had been an apprentice a long time ago, his boss had relied totally on manual labor and had made a fortune. The boss had invested in a pneumatic hammer from his accumulated profits and made even more money with it. Later, when the hammer broke from wear, they tied it back together with iron wire and still made big money from its operation. Who would ever have anticipated that forging would be a business that lost money? Yet now they had a several-thousand-worker mining machinery factory with a forging workshop that boasted several hundred workers. How could it be losing money? Where was the problem?

Lu Yongcun squatted on the foundation, his head in his hands. As he fixed his stare on the reinforced concrete foundation under his feet, one problem after another rose up in his mind. He did not find any answers to his questions; instead, he discovered a weak spot in the foundation. He knocked it with an iron rod, and a large lump of concrete fell off like cracked plaster. This triggered a thought in his mind, and he hastened to inspect the foundation more closely. The more he checked, the more apprehensive he became. The foundation of the speed press should have been the responsibility of the Department of Capital Construction. Though Lao Lu was not a construction worker, as an experienced blacksmith he could tell that the foundation had some real problems. He hurried back to his office and called the head of the Capital Construction Department.

"Manager Yu? A problem has arisen with the foundation of the five-hundred-ton speed press! I tapped it with a rod and a whole chunk fell off. How can it withstand five hundred tons of pressure?"

"How can you expect it not to chip if you hack away at it with an iron bar? You could probably shatter it to pieces if you used explosives!" The department head spoke sarcastically.

"Lao Yu, this foundation is not a laughing matter. Less than four years after we installed the speed press, we had to dismantle the foundation for an overhaul. What other country would have had to do such a thing? People use a foundation for decades—a century even. The foundation is still intact even after several hammers are worn out. If we go on this way, our country will suffer great losses! I suggest that your department test a piece of the foundation."

"There is no need. If problems eventually arise from the foundation, our department will see to it. You take care of the business in your workshop!" The head of the Capital Construction Department crossly hung up on Lu.

What a load of nonsense, endless haggling and arguments, repeated frustration. Lu Yongcun muttered to himself: "All right, keep arguing—argue till your hair turns white. The factory is going to collapse, and we will still be arguing. . . ."

4

Kang Tongyan bounced along lightheartedly. A while ago the political office had removed his label of "reactionary capitalist," and he was pleased and relieved. When he returned to the office of the workshop, he caught Lao Yongcun staring blankly at the telephone, deep in thought. He called out loudly, "Lao Lu!"

Lu Yongcun lifted his head and, detecting Kang Tongyan's delighted mood, asked: "Lao Kang, what's up?"

Kang Tongyan laughed: "Lao Lu, don't pretend you don't know. Isn't this all your doing?" He always knew the right thing to say. He knew clearly that the policy of removing political labels had been the decision of the party Central Committee, but he deliberately gave the credit to Lu Yongcun. All these years Lao Lu had been good to him. Even when he had been branded a reactionary, the forging shop did not treat him as one. When his advancing years made it difficult for him to do strenuous manual work, Lu Yongcun gave him the post of office clerk. The job not only maximized his special skills, it enabled him to wield a little power. Running about here and there, he had become noticeable enough to be listened to in the workshop. Deep down inside, he was grateful to this honest and ethical man Lu.

Lu Yongcun finally realized what Kang was referring to. He offered a cigarette to Kang Tongyan and said: "You should be grateful to the party for removing your political label. Lao Kang, what do you think we must do to manage the forging shop better?"

Kang Tongyan did not immediately grasp what Lu meant: "This . . . how should I put it. . . ."

"Suppose the factory were given to you, as though it were your private enterprise, what would you do?"

"Given to me?" Kang Tongyan's heart gave a start, blood rushed to his head, and his blood pressure seemed to rise. He knew his own capacities. He was also quite sure that Lu Yongcun knew he was no idiot. After all, he had bailed out the director many times. Was Lu Yongcun thinking of promoting him to deputy director since his political label had been removed? Heavens, was good news to come in pairs today? This sudden urge for power made him blush and sweat.

Sensing that Kang was on the wrong track, Lu Yongcun put the matter in a straightforward way: "In the past, your father operated Kang's Iron Works with only a few furnaces and men. You did nothing all day but play—catching rabbits and birds during the day, and visiting brothels at night. You only made a few quick visits to the workshop when you were in the mood; yet the shop made a great deal of money. Nowadays, the conditions are much better—more facilities, more workers. How come we are losing money?"

Kang finally understood. He knew the difficulties of the shop director facing him. In a sarcastic tone that he had not dared to use for a good many years, he said: "Actually, it seems to me that you have done a good enough job with the forging workshop. After all, this isn't your own factory."

"What do you mean? Are you saying that I did not work hard enough?"

"No, you have put in a great deal, but it was a wasted effort. If the workshop had been your own, you would have had to close it the way it is running now. Your own family would either have killed themselves or slept on the street, and the workers would have lost their livelihood. Could you imagine the situation being as comfortable as they have it now? Taking a nice salary just to sit around and shoot the bull. The Communist Party is so generous; the superiority of socialism means that everyone gets to eat, no matter what."

"I am incapable of managing the workshop well. . . ."

"Why are you incapable? It is because the workshop isn't yours. You have no power of decision. Therefore, you have no authority in the eyes of the workers. They can listen to you, or they can choose not to. None of you in the leadership appeals to the basic interests of the workers; instead, you try to appeal to their political enthusiasm. As a result, a side effect developed during those years when political movements proliferated, just as, when you've taken a drug for too long, you develop a resistance to it. Those who joined the party are less compliant than activists who have not joined. For the last few years, which small unit hasn't tried to recruit the "four black elements"* because they are more conscientious than the "five red elements?"† If the workers, supposedly the masters of the factory, do not consider the factory their own, can it be managed well? To tell you the truth, the factory at the moment belongs to no one—not to

* Landlords, rich peasants, counterrevolutionaries, and "bad elements," or their children.
† Workers, peasants, cadres, army men, and the revolutionary martyrs, or their children.

the factory managers; not to you, the workshop director; and even less to the workers. You would say that it belongs to the party, to the country. What national chairman could maange each and every factory?"

"You are talking nonsense again!" Lu Yongcun angrily glared at his former boss's son. Actually what made him angry was that there was a grain of truth in Kang's statements. It also reminded him of what the Party Youth League secretary, Xi Xiaoqing, had said before. That the two—with such completely different experiences, political background, and ages—could have made such similar points made him shudder.

Lu Yongcun's outburst sobered Kang instantly. "You old idiot," he cursed, "You forget yourself in your enthusiasm. Fortunately for you that Lu Yongcun is so honest and ethical. If it had been someone else, it would have been reported to the higher-ups, and your recently removed label would have been stuck right back on you."

Kang broke out in a cold sweat, and immediately forced a smile, saying, "Director, I'm only joking. Don't take it seriously."

"You don't have to give me that again. . . . Come off it!" Lu Yongcun said in disgust. "The quality of the speed press's foundation is problematic. The Capital Construction Department refuses to check it. Do you have any ideas on how to solve this dilemma?"

Kang Tongyan regained his spirits when he was asked this. He was always willing to help when Lu Yongcun encountered problems. Moreover, in this factory, he was confident that there was nothing that he could not manage. He took a pack of cigarettes from his briefcase, held it in his hand, and said laughingly, "Leave this matter to me. I will ask the people in the Capital Construction Department to do a test."

He turned to go, but suddenly remembered another matter. He pulled out a wad of money from his briefcase and pressed it into Lu's hands. With great seriousness, he said, "Give this to Lu Jie."

"What is this for?"

"His bridal suite still lacks a television. This is what I, the matchmaker, will help him out with."

Lao Lu was furious. Angrily he retorted: "I will have nothing to do with it!"

Kang Tongyan took back the money, displeased. "All right, I will give this to Lu Jie myself."

5

Lu Yongcun was paralyzed with anger after he read the test report that Kang Tongyan brought back. The foundation for the speed press was completely substandard. The blueprint demanded a load-bearing capacity of two hundred, and the actual product reached only ninety.

They had stopped production for seven months only to get this result. Over a hundred tons of cement and tons of reinforcing steel bars had all gone to waste. The most devastating thing was that seven months had been thrown away. Now they would have to use steel bars to chip away the few hundred cubic meters of the reinforced concrete foundation and build a new one from scratch. Another delay. . . . Who knew for how long?

Still, it was fortunate that Lu Yongcun was scrupulous enough to check on the quality of the foundation and to ask Kang Tongyan to do a secret test. If they had gone ahead and installed the press, the consequences would have been even more serious. Lu Yongcun immdiately reported the situation to the factory manager. The latter was furious too and called an emergency meeting. All the major department heads attended.

The head of the Capital Construction Department had been promoted from a dispatcher post. He was as skinny and shriveled as a monkey, but he had a loud voice. He was an energetic head of his department. Among the middle-level cadres in the mining machinery factory, he had the reputation of being competent, as well as being one of the four "smart mouths" in the factory—hence his nickname, Smart Mouth Yu. He was startled when confronted by the factory manager. He had not gotten wind of this at all. From the report passed on by Lu Yongcun, he recognized that his own men had done the test. Immediately, he swore inside: "Treacherous bastards, testing for others, and not even informing me."

Nevertheless, within a few minutes, while reading the report, he had already thought out an answer. Lifting his head, he spoke with perfect assurance, his face wearing an ingratiating smile: "This is not our responsibility. Our construction work was fine. This quality problem was caused by faulty cement. I must also make it clear to you all that the dormitory under construction is being built with this same batch of cement. If a future problem arises, our Capital Construction Department is not at all resposible."

How deftly he had wiped his hands clean. Nowadays, the strength of a person, the level of a cadre, all depend on how good he is at talking himself out of anything. Lu Yongcun was dumbfounded. His lips trembling, he had not yet thought of a way to retort, when someone responded for him.

The speaker was the head of the Materials and Supplies Department, a middle-aged man with a rough demeanor. His lips looked black and cold from too much smoking. The factory Supplies Department was similar to the department and food stores—that is, it was always others who asked them for favors and never the other way around. Therefore, those in the supplies trade had a great deal of clout. This department head enjoyed a celebrated nickname—Lin Dana.*

Lin Dana lifted his head up abruptly and coldly addressed the head of the Capital Construction Department: "Lao Yu, don't try to pass the buck. You may have a sharp tongue, but don't think you can slough off your own responsibilities. The cement we bought all bore bonafide certificates of inspection. How could it have gone bad? Why didn't you test it before construction? It is obvious that the cement was fine; it was you who messed it up. And now, you try to blame others for it!"

The meeting suddenly became lively as the two started a real verbal battle. An outsider observing this debate would have felt that all of them had good points, because both sides understood the art of arguing: it did not matter if you had good reasons or not; as long as you could argue your points forcefully, you were already halfway there.

The factory manager had a strong build and a look of well-being that gave people the impression that he was easygoing. He wished to settle the case as soon as possible. He wanted to push the responsibility onto the head of the Capital Construction Department, but Smart Mouth Yu fought back resiliently. Then the factory manager tried to pass the pressure on to the head of the Materials and Supplies Department. But Lin Dana was even more stubborn. The manager was anxious, but could not very well express his annoyance. He too felt powerless to resolve the situation. Things were strange these days. In theory, the manager had authority over the department heads. In fact, it was not always possible to exert this authority. It appeared as if the department heads occupied a lower position than the manager in the factory hierarchy, yet the former could stand up to the latter by grabbing hold of the latter's weak spots. In this way, they exploited each other's weaknesses, at times for mutual benefit, at times for a balance of conflicts. On the one hand, it seemed that all had power; on the other hand, it seemed that no one had power. In other words, if it were official business, nobody had the power to decide; even if one had power, one would not exercise it. But for private, individual business, everyone dared to throw his weight around as much as he could. Relations among the cadres were a nasty, muddled vicious cycle.

Lu Yongcun could only sit on the sidelines, feeling anxious.

It was a real dilemma. The factory manager could only signal the two heads to stop their argument saying: "All right, don't argue anymore. Drop the issue of responsibility for the time being. Let us first look into what we can do with the foundation."

* "The Boss."

Lu Yongcun agonized inside. He knew that the manager was giving ground. It was such an important incident and he was not even going to investigate who was responsible.

Lin Dana leaned back on the sofa, and said lightly, "Looking to see what can be done with the foundation has nothing to do with my department."

The manager asked Smart Mouth Yu: "Lao Yu, what is your suggestion?"

"I don't have any ideas either," Smart Mouth Yu responded listlessly.

Lu Yongcun could not hold his temper any longer: "The job must be done. Tear down this shoddy foundation and build a new one."

Smart Mouth Yu asked: "Who is to tear it down?"

"Naturally your department. This has always been your job, and, moreover, you are the ones who made a mess of it."

Yu glared at him, saying: "So whatever you say goes, right? The situation has not been analyzed, nor has the question of responsibility been thoroughly investigated. Even the manager has not made a decision on the matter. What right do you, Lu Yongcun, have, to say such a thing?"

"This. . . ." Lu Yongcun was speechless. His philosophy was that in a fight honesty would win out over dishonesty. However, other people had a philosophy diametrically opposed—that is, that dishonesty would win over honesty. When these two philosophies clashed, his was bound to be defeated. He could only say: "If you don't do it, who will? You can afford to drag this out, we can't. In the final analysis, the real loser is our country."

The head of the Capital Construction Department cut in sarcastically. "Don't you imagine that you are the only one who cares about our country's modernization. I am more anxious than you are. It is all right if you want us to work on the project, but at the moment I don't have any spare workers. If we are to tear down the foundation, we need to stop the dormitory construction first."

Hearing this threat, the manager became worried: "How can we possibly allow this?"

Smart Mouth Yu laughed: "I have an idea. Lao Lu, aren't your shop's workers idling around? I suggest you tear it down yourselves."

Arguing the issue back and forth, the burden fell back on the forging shop. Lu Yongcun burst out: "This is not our business. We are forgers, we can't do construction work."

"What is this 'you' and 'we.' Aren't we all working for the country's Four Modernizations?" The head of the Capital Construction Department also leaned back on the sofa: "All right, if you don't want to do it, you just have to wait."

Lin Dana reached over, took a filter cigarette from the factory manager's pack, and stuck it in his mouth. Smart Mouth Yu also reached out his hand, saying, "Hey, don't think only of yourself." Lin Dana took one more and threw it to Smart Mouth Yu: "You cheap fellow. Change your name from Smart Mouth to Shrewd Old Rooster from now on. You always cadge cigarettes off people during meetings!"

Smart Mouth Yu, not to be outdone, retorted: "According to what I have heard from your department, no matter how honest people are, after they work in Materials and Supplies under you for three months they would dare to cheat even their own fathers."

The two lit their cigarettes and laughed together. (Don't be fooled by their fierce argument just then. That was a sham fight, and would be forgotten as soon as the meeting was over. It would in no way affect their personal friendship.) How could Lao Lu ever be their match? His heart ached, and Kang's question flashed through his mind: "Who does this mining machinery factory really belong to?" The factory manager, the department heads—none of them acted as though the factory were under their care. They were not anxious even after such a serious incident! It looks like I, Lu Yongcun, am the only one who cares about it as if it were my own. No, the factory belongs to the party. But where is the party? Is the party real or illusory? Oh, party, you have been cheated. They would even dare to cheat their parents, so why not cheat you too. Nobody puts the party before himself. You have allowed them to occupy various positions, but they have abused you instead. They make a mess of our foundation, and they have all become perpetual liars. Xiaoqing, oh, Xiaoqing—the answer you were searching for is right here, isn't it?

Lu Yongcun often lacked sharp judgment when it came to evaluating people and situations; but today, he suddenly understood many problems that he had not dared to face in the past. The particular needs of a society created particular types of social personalities. If there was no need to haggle, there would be no sly bums. If there was the need for it, people would naturally have to haggle their way around. Take his own son Lu Jie—wasn't he emulating Lin Dana?

The factory manager pondered for a while, and finally put the pressure on Lu Yongcun: "This substandard foundation—it is better for your workshop to tear it down. You can send some workers to the Capital Construction Department first to learn the technique. . . ."

6

Lu Yongcun returned to the workshop, gathered the workers before the foundation of the five-hundred-ton speed press, and planned the task of tearing it down. The workers exploded. Aside from the fact that tearing down the foundation was an extremely unpleasant, tiring, and dirty job—it could not even really be justified. Since it was the Capital Construction Department that had made such an enormous error, the factory should dismiss the department head, suspend the department bonus, and compensate for the forging workshop's losses. On the contrary, not only did the Capital Construction Department disclaim responsibility, the forging workshop had to wash their shit off for them. Just now, the factory had suspended the forging workshop's bonus; when a nasty job needed to be done, it was handed over to the shop. How could the shop's workers swallow the assignment cheerfully?

Lu Yongcun was sympathetic to the workers' discontent, but he felt powerless about the whole situation. The seed of such bitter fruit had been sown ten or twenty years before. Now, Lao Lu had to take it all in one bite. The workers were angrily grumbling and swearing when suddenly someone discovered that Director Lu was deadly white, and that he was paralyzed in the pit of the trouble-causing foundation.

"Director Lu!" The workers gathered around him, startled.

Lu Yongcun did not know when it had all started. At first, he felt his heart pounding and his breathing become difficult. He felt constriction in his chest, and before long he could not stand on his feet. Xiaoqing and several other young fellows hastily lent him a hand. He had never detected any sign of abnormal blood pressure or a heart condition; but just now, inexplicably, it seemed that he had had a heart attack. A frightful shadow flashed across his face. He was forcing himself so hard to suppress the terrible pain inside that his face muscles were cramped with spasms.

Lao Lu tried to urge others to get on with their tasks, saying that he was all right. But Xi Xiaoqing refused to leave him. All of a sudden, he remembered his son's marriage plans. He could not help pulling Xiao Xi to his side and, in the faintest whisper, saying: "That young fellow Lu Jie is a good-for-nothing; he is not good enough for you. . . ." He was going to say more, but when he saw Xiaoqing blush and tears swell up in her eyes, he stopped himself.

After a while, Lao Lu suppressed the pain in his chest, and tried hard to raise his voice to address Xiaoqing: "Xiao Xi, please organize a task force in the name of the party Youth League. Try to have the foundation torn down within a month." As he spoke, he pulled out a wad of bills from his pocket and pressed it into Xiaoqing's hand, saying: "Put this money aside for a bonus. If there is not enough, after the next payday, I will give some more. . . ."

Xiaoqing was moved to tears. As she pushed the money back to him, she said with a sobbing voice: "Director Lu, don't worry. We do not want a cent of bonus. We assure you that the task will be done in good time!"

"No, you keep the money; the job is difficult; it is all my fault. I did not do my job well and now you are all suffering because of me." Lao Lu forced the money into the party Youth League secretary's hand.

The news spread. The forging workers were all upset. Gathering around Lao Lu, they said in voices trembling with emotion: "Director Lu, don't you understand us by now? What we say and what we do are two different things. Just now, when we were cursing and making a fuss, we were not really swearing at you. What we were cursing was the crooked style of doing things around here, of passing the buck without caring to see what is right or wrong. Please don't take it to heart! Though the Capital Construction Department is not willing to help our shop start production again, we are. After we finish our job, we will drag them to the party committee of the Electrical Machinery Bureau, to see who is in the right. We are all joining the task force in three shifts. We will tear it down nicely even without bonuses. We are really not working for a few bonus bucks!"

Lu Yongcun laughed gratefully; he laughed and laughed until the tears rolled down his cheeks. An intolerable constricting pain in his heart made him feel faint again. When the workers saw how the old director's sweating face had grown thin and gaunt during the past few hours, they felt terrible. Just as everyone was trying to take him to the hospital, Director Lu struggled to lift his head and growled: "Put me down, you are all so mixed up! You think I'm sick? It is our workshop that is sick. It is our factory that is sick. The root of sickness is in the foundation!"

The workers all comforted him, saying: "Don't worry. We are here to tear down the bad foundation, Old Director!" Someone brought a chair, and they sat him in it, saying: "Watch us set to work immediately to cure this foundation."

A trace of confidence glowed in Lu Yongcun's face. He murmured with sincerity: "The factory is the foundation of our country, we cannot afford to continue messing it up. . . . We must not leave hidden danger for the country. . . . The foundation, the foundation. . . ."

What the workers said, they did. The forging shop was suddenly bustling with activity. Strangely enough, today, the forging workers did a far better job than the experienced construction workers. Xi Xiaoqing led the Youth League members in taking on the most arduous tasks, and all worked furiously. At that moment, Kang Tongyan came in with a briefcase in his hands. The frenzy at the workshop literally dumbfounded him. With embarrassment, he glanced at the old director, seated in a chair, who, with an encouraging tone, pointed to a crowbar on the floor and said to him: "What are you waiting for? Isn't this a crowbar?" Kang squinted his little eyes, and his thin lips managed to squeeze out two words, "Yes, yes." Then, he dropped his briefcase, picked up the crowbar, and without looking back headed toward the crowd attacking the faulty foundation.

from *Shanghai Wenxue* (*Shanghai Literature*)
December, 1979

Trust
CHEN ZHONGSHI

I

A serious incident—a fight—had stirred every nook and cranny of Luocun* Brigade. The victim was Dashun, a member of the Youth League branch organization committee and son of Luo Mengtian, chairman of the Poor Peasant Association. The offender was Luo Hu, third son of Luo Kun, who had been branded a landlord in the Four Cleanups Campaign.† Early this year he had been rehabilitated and reappointed brigade party secretary.

According to eyewitnesses at the scene—the well-drilling site— the whole thing was the result of sheer provocation on the part of Luo Hu. For some days past, Luo Hu and a few of the offspring of cadres who had been the targets of criticism during the Four Cleanups Campaign had gone about railing against those who had been active in the movement. Dashun, who had participated in the campaign, was quite aware of what they were driving at with their gibes. However, he just let them rail on, didn't say a word, and carried on with his work. Later in the day, during a break at the well-drilling site, Lou Hu and his gang got more worked up. They came out with the vilest, most unbearable language. Dashun, his face red with chagrin, couldn't stand it any longer and blurted out: "Who are you cursing?"

Luo Hu stood up: "We're cursing whatever harmed people in the Four Cleanups Campaign."

Dashun, breathing heavily with anger, could not say a thing.

* Luo Village Brigade.
† The Four Cleanups Campaigns, also known as the Socialist Education movement, was a national movement to clean things up in politics, the economy, organizations, and ideology, 1963–1966.

Luo Hu strode up to him. He pointed at Dashun's red face and said even more brazenly, "I'm cursing the one with the feverish face!"

"It's too uncivilized!" Dashun said, "Barbaric—"

Before he could finish his sentence, Lou Hu's fist had struck him heavily on the forehead. Dashun fell back a few steps, then steadied himself and came back at him. The two went at it. The other youths who had been behind Luo Hu all went up to them, pretending they were trying to break up the fight, but actually helping one side. Si Long, the son of the brigade leader, took a firm grip of Dashun's right arm and someone else held back his left, allowing Luo Hu to punch and kick freely until a stream of blood shot from Dashun's face, and he fell to the ground, unconscious. That it had been a premeditated incident was only too obvious to eyewitnesses.

All at once, this affair became the chief topic of discussion all over the village. Relations between those that had participated in the Four Cleanups Campaign and those who had suffered in it became more tense than ever. A feeling of unease pervaded the streets of Luocun. . . .

II

In the evening, after the spring rains, the mountains looked green, the water was pure, and the air was fresh. Patches of cloud floated at leisure; the ears of wheat were filling out, and the ripe pods were forming; the snow-white blossoms of the honey locusts on South Hillside exuded wafts of fragrance. At the bottom of the hill, by the mouth of the ravine, the party secretary Luo Kun and five or six commune members, whips in hand, were plowing the soft earth of the sweet potato field.

Suddenly, Luo Kun's wife stumbled up the slope to the field in disarray, shouting in an unsteady voice: "Quickly, it's terrible! . . ."

Luo Kun whoa'd the oxen, stuck the plow in the field, and rushed over.

"Something dreadful has happened!"

Luo Kun, greatly alarmed, asked, "What is it? Speak up!"

"Our third child and Dashun had a fight. Dashun . . . finished. . . ."

"How is he now?"

"Carted off to hospital . . . no saying."

"Oh! . . ."

It was as though Luo Kun had been struck a blow on the head; his ears hummed. He stuck his whip in the earth and went down the slope, heading for the well-drilling site by the riverbed. As he walked, the tails of his shirt brushed the waist-high wheat and made a rustling noise.

At the work site, wooden staves, leather cord, picks, and shovels were strewn all about. A patch of young wheat nearby had been trampled. These were signs of the fight. Not a soul was to be seen; only the drilling frame loomed in the air.

From the temporary shelter made of rice straw where the tools were guarded at night, reckless words could be heard. Luo Kun turned to see: his third son Luo Hu was sitting there on a bed board with a few of his friends, playing cards.

Luo Kun fixed his gaze on him and said: "You had a fight with Dashun?"

His son answered, "Yeah."

"Had he insulted you?"

His son was unconcerned: "No."

"Then why did you fight?"

His son gave a full account of what had happened, without hiding his acts of provocation. He was quite willing to own up to what he had done.

Luo Kun heard his son out with a stony face. Then he said with a sardonic smile, "It was sheer provocation on your part. You sought to vent your rage on Dashun!"

His son rolled his head and blinked in silent acknowledgement. His air proclaimed to all—he wasn't scared.

Luo Kun asked, "Have you forgotten what I said to you at home?"

"Not at all!" his son replied. "During the Four Cleanups Campaign his father did us in good and proper. Now I'm no longer afraid of him! He. . . ."

Luo Kun could bear it no longer. Hearing this, he raised one calloused hand and slapped it across his son's slightly flushed white face.

His son ducked from the waist and turned his head to one side.

Luo Kun turned and strode from the well-drilling site along the machine-plowed main road to the village in the dusk.

What a terrible business! It couldn't have come at a worse time. Luo Kun, with hands clasped behind his back, walked along the road laced with green grass. He just couldn't calm his feeling of frustration. During the Four Cleanups Campaign the old fellow, Poor Peasant Association Chairman Luo Mengtian, was someone the work team relied on. In the matter of branding Luo Kun a landlord, they had had the old man's seal of approval. During the ten years when he was an object of dictatorship, Luo Kun had hated Old Man Mengtian, thinking: You and I played together as kids; together we ran away from the press gang; we worked together in the land-reform and set up cooperatives. Don't you know me, Luo Kun, well enough? How could you put your seal to all that fabricated "evidence?" Feeling this way, he just didn't want to even speak to the old man. But then, sometimes, he would think: When the high and mighty Four Cleanups Campaign work team showed up, how many could resist them? Whereupon he would forgive him. But whether he hated him or forgave him had not mattered, for while he was an object of dictatorship, he had had no dealings with the old man. Then, this spring, his case had been cleared: he was taken back into the party. In elections in the party branch, he had been unanimously elected by party members to the highest position of leadership in Luocun Brigade. He had wept.

He had wanted to seek out Old Man Mengtian and have a talk with him, but he never succeeded. The exceptionally stubborn old man just would not talk with him. Not long before, Luo Kun had gone over to the old man's place, but his wife had claimed he was out, and had turned Luo Kun away. Not only was the old Poor Peasant Association on guard against him, but all those who during the Four Cleanups Campaign, under the "guidance" of the work teams, had criticized the cadres were now feeling guarded toward those who had resumed power. And this is what troubled this party branch secretary, Luo Kun, most. After all, he thought, people are not of the same mind—and if everyone is on guard against everyone else, how can we promote production? How can we achieve mechanization? And precisely at the time when he was disturbed by the complexity of human relations in Luocun, his son had to go and get him into this terrible mess.

III

Luo Kun headed straight for Old Man Mengtian's place. As he stepped over the threshold, he braced himself for the worst; he was prepared to look upon the very worst face the old man could make and listen to the worst things he could say.

In the courtyard there was a bicycle, its carrier laden with a sack of rice, bread, clothing, and the like, probably destined for the sick man. From the central room, a hubbub could be heard.

"Obviously trying to get his own back. . . ."

"And his father had promised he'd 'forgive and forget!' What a lot of hot air!"

"Sue him! Take him to court. We can't go on like this. . . ."

The voices were familiar: some of them belonged to a few who had been active in the Four Cleanups Campaign; the others were those of relatives of Mengtian. Luo Kun paused. To go straight in would em-

barrass everyone. He stood in the yard and shouted, "Brother Mengtian!"

The talking in the room stopped.

Old Man Mengtian came out and stood on the steps, but did not
come down.

Luo Kun walked up to him and asked, "How is Shunwa* doing?"

"Let him die and have done!" the old man countered angrily.

"But Brother, the child must be seen to at once!" Luo Kun continued, "Just so long as Shunwa is okay, the matter can be settled by
the authorities right away. . . ."

"Come off it!" Old Man Mengtian waved one arm. "First you
strike with a hammer, then you stroke with your hand! Why bother
pretending!"

So saying, he went down the steps, took his bike, and went out the
gate.

Luo Kun stood there in the yard, feeling numb. The blood rushed
to his face. He felt acutely uncomfortable, for he was a man of over
sixty, an age that *should* be treated with a little dignity and respect!
As he walked out the gate, he actually bumped into it.

He walked in his own door. The room was filled with people, men
and women. Luo Kun swept his eye over the crowd and saw at a
glance that those standing there were for the most part cadres like
himself who had suffered "rectification" during the Four Cleanups
Campaign—or their families. They were trying to allay his timid
wife's fears:

"Don't be afraid! What if he did beat him up!"

"His father shouldn't have gone about doing people in in the Four
Cleanups Campaign."

"To be honest, Old Man Mengtian has become a stinker!"

Call this patching things up? More like adding fuel to the flames!
Luo Kun got quite fed up with their talk. Then he looked around and
saw the brigade leader Luo Qingfa sitting there listening to all this
kind of talk and feeling good about it! He tried talking to the brigade
leader, but Luo Qingfa just poked fun at him, saying, "So you went
to make up with Old Man Mengtian, eh? I bet he just threw it straight
back at you! My dear older brother, you are too timid! What a softie!"

Luo Kun sat on a wooden stump before the stove and would not so
much as look at him. Recently, he had found quite a lot to resent in
the brigade leader. As soon as he was appointed, he acquired for
himself a nice plot of land in his own Third Team.† This team had

* A diminutive for Dashun, rather like "Shunnie."
† A team is a collective unit of land and people.

planned to build an electrically powered flour mill there, and so had turned down applications from several commune members. But when the brigade leader applied, the team leader was at a loss, and finally gave in. The kindhearted commune members felt that since the bridage leader had suffered wrongfully for several years, he ought to be given special consideration. And so it was passed. Soon afterward, the commune factory asked for a worker from the team, and it was the brigade leader's daughter who went. The commune members for the most part didn't object. This was also out of special consideration for him. Surely this was enough? But no, his son had to team up with Shunwa to beat people up and create a scene! After which, instead of sorting things out, he had rushed over to support and bolster Luo Kun's wife! Took him for a gold leaf, but find he's a copper shard, he thought to himself.

Luo Kun put a scowl on his face to show his coolness to the well-intentioned morale-boosters. Paying them no attention, he said to his wife: "I want to take out fifty yuan."

"What for?" the wife asked.

"I'm going to the hospital."

The brigade leader was taken aback, stared, and then understood. Snorting in contempt, he jumped off the kang and left. The others in the room, sensing something was amiss, went off sheepishly.

Luo Kun said to his young daughter cowering by the table, "Go and get the party security representative and the Youth League secretary. Tell them to come right away!"

His wife got money and grain coupons out of the chest and handed them to her husband. "Look after yourself on the road."

Luo Kun comforted his wife saying: "Don't worry! You've nothing to fear either. No use worrying, anyway. You must carry on as usual: sleep when it's time to sleep; eat when it's time to eat."

The security representative and Youth League secretary hurried in.

Luo Kun said, "You two look into this business of today's fight and make a report of it to the local police station."

The security representative said: "Let's keep this matter in the brigade. We can deal with it!"

"No! This must be left to the police! This is no ordinary brawl!"

The Youth League secretary was about to say something, but Luo Kun turned to her and continued: "You know your uncle [the security representative] is no good at writing! You'll give him a hand, won't you?"

So saying, he stood up, picked up the sack of bread his wife had got ready for him, pushed off on his bike, and left without even a look back. In the faint moonlight he rode off along the main road.

IV

For a full five days the old party secretary sat by the sick bed, feeding Dashun and emptying his bed pan. The young man was so moved he shed tears.

Old Man Mengtian sneered at all this: "You're just putting on a show! Your son goes and practically beats someone to death, then you put on an act—all kindly and concerned, how two-faced!" If Luo Kun ever sat down to chat with him, he would stiffly walk out of the sick ward. Later, when he saw his son act chummy with Luo Kun, showing no sign of the anger of the beaten, in his heart he cursed his son as a "spineless wretch." Spurred by anger, he got on his bike and simply went home.

With sadness, Dashun told Luo Kun how his father had been used by the Four Cleanups Campaign work team, which was out to get people. After the campaign, people in the village cursed him, and his father felt terrible. But he had an obstinate streak in him—he had made his bed and he would lie in it. On the matter of the Four Cleanups Campaign, if you discussed it with him calmly and nicely, he would admit he'd wronged some people. But if you cursed him, he would bristle, "Why blame me? I didn't make anything up! I didn't organize the Four Cleanups Campaign! You say my seal was on it? Well, my head was not mine to shake! If anyone's been wronged, go to the work team!"

Luo Kun explained to the youth how Old Man Mengtian had suffered greatly during the old regime, was filled with love for socialism and for the party; if he had not withstood the pressure, it was not entirely his fault. Besides, the old man had always been a good worker, a pillar of the collective. . . .

On the seventh day, Dashun had his stitches out and was discharged from the hospital with a bandage around his head. Luo Kun insisted that the young man ride on the carrier of his bike, and the latter kept refusing. But Luo Kun said: "Your wound won't stand any strain. The doctor said to rest!" So he carried him off.

"Uncle!" Dashun murmured from the back of the bike, a quiver in his voice: "When you get home, don't be hard on Huer.*

Luo Kun did not answer.

"All those years when you were being wronged, Huer also suffered. If any child got angry at him, they called him "landlord" and made him feel inferior. I can see why he's angry. . . ."

Luo Kun felt a sudden pang, and a lump constricted his throat. During the ten or more years when he had been branded a landlord

* Pet name for Luo Hu.

element, all the hardship and humiliation that he and his family suffered—it didn't bear thinking about.

The youth continued from behind his back, "I've heard that my Dad and you, as well as Brigade Leader Uncle Qingfa, were all poor kids in the old society. After liberation, you carried out land reform together, organized cooperatives together, and were so close you were like one man. It is only with the turmoil of the past few years that things have come to such a wretched state. Even the children have become enemies!"

Luo Kun couldn't contain himself any longer. He felt two warm streams flow down either side of his nose and a salty taste in his mouth. How well put! Wasn't this precisely what he felt deep down? He just wanted to hug this darling youth and kiss him! He jumped off the bike and grabbed Dashun by the hand. "My child, you're right!"

"I want to see Huer as soon as I get back. He may avoid me, but I'll seek him out!" the young man said. "We must put an end to this hatred!"

The two mounted the bicycle once more and, along the highway thickly lined with poplars, as though he'd been injected with some spiritual hormone, this man who was over sixty flew along on his bicycle, carrying a young man at his back.

The houses and trees of Luocun came into view.

V

When, pushing his bicycle, Luo Kun walked into the village side by side with Dashun, clusters of people deep in discussion were scattered here and there on the streets, and there was an unusual air about the place. A large crowd had gathered outside the brigade office. As they were passing the office, someone called him in.

In the office were seated the chief cadres of the brigade committee, as well as Old Jiang, the local police chief, and two policemen. The air was tense. Brigade Leader Qingfa, his hair bristling, was expressing his views: "As for my view, I'm firmly against it! It would be too harsh a blow for the comrade recently reinstated! His father suffered wrongly for ten years!"

Luo Kun understood. He glanced at Qingfa and said, "Comrade, the law is the law! It knows no one, takes no account of people's feelings!"

Luo Qingfa angrily broke off and turned his head to one side.

Luo Kun said to Police Chief Jiang, "Do it according to the book! That's not attacking me, it's supporting me in my work!"

Police Chief Jiang told Luo Kun that, with the approval of the security authorities, Luo Hu would be dealt with according to law: dentention for fifteen days. He had come to inform the brigade cadres and Brigade Leader Qingfa had staunchly opposed the sentence.

"Go on, put it into effect! There's nothing to say. The law knows no one!" Luo Kun said.

Some militia brought Luo Hu into the office. The young man stood with haughty visage, planted in front of the masses, quite fearless. Even when the police chief showed him the warrant for his arrest, he was still bolstered by a certain feeling, and was not at all afraid.

Qingfa let fall a great smack on his thigh and turned his head to the other side. The veins showed blue in his neck; they throbbed.

Luo Kun glanced at his son, turned away, and got out his pipe with slightly trembling hands.

At the precise moment when the militia pushed Huer out the door, the Poor Peasant Association Chairman, Old Man Mengtian, who had been sitting in the corner, eyes staring and mouth pouting, suddenly stood up, threw himself down on his knees in front of Luo Kun, and said weepingly: "Brother, I have wronged you!"

Luo Kun quickly helped the old man up and settled him down on a bench. Then Old Man Mengtian threw himself in front of Police Chief Jiang and said tearfully, "Please, Chief! Let Huer go. I . . . oh!"

At this, Dashun, standing by the door, began to weep, his arm around Huer's neck. Huer, looking at the white bandage on Dashun's head, let his eyelids droop; his nostrils pulsed quickly.

Huer broke away from Dashun's arm, turned back in the door, and stood in front of his father. Two shining tears rolled out, "Dad, now I know why the people of Luocun support you." So saying, he went out. The cadres of Luocun sat down once again in the office, smoking. No one said a word, yet no one would leave. The commune members gathered from the streets in front of the doors and windows of the office. They strained to gape at party Secretary Luo Kun—his dark, square face; the hair and stubble streaked with white; his sunken eye sockets. They gazed as though they had just come to know him.

Luo Kun sat there, looking at the brigade leader who had subsided and seemed slightly ashamed, and at the other cadres. He said, "Comrades! The party rehabilitated me. Why? The commune members brought us back to power. Why? Think about it! What were relations like between cadres and commune members in Luocun during the cooperative movement? Or even during the three hard years?* When life was hard, how were relations then between cadres and masses in

* Three hard years (1959–61) right after the Great Leap Forward, when there was widespread famine.

Luocun? You all know! These last ten years or more, Luocun has been torn asunder. Among cadres, among commune members, between cadres and commune members, it was here a clique, there a clique, here a faction, there a faction. How many trenches have been dug? If this matter is not cleared up, no one can sort out the mess in Luocun. You want to promote production? Achieve mechanization? Impossible when people's minds are not set on the task at hand and their energy is not focused on promoting production but on intrigue, on being suspicious, and on guarding against one another."

"Comrades! Our Luocun has suffered a serious internal injury. I believe that those who have made mistakes will gradually learn from them. We who have suffered "rectification" should be big-hearted, and not pass this enmity on to the next generation."

"It hasn't been easy for Luocun to come this far. It hasn't been easy for us to come this far. I am over sixty. When it's time to hand things over to the next generation, we should not only hand over to them a prosperous Luocun, but also a united Luocun. . . ."

Inside and outside the office, all was silent. Many, many people—cadres and commune members, men and women—had tears in their eyes. Through the glistening tears shone hope, trust. . . .

from *Shanxi Ribao* (*Shanxi Daily*)
June 3, 1979
Translated by Michael Crook

Inge Morath/Magnum Photos, Inc.

V. Politics

All of the selections in this book could be included in this chapter, for China's New Realism writers blame flaws in the political system for problems in every sphere of life, from work to love. The selections that follow reflect recurring themes of the New Realism literature: the abuse of power by individuals in leadership positions, the capriciousness and arbitrariness of Chinese politics, and the human cost of political experiments conducted in the name of "the people."

The two long poems that begin the chapter—"General, You Can't Do This" and "In the Wake of the Storm"—expose blatant abuses of power and privilege by individuals who held high positions in the Chinese bureaucracy in 1978–79. "General, You Can't Do This" is only one of many scorching exposés written by Ye Wenfu. "In the Wake of the Storm," by Shu Ting, is a memorial to the seventy-two people who drowned in Bohai Gulf when an offshore oil-drilling platform capsized due to the negligence of those in charge. As a result of this scandal, which also involved a cover-up attempt, an oil minister was forced to resign and other officials were sent to jail after a public trial.

Wang Peng's "At the Denunciation Meeting" is a satire of the struggle meetings that were common occurrences under the rule of the Gang of Four. A form of party discipline in which the target of struggle was subjected to criticism, cross-examination, insults, and sometimes blows, the denunciation meeting was used to correct the ideological thinking of someone who was considered to have deviated from the party line. In this story, an innocent old harnessmaker is called in to be struggled against for the crime of "following the capitalist road." The accusation is so ludicrous that the meeting becomes a mockery—a denunciation of a system in which political ideas and slogans are manipulated by individuals for their own ends.

In Gu Cheng's poems "The Two Realms of Love" and "Epigraph," the people are the pawns of those in power; all they can do to ensure survival is "ride the waves."

Political capriciousness is also the theme of Jin He's "Second Encounter," a story about a former Red Guard who is put on trial for a "crime" he committed during the Cultural Revolution. Through a series of flashbacks, a high-ranking cadre who presides over the trial remembers the crime, in which he himself is implicated. "Second Encounter" raises the question of responsibility in a society where violent acts have been committed for vacillating political ideals. Who is to blame? The Red Guard who was urged to fight for an ideal at all costs? The cadre who should have dissuaded him from the deed? Or a political system that makes today's revolutionary deed tomorrow's political crime?

The characters in "The Get-Together," by Gan Tiesheng, are those of the Mao Generation who have suffered the worst fate—the urban youths sent to the countryside during the Cultural Revolution who, because of "problematic" backgrounds, must remain there, perhaps for life, after most of their peers have been allowed to return to the cities. These young people are the casualties of a grand political experiment; their lives, the tragedies played out long after the official drama is over.

The unconvincing tag-line, in which the author sees in the distance "a patch of blue," is a throwback to the convention that is required in socialist realism of ending every story, no matter how tragic, on an optimistic note; it was probably added so that the story could be published in an official journal. Another version of the "The Get-Together," which appeared in the underground publication *Jin Tian* (*Today*), ends the story instead with the narrator standing by Quixia's grave, vowing that no matter what, he will leave the countryside and return to his parents in the city. Seeing that Quixia's tombstone has fallen sideways, he tries with all his might to push it upright, but it cannot be moved.

General, You Can't Do This!
YE WENFU

History always advances by laboriously solving one new problem after another.

Allegedly, a high-ranking general who had been returned to a leadership post after having been persecuted by the Gang of Four ordered a kindergarten demolished in order to build himself a mansion. Complete with modern facilities, the house cost several hundred thousand yuan in foreign exchange. I . . .

What should I say?
How shall I say it?
You
Are a respected senior,
I am but a late comer.
Between you and me
stand the gunsmoke-filled
Thirties and
Forties,
I had never thought
of criticizing
you.
Because
It was perhaps your very hand,
The hand that fiercely
machine-gunned the Old World,
That snatched
The whip slashing my back—
You held me next to
Your blood-stained
Sweat-soaked chest,
Your tear drops
Fell with a bang!
Sobbing,
You caressed the scars
That covered my body,
Your thick lips
trembling,
You said:
"Child,
We are
li-
ber-
ated—"
And so,
With little bare feet
Treading in your
Large, deep footprints
I entered
New China. . . .

No! General,
Even so,
I shall say,

In fact I must say!
Remember?
That year
You charged the Luding Bridge*—
Behind you: pursuing soldiers!
Facing you: consuming flames!
A river of devouring, towering waves,
A few ponderous iron chains suspended. . . .
The Revolution
Burned with anxiety
On a precipice—
Were the sparks of Jinggang Mountain†
To be ruthlessly engulfed
By the torrents of Dadu River?
Your bloodshot eyes
Glared.
Abruptly, you thrust
Your mauser pistol
Into your waistband.
With a shout
Like thunder
Bearing mighty winds,
You charged into
The heroic annals of
The Chinese Revolution!
At that time,
General,
What was in your mind?
I dare say,
You were thinking:
"I seek
A better life
For generations to come!"
You said:

* A narrow suspension bridge over the Dadu River in Yunnan province. Refers
to a famous incident during the Long March (the 6,000-mile journey from the
southern province of Jianqxi to the northwest province of Shanxi made by the
Red Army in 1934–35 during the civil war between the Nationalists and the
Communists) in which the Communists were trapped at one end of the bridge
by a Nationalist force pursuing them and a Nationalist garrison on the opposite
bank. Throwing hand grenades, a small detachment ran across the bridge and
managed to overcome the garrison so that the entire Communist force could
cross the bridge.
† Jinggang Mountain was where the Communists established their first base.

"Give me!
"Give me!
The most arduous tasks. . . ."
How unfortunate!
My bullet-scarred General,
That forty years later,
Your hero's body
Has been lamed
By the weight of honors.
Your thundering voice
Has been eroded to such weakness
By the flow of time:
"Give me. . . .
"Give me. . . ."
Give you the moon,
You would think it too cold.
Give you the sun,
You would think it too hot.
You want to hold the earth
In your lap
You want everything
For your pleasure
For your fancy. . . .
Want everything,
You want everything!
Why
Do you simply not want
The oath you took when you joined the party?
Why
Do you simply not want
The true colors of the proletariat?
Must the sparks of Jinggang Mountain
That even the torrents of
Dadu River failed to overwhelm
Be extinguished in
Your glass of maotai wine?
Must the red boat that sped along
In the stormy Nan Hu*
Be allowed to run aground, anchored at
Your easy chair?
Must a Communist

* The first meeting of the Chinese Communist Party took place in a boat in
Nan Hu (South Lake) in 1921.

Repeat Niu Jinxing's*
Tragic history?
Were generations of
Desperate struggles
And uprisings
Only for your family's
Endless pleasure-seeking?
If this is true,
General,
How can you be worthy of
The last wishes of
The comrade who died in your arms?
How can you be worthy of
The hoary-haired
Author of *The Communist Manifesto?*
Go, General,
Put on the
Red-tasseled straw sandals you once wore,
Kiss the earth for which you once bled—
The Earth
Snatched, inch by inch,
From the enemy's hands.
The Earth
Dredged up, inch by inch,
From the ravine of suffering.
The Earth
Stamped, inch by inch,
With the mark of revolution
The earth that
Inch by inch
Once nourished
The Red Army,
The Eighth Route Army,
The New Fourth Army,
The Liberation Army.
The wooden ladle in the hands of
That mother in Taihang
Who fed you millet soup
Is still in the bowl
Stirring wild vegetables;

* Niu was one of the urban literati in Henan, adviser to the peasant leader Li
Zicheng at the end of the Ming Dynasty. Niu and Li conducted progressive social
reforms during the 1639 famine, but they were later crushed by the Manchus.

The three-generation family of
The dear woman in Luoyang
Who dressed your wounds
Is huddling in a six-meter-square
Hut;
Cooking pots propped up on the bed. . . .
My high and mighty General,
You rode in battle for decades,
What was it ultimately for?
Ignoring people's sufferings,
You!
Is not the conscience of a Communist
Rebuked by truth?
Could it be that you firmly believe
That the law
Is but a card in your hand,
Or at most
A gentle breeze on a summer night?
Could it be that
All the pores of your body
Are now impermeable to even a drop
Of Premier Zhou's virtue?
For your own Modernization
The Kindergarten was torn down
The children forsaken!
Snowy-haired one
How many more years of comfort can you have?
Tomorrow is the children's.
It is theirs!
If the children are forsaken,
Who will hold your box of ashes?
Maybe
You proudly say:
"I have a son. . . ."
Yes, you have a son—
If your son
Is a
Revolutionary,
He will
Leave
Your mansion in disgust.
If he is an
Unworthy descendant,

His lily-white hands
Will forever hold
The people's accusations against you!
I have a friend,
A purchasing agent,
If he knows of
Your generous act
How bad
Will he feel!
When he learned that
The hair inside the ear of an ox
Will earn foreign exchange
For the past few years,
He has been diligently
Snipping
And snipping
Hair
After hair
Until he has actually accumulated more than ten catties. . . .
Like silkworms spinning silk
The people accumulate wealth for their mother country.
What right do you have
To brazenly squander
The blood of martyrs
The people's faith in the party
The hardworking sweat of the laborers?!
Must the Four Modernizations,
Solemnly proclaimed
By Premier Zhou,
The Four Modernizations for which
The party and the people,
Enduring ten years' wounds,
Are sweating and bleeding
In front of furnaces,
In the fields,
Be the greasy crumbs
And
Spittle,
That you,
Belching,
Casually toss to us?
How unfortunate—
My General!

On the first Long March
You conquered Dadu River
Yet today,
On the new Long March,
Has it crossed your mind—
That one more step backward
And you will become Dadu River?
No!
The tragedy of Niu Jinxing
Will never be repeated—
Because the people
Will never be silent!
May my poetry
Become crackling thunder
And bearing mighty winds,
Rush into your ears,
Rush into your heart,
On the road of this new Long March,
Listen to the progressive young
And progressing laws
Cry:
"General,
You can't do this!"

from *Shikan* (*Poetry*)
August, 1979

Whom Are You Writing About?
How "General, You Can't Do This!" Was Written
YE WENFU

After writing a popular work, I never like to show off by writing essays or giving talks about how the work was created. This time I feel compelled to.

After "General, You Can't Do This!" was published, I received many letters from readers and I became the object of the serious attention of my work unit. Questions rained down on me. All revolved around one distinct question:

"Whom are you writing about?"

This reminded me of Lu Xun's Ah Q.* Who was Ah Q? If we were

* The ignorant, exploited, suspicious, self-deceiving, bullying antihero of *The True Story of Ah Q*, a satire written by Lu Xun in 1921 in which the author—one of modern China's greatest writers—sympathetically caricatures the mentality of the Chinese peasant around the turn of the century.

going to ask Mr. Lu Xun, we might as well ask Ah Q or, more directly, ask those who, after reading *The Story of Ah Q*, were dumbfounded and rushed out like a tornado, foaming at the mouth, pointing at Mr. Lu Xun's nose, howling and stuttering, "Why—why—why . . . write—write—write—write about me?"

Originally, I did not want to respond to these ridiculous questions. However, when comrades from the concerned central department also demanded to know whom I was writing about, I was confused. At first, I could not believe my ears, then I was speechless; pain clutched my heart.

If I were a profound, cultivated poet, I could have sharply refused. Unfortunately, I am not. I am a soldier. Soldiers are used to answering their superiors and accustomed to unquestioningly carrying out their superior's orders. If this were not so, then why did Comrade He Long* receive such inhuman treatment? Why would martyr Zhang Zhixint have fallen in front of the guns of the unseeing sharpshooters? But I do not want to write a report. I only want to let my superiors know whom I was writing about. I also want our people to know. It is because I feel that they should know more about the real situation. Therefore, I decided to publish the story of how I came to write this poem.

It was a painful experience.

During these years, on different occasions, like every comrade everywhere, I would hear the grumbling voices of people who have housing problems. But for a long time this did not arouse my attention—I, whose thinking was rigid to the point of numbness.

I saw many different kinds of houses added on to the sides of residences, built wherever there was space.

I saw many families quarreling or fighting over housing.

I saw many upright people who wept at not having been allotted housing, or who, having been allotted housing, were as jubilant as Du Fu‡ was when he heard that part of the country had been recovered from the rebels.

I saw many leading administrative units swallow different kinds of capital belonging to their own subsidiary units, even spending emergency funds set aside for people in disaster areas, in order to build houses for themselves.

I saw the professional "construction teams" of some large units

---

* A famous old general who was severely persecuted during the Cultural Revolution.

† A low-level cadre who insisted that Mao's Cultural Revolution was incorrect. Brutally shot in 1974, she is now considered a "model martyr."

‡ A famous poet of the Tang dynasty. This incident took place during the An Lushan Rebellion.

working on "repairs" on the magnificent residences of several leading cadres for months and even years. (Frankly speaking, it was expansion—bit by bit.)

I saw "guerilla fighters" for long periods sleeping here one night, there another. . . .

But all these did not arouse my serious attention—I, whose thoughts had been rigid to the point of numbness!

This April, when I heard that a certain commander had actually ordered a kindergarten to be torn down in order to build himself a modern mansion, I was finally startled awake!

I was finally startled awake!

I finally ended my painful numbness; I tasted pain!

I am grieved! I am angry! Troubling thoughts surge in my mind!

An old revolutionary soldier who charged enemy lines during the twenty-five-thousand-mile Long March, a high-ranking general who was brutally persecuted by the Gang of Four—the party and the people had wished so much that, bearing in mind his deep hatred for the Gang of Four, he would contribute his remaining years to what history requires of him in the new Long March! But he—

A series of questions triggered my painful thoughts:

Must the sparks of Jinggang Mountain
That even the torrents of
Dadu River failed to overwhelm
Be extinguished in
Your glass of maotai wine?
Must the red boat that sped along
In the stormy Nan Hu
Be allowed to run aground, anchored at
Your easy chair?
Must a Communist
Repeat Niu Jinxing's
Tragic history?
Were generations of
Desperate struggles
And uprisings
Only for your family's
Endless pleasure-seeking?

What puzzles me most is this: these high-ranking cadres, groomed by the party for decades,

What rights do you have
To brazenly squander

The blood of martyrs
The people's faith in the party
The hardworking sweat of the laborers?

Yet, when they have done this, or are in the process of doing so, why does nobody question them? Where are our laws? Where have the laws gone—to play hide and seek? Is it true that the law, raped by Lin Biao and the Gang of Four, can no longer regain its dignity? Oh Law, Law, why are you always so coy, sitting alone, holding a pipa,* half-covering your face. To put it another way, why are you always like the delicate hands of a fine maiden, only fit for needle-work?

I really want to have a talk with that general:

The wooden ladle in the hands of
That mother in Taihang
Who fed you millet soup
Is still in the bowl
Stirring wild vegetables;
The three-generation family of
The dear woman in Luoyang
Who dressed your wounds
Is huddling in a six-meter-square
Hut;
Cooking pots propped up on the bed. . . .
My high and mighty General,
You rode in battle for decades,
What was it ultimately for?
Ignoring people's sufferings,
You!
Is not the conscience of a Communist
Rebuked by truth?

With such extremely disturbing thoughts, in a fit of temper I wrote this draft of the poem. Yes, I wrote with tears in my eyes. I wrote feeling distressed over my own contradictions, and cherishing my deep, complicated love for the party. After finishing it, I could not help myself and, without a second's delay, gathered a few friends, and loudly recited it to them. When I finished, my friends and I could not help weeping together.

But that was during the cold spring of April. There have been some

* Chinese musical instrument.

who believed that "the party's line has been too far to the right," that thought has been too "liberalized," that "there is the need to hold back a bit," and so forth.

To play safe, I read the draft to more friends. On one of these occasions, in a military unit, it created a stir. It happened that the political officer of that military unit (also an old cadre who had been severely persecuted during the Cultural Revolution) had also torn down the unit's Kindergarten to build his own house.

During the Fifth People's Congress, I heard that some high-ranking leaders occupied several hundred houses!

I am surprised to the point of—

I wonder, was there not one among the members of those huge households—sons, daughters, daughters-in-law, sons-in-law—who would protest as a true Communist? Were they so complacent, buried in the socialist buildings supported by martyrs' remains, sitting on sofas, leisurely blowing rings of cigarette smoke?

At last, I tortuously woke up to reality: houses! houses! These two totally different situations so clearly contrast with each other. They have become an extremely serious social phenomenon!

I decided to revise the first draft!

I gathered the opinions of some friends, and revised it once more. But in the end, I did not make it known. I was afraid that my thinking had gone too far. See how unbearably rigid my thinking had become! Originally I sorely felt the social problem, yet a gust of wind had made me doubt myself! Because of this, I kept the draft to myself for more than a month.

One day, I came to town and accidentally passed the neighborhood of Beihai.* Huge trucks were busily shuttling to and fro on a dusty street. I stood by the roadside in the dust, and peered over the wall at the busy cranes. Rows of modern houses now replaced the spot where the Empress Dowager had once lived. Tears blurred my eyes instantly. Though some time earlier I had heard that a great deal of construction was going on in the area, at a cost of several hundred million yuan, I had never really paid such close attention to it. I was standing right in front of this magnificent modernization!

I was stupefied!

I was transfixed!

Like a spring flood breaking loose on my face—a soldier's face—the tears painfully gushed forth.

At last I understood why, at every level of the party hierarchy, some cadres dared to squander the people's sweat and toil. Suddenly

* A neighborhood near the Forbidden City where most of the highest party officials in the country live.

I was reminded painfully of Chin the Second and Yang Guang.* My heaven, we are proletarians. Yes, proletarians. Can it be that even grand proletarian revolutions cannot escape the lamentable fate of decayed feudal dynasties because of historical limitations? Our national economy has not yet recovered from near collapse. Our people still lack sustenance. How can we tear down the fine houses of the Empress Dowager in order to build modern houses?

Standing in the dust, I missed Chairman Mao; I missed Premier Zhou. They were reluctant to spend money on their old houses, though they were in need of repair. The papers in the past were full of heartfelt praise for the simple life of the leaders. Why is it that today they keep silent?

I recalled the skeletal hands of mothers carrying their babies, reaching toward my bowl in the Taihang Mountains, on the streets of Chongqing, in county towns.

I thought of the sharp confrontation between democracy and privilege.

I thought of the sharp confrontation between the Four Modernizations and a bureaucracy immune to the needs of the people. . . .

I thought, the first generation of proletarian revolutionaries armed our party with Marxism-Leninism. Originally, peasants were the allies of the proletariat. However, since China's revolutionary path began in the countryside and ended in the city, our party has largely been composed of peasants. These peasants were small-scale producers. They urgently sought to liberate themselves from the exploitation of the three pillars.† Under the leadership of the party, they bravely fought against the old society. Nevertheless, with regard to realizing communism, some of them did not have clear vision. Today, after several decades, they have become leaders of our party at many levels. But are they proletarian revolutionaries? The backward nature of their class has finally stubbornly revealed itself. They would like to erode our proletarian party with the short-sightedness of generations of peasant rebels.

This is a dangerous signal.

Our party must consciously struggle with this backward small-producer's mentality.

I have not exaggerated. I speak truthfully as a Communist Party member. In China, honest people often bear risks. But I must say it. I firmly believe that, today, those who speak the truth do not necessarily perish.

* Emperors who had risen as peasant leaders and whose reigns marked the end of dynasties.
† Imperialism, capitalism, feudalism.

With lavishness on such a scale, can modernization proceed along the rough path of history from Changan Street* to the remote mountain village?

I could not tolerate it any longer. Tears in my eyes, I left that dusty street. Not daring to take another look at the rows of proud buildings, I hurried home. I completely revised the long-suppressed draft, and determinedly delivered it to the editors of Shikan [Poetry].

I think it is a good thing for concerned units in the central government to inquire as to whom I am writing about. They must seriously deal with those who wasted the people's sweat and toil. I also ponder: Are the leaders in these units not aware of such large-scale construction? It puzzled me that they have to ask a poet seriously about such an important matter. Nevertheless, I hereby provide all the background for my writing "General, You Can't Do This!" I believe that I am speaking the truth—a Communist Party member boldly facing reality and being honest.

from Yalu Jiang (Yalu River)
November, 1979

In the Wake of the Storm
SHU TING

In memory of the seventy-two comrades killed in the "Bohai Number 2" oil-drilling platform accident.

1

In Bohai Gulf
Where leaden clouds suspend the memorial couplets
Are my seventy-two brothers

On the road where spring must pass each year
Sea billows and dying winter conspire
To cut off the breaths of seventy-two

2

Seventy-two burning lines of vision
Could not raise the sun
From the horizon
Seventy-two pairs of steel-cable arms
Could not steady

* In Beijing.

A stretch of capsized land
They sank like anchors
A violent blizzard
Had temporarily won

3

Seventy-two sons
Dim their fathers' last years
Seventy-two fathers
Become their young sons' distant memories

Those standing on shore gazing into the distance
Finally, sorrowfully, lower their heads
Like bold question marks
Towering in the harbor, written in the dusk
Filling in future log books

Hope's flag
Lowered to half-mast

4

The typhoon has long since landed
But seventy-two drowned appeals
Still tortuously wind
Through lead type
And finally through the microphone
Strike the echoing wall of justice.

In midsummer
Millions of hearts
Suddenly chill

5

No, I am not improvising
An ancient Roman tragedy
I plead for people to think deeply with me
My grandfather's worth
Was once the landlord's two measures of millet
Father, for "humanity" writ large,
Blocked the enemy's fire with his chest
Am I scarcely more fortunate than grandfather
Worth two rivets, a machine

6

Who says that life is a leaf
If it withers, the forest is still full of life
Who says that life is a spray
If it disappears, the ocean still churns on
Who says that after heroes have had conferred posthumous honors
Death can be forgotten
Who says the future of mankind's modernization
Must offer life as a bloody sacrifice

7

I hope when the whistle calls me
Mother won't have cause to worry
I hope the treatment I receive
Will not twist my child's spirit
I hope I live and labor
For others as well as for myself
I hope if I die
No longer will someone's conscience quiver

Finally I sincerely hope
That future poets
Will no longer have this powerless anger
When seventy-two pairs of eyes
Overgrown with seaweed and red coral
Tightly fix their gaze on your pen

from *Shikan* (*Poetry*)
October, 1980

At the Denunciation Meeting
WANG PENG

One night, when everyone was fast asleep, the team leader, Deyuan, let Old Man Niu Sheng* in on a secret. "Best be on guard, Elder Uncle! The 'Thunder God' is planning on holding a denunciation meeting just for you!"

Deyuan left Old Man Niu Sheng scared witless. The old man knew that "Thunder God" was the nickname—given by general consensus—to Comrade Lei† who had come down with the work team.

* *Niu Sheng* means "ox tether."
† *Lei* means "thunder."

The man was not old—he looked around thirty at most. But he had an awesome brusque way with him when it came to work. Early in the spring, he just dug in his heels and wouldn't let anyone plant any ginger in their private plots; then when the hot weather came, he rounded up all the team cadres and made them uproot all the tobacco plants the commune members had grown.* In the end, he made all the private plots barren, and everyone felt very frustrated.

Now Old Man Niu Sheng had fallen into the hands of the "Thunder God." He was probably done for. He was so bothered he did not get a wink of sleep all night. All his life, this old man had been respected: he had never squabbled with anyone, or done anything to be ashamed of; how could he face a denunciation meeting? Denunciation meetings—this old man had seen plenty of them these last few years; the dunce cap on the skull; bricks hung around the neck; the body blows with the willow, et cetera. When, in the past, the old man had seen these things going on, it had made him tremble all over. Who would have thought it would now be his turn. The old man sighed. Feeling the wrinkly skin on his body under the blanket, he thought to himself: I must shave myself bald—to save having the hair pulled; on my body I'd best wear my padded vest under the shirt—it would be good padding against the stick. . . .

The denunciation meeting was even worse than Old Man Niu Sheng had imagined. The atmosphere was frightening. The great big storeroom—originally used to store grain, only now there was no grain to store—was crammed with people. There were a few tables in the front of the room. Comrade Lei was sitting in the middle. From the beam hung a gas lamp—so bright the old man could scarcely open his eyes. Comrade Lei announced in a booming, unusually awesome, frightening tone of voice—a tone reeking of gunpowder—the opening of the meeting. It was as though a whole string of firecrackers had been set off right behind the old man. Comrade Lei called upon Old Man Niusheng to make a complete confession of his crime of taking the capitalist road.

What was there to confess? Old Man Niu Sheng did have a skill that had been passed down through the generations—the skill of cutting leather cords. But this made him different from other countryfolk: besides doing farmwork, they could all do a bit of carpentry, odd construction jobs, and so on. In the slack season, it was a way of covering losses, and getting a little pocket money. In the old days, this job, which involved dealing with dead horses and ox carcasses,

* An example of Lei's political extremism, interfering with people's private plots. Tobacco and ginger are cash crops and therefore "smell of capitalism"— a party line in the early seventies under the Gang of Four.

was looked upon as a most lowly skill. It was not until cooperativiza-
tion that Old Man Niu Sheng became renowned far and near for the
straps he cut, which were strong, even, and durable. He became
known for miles around as "Old Man Ox Tether," and County Commissar Liu even came in person and presented him with a framed
glass "certificate of merit," which he received with trembling hands.

But now, Old Man Niu Sheng had become Comrade Lei's "Capitalist Model." It was said that Comrade Lei had made some calcula-
tions: three yuan to cut up an ox hide. At a hide a day—why, that
would bring an astounding ninety yuan a month, or one thousand
eighty yuan a year! That, plus the work points he made, and the
grain and firewood and all that they got at the year's end—why, he
would have struck it rich! When Comrade Lei's theoretical article was
broadcast over the speaker system and carried in the newspaper, it
became known far and wide that in Hu Yang Village someone had
"struck it rich." Old Man Niu Sheng had not known whether to
laugh or cry. From the time he had inherited his father's set of tools
all those decades ago, the most hides he had ever cut in one month
was three and often there would not be one in four or five months.
He couldn't understand: Comrade Lei had come as part of the work
team from on high; how could he wish oxen to die every day in
his team?

Of course, Old Man Niu Sheng was ashamed about the three yuan
per hide. But that was because the peasants insisted. They would
look on as he undid his shirt and practically kneel on the stinking
hide—which might be days old—spread out in the yard, to scrape
away remnants of bloody tissue. Any ordinary person would be
unable to eat for three days after a sniff of the smell. After the scrap-
ing, he would put his hands in the boiling hot alkaline water to treat
the hide. Then he had to cut it into strips, rub the strips, and so on.
Why, the one hide would keep him busy right through the night. In
order to overcome the horrible smell, he always had to buy a bottle
of liquor. And furthermore, those peasants who had come a long way
would stay the night at his place. And when the old man ate, how
could he let others just look on? With his old friends and acquaintances it went without saying—even strangers on their first visit
would be treated like honored guests. When they took their leave the
deeply moved peasants might come out with five- or ten-yuan notes,
but old Niu Sheng would always say, "That'll be three yuan." No
wonder Lao Liu the carpenter had worked it out and said, "All you
can show are losses! If it were me, I'd have washed my hands of the
business years ago!"

But that Comrade Lei, who was forever going on about his "all-around dictatorship" and his "restricting bourgeois rights," had all but made Old Man Niu Sheng's peasant dwelling out to be a landlord's mansion, and was set on banning this kind of "capitalist activity."

As it turned out, the very day after the ban was announced, Old Man Lu Ziming from Shishu Ling* turned up at his door with an ox hide. As whenever old friends meet, there were the usual inquiries made of each other's situation. Lu Ziming was still as forthright as he had been when he was young. Full of gripes, he described how a few years back, when they had harvested their cash crops, every family in Shishu Ling was fairly prosperous. But now, with their struggle meetings and denunciation sessions, the place had gotten so poor even the devil wouldn't pay a visit there. "Just imagine! We're so poor we can't afford to buy anymore." Pointing at the ox he had carried over, Lu Ziming continued, "So I had to come and trouble you."

What can I do? They only proclaimed the ban yesterday! Old Man Niu Sheng thought to himself. But he did not have the heart to tell his friend his problems. Look at that! What a first-rate hide! Big and perfect. There is enough for eight pairs of center harness and six pairs of side harness—enough to last Shishu Ling several years, he thought. What the hell! I'll do it. The old man got busy as he had always done: he worked through the night, and just before dawn he saw his old friend off.

It is said that even a sparrow flying by casts a shadow, and so some "theoretical backbone" reported this "new trend in the class struggle" to Comrade Lei, which is what had led to the denunciation meeting.

". . . and that's the whole of it. There's nothing more. . . ." Old Man Niusheng was saying, his lips trembling a little.

"No! That won't do! You've got to give a thorough account!" Comrade Lei exploded, banging the table.

"What? The rubber tire of the cart?"† Old Man Niu Sheng was scared witless by the shouting. He knew that Comrade Lei had just confiscated everyone's handcarts and, to prevent the "sprouts of capitalism" from shooting up again, had demanded that even old tires and wheel rims be surrendered. So he quickly answered, "But I have no cart! If I did you can be sure I'd give up the tires, wheels and all!"

Immediately all the commune members, regardless of the fact that this was a solemn denunciation meeting, burst out laughing, and order was thrown to the winds in the meeting place.

* Persimmon Ridge.
† Here there is a pun: *jiao dai* ("to confess") sounds the same as *jiaodai* ("rubber tire").

Comrade Lei got so annoyed he began to gesture with his hands and stamp his feet. He glared at Old Man Niu Sheng, whereupon a few of the jokers among the crowd started whispering. "This fellow is thoroughly unrepentant! His confession is just a hoax. We mustn't let him spread any more poison!" This led to more laughter. For these were the words Comrade Lei always used to sum up a confession, regardless of what the accused had said. Sure enough, before the laughter had died from everyone's lips, Comrade Lei announced, "This fellow's thoroughly unrepentant! His confession is just a hoax. . . . Now let us begin exposing his crimes and denouncing them!"

Old Man Niu Sheng knew that once the denunciation had begun, he should prepare to be beaten. He unthinkingly felt the padded vest he was wearing under the cotton jacket.

At first, Comrade Lei just waited and bore with it; then he started to fix empty stares on the "theoretical backbones" and the team cadres. Those that were stared at either were busy puffing away on their pipes or pretended they were thinking, searching for something. All avoided those eyes that put a certain pressure on them. Finally, when no one could bear the silence any longer, someone got up to denounce. Comrade Lei breathed a sigh of relief. He nodded, saying, "Good. Let's have Team Leader Deyuan lead off on the denunciation."

"What? My old chum Deyuan whom I've known for decades?" Old Man Niu Sheng practically shook.

"Listen, Old Grandad. You're coming up to sixty you know! Everyone knows you're an old man without kids or anything—a "five guarantees"* recipient. So why do you bother cutting ox hides? You could sit there without moving a muscle and the team would have your white rice and refined flour brought to your door. There! You have it cushy, and you won't just enjoy it! Why go to all that bother to take the "capitalist road?""

Deyuan kept denouncing old Niu Sheng. Yet the masses at the meeting, feeling sad and surprised, began to exchange meaningful glances. As soon as Deyuan finished speaking, several people raised their hands, all eager to denounce Old Man Niu Sheng. Comrade Lei busily nodded his head. The "theoretical backbone" who was acting as notetaker wrote busily.

It was the turn of Shengcai—the team's well-known joker—to denounce. "This day, we must thoroughly denounce old Niu Sheng's capitalist thinking. The old fellow hardly ever reads the papers or studies. All he cares about is working with all his might by day; then at night, instead of sleeping, he's got to tan hides and cut harness.

* Childless and infirm old persons in a rural collective are guaranteed food, clothing, medical care, housing, and funeral expenses.

What do you want to cut harness for, I ask you? What we want now is revolution, not production, and when it comes to farming, what do you want harness for anyway? Hmph! Why can't you be like Comrade Lei: sleep in the morning, read papers at noon, sort out capitalist roaders at night. . . ."

Hearing Shengcai's "denunciation," everyone in the room had to bite their lips to stop themselves from laughing out loud. A forest of fists were raised by people wanting to "denounce." The speeches went on and on:

"Yes, and we also have to work out how many hides he's cut since Liberation, and just how many work teams are using his 'capitalist wares!'"

"Right! Total up just how many sets of harnesses hitched to how many team of oxen, and just how much grain they have produced—all this is 'evidence' of his capitalist crimes!"

More and more people spoke up, the denunciation became more and more heated.

As for Old Man Niu Sheng, he gradually calmed down. He no longer felt uneasy or frightened. In fact, it occurred to him that the feeling within him at this moment was not unlike what he had felt as he received the framed glass plaque from County Commissar Liu all those years ago.

from *Renmin Wenxue* (*People's Literature*)
November, 1979
Translated by Michael Crook

The Two Realms of Love
GU CHENG

Over there
Power adores Gold,
Over here,
Gold woos Power.
But what about the people?
The people
Have always been their gifts of betrothal.

from "A New Subject for Study," an essay by Gong Liu, published in *Xingxing* (*Sparks*)
October, 1979

Epigraph
GU CHENG

In the sea of life,
Hold firm the rudder
Don't, because of a favorable wind,
Be drawn into a whirlpool
For the time being, let running aground
Be a precious little rest.
Calmly watch the complacent sails
Ride with the waves.

from *Yanhe* (*Yan River*)
July, 1980

Second Encounter
JIN HE

The incident took place in the pretrial room of the district's Public Security Bureau.

After a criminal element had been interrogated and led away, Li, the head of the pretrial department, handed a new file to the district's deputy party secretary beside him, Zhu Chunxin.

Zhu Chunxin was about fifty—with a strong build and slightly stout. His hair was well trimmed; his eyebrows were thick and dark, and his eyes always looked thoughtful. His square jaw looked dark even when he had just shaved. He impressed people as being solemn, experienced, and energetic. In the allocation of responsibilities of the standing committee of the district committee, he was in charge of organization, personnel, and the system of public security, prosecution, and courts. After the Gang of Four was smashed, when disorderly elements* were being thoroughly investigated, he came personally to the district's Public Security Bureau. He intended to seize on a few typical cases and conduct a public trial of the most serious disorderly elements that would be broadcast throughout the district in order to promote the investigation campaign. However, it required a great deal of effort to set up these sample cases; they had to be backed up by solid, accurate evidence that would stand the test of time. The investigation of the first criminal element had not been satisfactory: both the investigation material and the prosecution material differed greatly from the account of the accused. Zhu Chunxin

* Those who had engaged in beating, vandalism, and looting.

knit his brow. Before the second criminal element was brought in, he took a moment to shift his thickset body and stretch a little without being noticed. Then he leaned back in his chair and glanced at the second file handed to him by Department Head Li. An abstract of the case was written on the front:

"Ye Hui. Male, twenty-eight years old. Class background: worker. Student status. At the time of arrest, a furnace worker in our district's power plant. Criminal Ye followed Lin Biao and the Gang of Four during the Cultural Revolution, and engaged in beating, vandalism, and looting. Most seriously, during a fight in September of 1967, he personally crippled a worker and stabbed a student—Shi Zhihong—to death with a spear. Without doubt, he is one of the most serious types of disorderly elements. . . ."

As Zhu Chunxin read the file, his thick brow suddenly jerked up, and he lifted his head as if to ponder something. Then he shook his head to himself, and continued reading.

Department Head Li pointed to the file and asked Zhu Chunxin with a smile: "Secretary Zhu, do you know this person?"

"No." Zhu Chunxin shook his head, "I only came to this district in 1970. I was still in Beining municipality in 1967."

"Ye Fei was a sent-down educated youth* from Beining municipality. He was recruited by our district's power plant in 1972," Department Head Li continued.

"Oh . . ." A shadow of surprise and anxiety appeared on Zhu Chunxin's solemn face. Sensing this, he immediately calmed himself, laughed lightly, and said: "I was being struggled against at the time. As for the fighting, I only heard of it later. I don't know this person Ye Hui. Both sides suffered casualties—what a terrible thing!" Zhu Chunxin shook his head sadly. Then, lifting up his square chin, he asked, "What did Ye Hui do then?"

"He was the leader of a Red Guard organization in a middle school."

"A Red Guard leader in a middle school?" Zhu Chunxin's eyes rolled a little, as if he were muttering to himself but also as if he were asking Department Head Li.

"Yes."

"Hm. . . . These disorderly elements with blood on their hands should be dealt with severely," Zhu Chunxin said with a solemn air. Then he thought of another matter, "Did he go by another name?"

"I don't think so. . . ." Department Head Li was about to say something else when the door of the pretrial room opened, and a

* Sent down to the countryside.

young worker in his late twenties was brought in. Li quietly said to Zhu Chunxin, "There, here he comes."

The accused had old work clothes on. His oil-stained jacket was patched at the elbows. His shoes were old and discolored. Though the young man seemed not to care about his appearance, he was not sullen. Coarse, thick hair covered half his forehead. His sharply defined mouth was slightly open, revealing a neat row of clean teeth. He was a handsome fellow. Before he sat on the square stool for the accused, he glanced at the examiners in front of him with his clear, dark eyes and smiled mockingly. He appeared calm and relaxed. However, when the criminal's eyes met those of Zhu Chunxin, the latter was startled—it seemed he had this expression, this smile, somewhere before.

Is . . . that him? A secret suspicion flashed through Zhu Chunxin's heart.

"What is your name?" Department Head Li started the examination.

"Ye Hui," the criminal answered.

"Have you used other names?"

"No."

Department Head Li nodded at Zhu Chunxin, confirming his previous answer. The latter completely ignored the gesture. He knit his thick dark brows and fixed his gaze on the face of the accused. Then, in an unusual move, he left his seat, locked his hands behind his back, and paced beside the criminal. On returning to his seat, Zhu Chunxin acted as if he were pondering a question, but his eyes were searching the criminal's forehead. Obviously, he was looking for a certain physical characteristic in the criminal.

"It is necessary to inform you of the party's policy. . . ." Department Head Li repeated the routine talk to pretrial criminals. "Please give an account of your crime."

The interrogation was conducted in a solemn atmosphere, but Zhu Chunxin remained silent, his eyes staring at a line in the file: "Ye Hui: charged with the crimes of beating, vandalism, and looting."

Yes, it must be he—Ye Weige! Zhu Chunxin cried inside. I wish that it were not, but I saw the scar on his forehead! I wonder why he refused to admit to having used the name Ye Weige.

"Confess the major facts of your crime. Don't try to gloss over anything. Honesty will be treated with leniency, but resistance will be dealt with severely. . . ."

The sound of the interrogation faded in Zhu Chunxin's ears, and an incident from the past that he did not want to remember unfolded vividly before his eyes.

It had been in September, 1967—a harsh, chaotic, painful autumn.

The mass organizations of Beining municipality had already polarized into two major factions. One faction was the "East Is Red" Command, which claimed that it was the "revolutionary rebel organization," and that the other faction was only a "mass organization." Zhu Chunxin was made the "revolutionary leading cadre" of the "East Is Red" faction, as a consequence of "revealing his stand," and so he naturally became one of the Red Alliance faction's "three anti-elements," which aroused more clamor to bring him down and more cruel struggle. To avoid being dragged out and struggled against, he had to live the life of a fugitive. Since living at home was not safe, he had hidden in workers' dormitories, rural team offices, Xinguang Studio's darkroom, and even the major departments that nobody could touch—the Power Distribution Office as well as the offices of the labor reform teams. No matter where he went, he was constantly troubled by fear, irritability, and shame. He felt extremely uneasy with the contradiction between his status as deputy secretary of the Beining Municipal Committee and his fugitive life.

What else would I do? I did not wish it so! Zhu Chunxin thought. If I am arrested by the opposing faction, I may lose my life! What a mess, what a mess! What kind of drama is this?" He secretly grumbled. The People's Daily once wrote satirically: "How could there be leading revolutionary cadres who are afraid of the masses?" Zhu Chunxin retorted secretly: How could you not be afraid? These "scholars" put it so lightly. Let them try it themselves!

One evening in September of 1967, after several tortuous relocations, Zhu Chunxin quietly moved into an office building in a room away from the street on the second floor. Two beds were temporarily placed in the office. There was no mosquito net. The bedding looked as if it had never been washed: it was greyish, slimy, and stale-smelling. But to Zhu Chunxin, who had worried all day about his safety, it seemed a precious haven. It was fortunate that the September night was cool, but not chilly. A refreshing autumn breeze blew in from the window. The light from the room shone on the fluttering leaves of the old birch trees, creating flickering patches of silvery light. Whether because the broadcasting personnel had lost their voices, or the tubes of the amplifier needed a rest, the loudspeakers set up at opposite corners of the tall building were not broadcasting "the stern statements" and "the strongest protests," "quotation songs," or the songs of the "three loyal-to's."* Therefore, Zhu Chunxin's new home seemed serene and quiet.

* Cultural Revolution dogma. The "three loyal-to's" were "loyal to Chairman Mao, his thought, and his revolutionary life."

Lin Fengxiang, the deputy director of the Municipal Committee Office, who had been accompanying Zhu Chunxin from place to place, pulled the curtains and gave a bitter smile, saying, "We may finally sleep safely tonight."

"Perhaps." Zhu Chunxin scratched his unshaven chin with his finger nails, making a coarse sound on his beard. "But if there is trouble, our staying on the second floor means that there is no escape route through the back. . . . Oh no!"

Though not yet forty, Lin Fengxiang was a favorite cadre of the leadership of the Municipal Committee. He knew just what his leaders needed, both in work and in arranging for their daily needs. Furthermore, everything was done with style and restraint, just right. Even the most demanding, most reserved leaders were quite willing to put themselves in Lin Fengxiang's skillful hands. Though his relationship with Zhu Chunxin was that of a junior to his superior, the Cultural Revolution had made them close friends-in-distress. Lin Fengxiang had also noticed what was worrying Zhu Chunxin, but what else could they do? Nevertheless, he had his ways to make the leader feel easier: "There shouldn't be any trouble, at least not tonight. . . ."

Bang! Bang! Bang! Someone knocked.

Lin Fengxiang swallowed his unfinished sentence and his face turned pale. Zhu Chunxin fixed his gaze on the door, his mind racing, trying to decide whether the person knocking at this late hour was angel or devil. Nobody knew where they were staying, except for a few concerned leaders at the headquarters and a few of the trusted staff. Moreover, the leaders at the headquarters had already made clear that they would not come tonight, and would only come tomorrow to take them to a meeting. Then who could the visitors be at this late hour? Could it be the Red Alliance faction following them? If so, the situation could be really sticky.

Bang! bang! bang! bang! The knocking continued.

Zhu Chunxin wanted to find a place to hide, but there was nowhere to go. The roof had no air hole, and the bed wasn't big enough to hide anyone underneath. He shot Lin Fengxiang a questioning look: Should we answer or not? Open up or not? Lin Fengxiang stared back blankly, not knowing what to do. Realizing that he might have to die with Zhu Chunxin, he shivered inside.

"Bang, bang, bang!" The knocking resumed with more force. Whoever was knocking seemed impatient.

It looked as if they would have to open the door. Zhu Chunxin unwillingly gave Lin Fengxiang the signal.

"Oh . . . Oh . . . yes!" Lin Fengxiang answered with the tone of one who had just been wakened. He came to the door and, his teeth chattering, asked, "Who is it?"

"Open the door quick!" a young man outside answered.

"We are friends," another young man said.

"Cowards!" This was the voice of a third young man.

"Who are you looking for?" Lin Fengxiang asked.

"The people in this house!"

This kind of answer still made Zhu Chunxin and Lin Fengxiang nervous. Acting on Zhu Chunxin's eye signals, Lin Fengxiang said: "We have already gone to bed. Whatever it is, it can wait till tomorrow!" He forced his body against the door, his legs trembling.

"Having an easy time of it, eh?" Sarcastic laughter came through the door, "Don't babble anymore. If those Lao Bao* come, this door won't be of any damn use! Open up quickly. This is an emergency!"

Zhu Chunxin, seeing the sense in what the person outside was saying, exchanged a glance with Lin Fengxiang. Lin Fengxiang figured that it was useless to try to defend the door by himself, and so he finally opened it.

A dozen or more young men around the age of eighteen and nineteen barged in and stood in the middle of the room. Some held long wooden rods; some carried spears. Daggers and knives of different shapes were stuck in their belts. All of them looked bold and threatening. Zhu Chunxin watched this group of unidentified intruders with surprise. Without even knowing it, he had gotten out of bed; his heart was pounding violently.

"Are you Secretary Zhu?" A young man without a weapon stepped forward and asked in a gentle, courteous voice.

"Oh . . . hm . . . I am Zhu Chunxin, Zhu Chunxin." Zhu Chunxin was annoyed at his own cowardice and humble manner of speaking.

"We have been sent by the 'East Is Red' Command to protect you." The young man without weapons smiled calmly and said, "I am Ye Weige.† Your safety here is the responsibility of the third detachment of our military unit."

"Protect? Oh. . . ." Zhu Chunxin's eyes instantly lit up with appreciation and excitement, and his thick, dark eyebrows twitched. He scratched his beard lightly a few times with his fingernail, examining this young man named Ye Weige. The latter's thick, coarse hair was cut very short, and his sharply defined mouth parted naturally, revealing a set of clean, white teeth. His quick eyes expressed the gen-

---

* Epithet used by the radical factions of the Red Guard for the more conservative factions who allegedly supported Liu Shaoqi and the established party cadres.
† "Defend-the-Revolution" Ye.

erous, eager, innocent, unabashed wildness characteristic of the young people of this period. His green attire, typical of a Red Guard's, made him look all the more brave and competent. Not until this moment did Zhu Chunxin's fear-stricken heart finally stop beating wildly. "Have a seat—please be seated!" He pointed at his bed and Lin Fengxiang's. "Please sit over here; do sit down."

After the Red Guards had sat down, Zhu Chunxin again said in a sincere tone: "The revolutionary rebel comrades-in-arms at the command headquarters are so considerate! It must have been hard for you young generals—I suppose this place is quite safe."

"No, a problem has arisen," Ye Weige said with genuine solemnity. "The command headquarters said that the Lao Bao have detected a pattern in your movements. They may start trouble."

"Oh!" Zhu Chunxin was startled; his eyebrows drew together. "So quickly! What should we do? Your dozen or so men. . . ." Zhu Chunxin was about to say, "How can you manage?" But he caught himself and said instead, "Your responsibility is gigantic!"

Ye Weige smiled. He habitually squared his shoulders and held his hands in tight fists. "Secretary Zhu, don't worry. Though we are only a handful, as long as there is a third detachment, your safety is guaranteed. In the slight chance of an emergency, headquarters will send reinforcements." His solemn manner of speech made one think of a brave soldier taking an oath of loyalty to his leader. "Since you stand by our side, you are standing on the side of Chairman Mao's revolutionary line. To defend Chairman Mao's revolutionary line, we revolutionary rebel fighters are prepared to risk our lives and shed our blood!"

Watching this excited, generous young man, Zhu Chunxin was speechless. He tried to restrain the impulse, but then stepped forward and shook Ye Weige's hand: "Thank you, young generals! I thank you, thank you."

Ye Weige stared at Zhu Chunxin's face, startled, and slowly withdrew his hand. He was surprised by this act from a leading cadre. It had never occurred to him that his words and deeds might gain someone's appreciation. He was only expressing his sincerity and steadfastness in following a great faith; he was only doing his duty—a duty of unequaled, exalted sacredness.

"If something does happen, don't panic, and don't go near the window. Block the door—there, use this office desk. . . ." Ye Weige clarified a few important points. As he was leaving, he said, "Our signal is one knock followed quickly by three knocks: tap, tap tap tap. . . ."

Tap tap tap.

The sound of something knocking on wood pulled Zhu Chunxin from his reverie and back to the pretrial room.

"Why did you participate in the fighting? Hm?" Department Head Li was gazing severely at the criminal, and knocking on the desk. "The 'Sixteen Points'* have long decreed that one must 'struggle with words, not force.' Then why did you fight? You made your motivation appear so pretty; this is pure sophistry!"

The criminal sitting on the square stool smiled calmly and said, "I am relating the facts."

"Facts, facts! You are trying to hide something—otherwise why won't you reveal the name of the leading cadre you were protecting?" Department Head Li retorted.

Hearing Department Head Li's interrogation, Zhu Chunxin's heart gave a start and his ears hummed. Secretly, he resented him for asking such a question. He was worried that the criminal might say "Zhu Chunxin" under pressure and put him in an extremely embarrassing situation.

"I have forgotten," the criminal replied.

"No, you have not forgotten—you are lying," Department Head Li said. "No leading cadre would have connived with your fighting! Continue with your account of the crime!"

Not until then was Zhu Chunxin able to sigh with relief. He had never imagined that he would meet Ye Weige again under such circumstances. His heart was just as heavy as that of the accused.

The cross-examination continued, but Zhu Chunxin could no longer sit still. He felt chills crawling up his spine, his face was burning, and his limbs were stiff. So he quietly had a few words with Department Head Li and went out of the room. Hands behind his back, he strolled around the little courtyard outside. It was September, 1977; the autumn air was refreshing, though the sun around noontime was still scorching. The breeze brushed past the lush green leaves of the old birch trees, making a whooshing sound. Zhu Chunxin stood in the shade of the old birch tree and looked up, listening to the rustling. Somehow, he felt that the old birch tree was talking to him in a sarcastic tone: "Congratulations on your reunion with Ye Weige! After ten years of stormy weather, the changes for both of you have been dramatic!" Zhu Chunxin was startled, but, calming himself, he smiled bitterly: What else can I do? I did not wish him to become a criminal!

The rustling sound of the leaves gradually faded away, but the noise of a car in the distance drew closer, and entered his memory. . . .

* Guidelines adopted by the Eleventh Plenum of the Central Committee in 1966 with regard to the Cultural Revolution and Red Guard activities.

It was near daybreak. The sharp braking noise of a car was suddenly heard outside the building, followed by the noise of a crowd and the sound of metal instruments knocking on the door.

"Open the door!"

"Quickly, open the door!"

There was a loud clamor outside.

"What do you want?" the people in the building asked.

"To catch a thief."

"You came to the wrong place. There is no thief here!"

"Someone saw a thief sneaking into this building!"

"Nonsense!"

"Yes or no, are you going to open up or not?"

"Don't kid yourself, who knows what kind of people you are!"

Smash! Crash! It was the noise of shattering glass.

Though the scene took place at the front entrance, facing the street, Zhu Chunxin and Lin Fengxiang, who were in the back of the building on the second floor, could hear all of it very clearly. They were thunderstruck by this sudden event. Those claiming they were there to catch the thief were obviously coming for them.

"Comrade fighters upstairs, pay attention—" Ye Weige shouted in a firm, low voice. "Gather quickly! The Lao Bao are here!" Then something heavy was thrown on a table, and Ye Weige was swearing, "Damn, the telephone lines have been cut!"

After a rush of footsteps, Ye Wiege skillfully assigned combat positions to members of the third detachment. Ye Weige was heard shouting: "Attack with words, but defend with force. The time has come for us to defend Chairman Mao's revolutionary line with our blood and our lives! Never let the Lao Bao enter the building! Comrade fighters, let's go!"

"Only a few birds are in the building. Comrade fighters, charge!"

"Charge in, and dig out the three-anti element, Zhu Chunxin!"

"Charge!"

Instantly, there was a loud commotion outside. Bricks and rocks were thrown at the door. The banging on the windows, the noise of shattering glass, the crude swearing and shouting, all blended together.

Zhu Chunxin and Lin Fengxiang sat on the bed in the corner, staring blankly at each other. Zhu Chunxin took another look around the office, and still failed to find a hiding place. He cautiously walked to the window. A few old birch trees outside were all seven to eight meters away; they provided no escape route. What could be done? Fear, despair and anxiety overwhelmed him. At that moment, he placed all his hope in Ye Weige and the dozen or so brave, experienced little generals. He even began to worry whether the young men had enough weapons.

"Ye Weige, someone has entered the first floor!" Somebody yelled.

"Where?"

"The window."

"Carry out the second plan—retreat to the second floor and guard the stairs!" Ye Weige gave the commands, showing the brilliance of a fearless commander in the face of danger.

"Zhang Jihong was hurt, Ye Weige!"

"Quickly, move him to the second floor. . . ."

Whatever else Ye Weige said was drowned out by the flood of human voices pouring into the building.

"Charge, charge upstairs!"

"Arrest all the bastards in the building!"

Following this commotion was another wave of fierce fighting and a storm of bricks, interrupted by the cries and groans of the injured.

Zhu Chunxin sat on the bed in a daze, his heart pounding violently. He had experienced these scenes before, and he could imagine the fierceness of such close combat. However, he had another combat going on in his mind—the battle between the two Zhu Chunxins. One Zhu Chunxin said: "As an old cadre, I should ask the two factions to stop this unnecessary bloodshed. But what can I really do? Maybe I will have to shed my blood too." The other Zhu Chunxin contradicted the former: "This is a struggle between two lines; therefore, one should not be at all softhearted about it!" One said: "This is extreme selfishness!" The other said: "This is the firmness of revolution!" One said: "This is shameful!" The other said: "What else can I do? I didn't wish it this way!"

Some groaning was heard outside the door in the corridor. Zhu Chunxin felt that he must do something.

"Lao Lin!" Zhu Chunxin called Lin Fengxiang.

Nobody answered. Zhu Chunxin looked around the room. There was not a trace of Lin Fengxiang. He might have slipped away.

If not, he might have gone to help! thought Zhu Chunxin. He gently opened the door and poked his head out to take a look around. He nearly yelled with a start. Some time ago, Ye Weige had gathered a large basket of bricks, a pile of rocks, and two bundles of wooden rods of different lengths in the corridor. Zhu Chunxin shivered uncontrollably. Then he suddenly discovered that a few meters down the corridor a young man was lying. Bright red blood had spilled on the slippery floor and was glittering in the morning light. Totally outnumbered in the intense fighting, his protectors had had no chance to bandage their injured. He guessed that this might be the Zhang Jihong mentioned earlier.

Zhu Chunxin quickly went over, unbuttoned the young man's shirt, checked his injury, and bandaged the wound. Just as he had finished the simple bandaging, he heard Ye Weige shouting anxiously: "Quickly, drag the basket of bricks over here!"

Zhu Chunxin looked back uncertainly.

"Don't look stupid, I am addressing you!" The commander's voice was decisive and stern.

Zhu Chunxin realized then that Ye Weige was giving him a combat order. He had become a true comrade-in-arms for these little generals. Without further thought, Zhu Chunxin walked over to the basket filled with bricks and grabbed the edge. But as soon as he touched it, he drew back his hand as if it had been scorched. He felt the bricks flying in front of his eyes and dropping back into the basket. The basket no longer contained bricks—only many bashed and swollen heads dripping with blood. . . .

Should I do this? Zhu Chunxin asked himself. Isn't it a criminal act for the leading cadres to participate in the fighting?*

"What on earth are you doing? Do you want that gang to come up here?" Another young man guarding the stairs came over, fuming.

Zhu Chunxin could hesitate no longer. What else can I do? I never intended this to happen, he murmured to himself, while he dragged the basket of bricks with all his might toward the stairs. Fortunately, the young man took the basket off his hands halfway down the hall. The attackers downstairs could not have seen what he was doing.

Every charge of the attackers failed under the brilliant defense organized by Ye Weige. Though a few more of his comrades-in-arms had been injured slightly, it was obvious that the attackers had suffered several times more casualties. A stalemate was reached on the battlefield. The attackers started to call names. On the one hand, they swore at "the small bunch of thugs in the 'East Is Red' Command—the 'monarchist dogs'; on the other hand, they cursed Zhu Chunxin for "inciting the masses against the masses" and for "generating fighting and bloodshed." They also vowed to "deal with him severely."

The defenders upstairs returned their verbal abuse while taking a breather to regroup their forces. It was then that Zhu Chunxin discovered that Lin Fengxiang had not helped to guard the stairs. Nobody knew where he had gone. Zhu Chunxin finally understood: Lin Fengxiang was afraid that if the gang charged upstairs, he might be

---

* Fighting had been forbidden by Mao's "Sixteen Points."

victimized with Zhu Chunxin, and therefore had long ago slipped away to hide somewhere. However, in front of the young men, he did not mention the matter. It was only when he had returned to his temporary abode and had sunk down onto the bed that he ground his teeth and muttered: "What hypocrisy! What a dirty trick!" Lin Fengxiang's desertion made him feel disappointed and empty, but it pushed his appreciation and love for the young people to new heights. These little generals are hard to come by! In time of war, they will be loyal soldiers and officers! he murmured appreciatively to himself.

Suddenly, he heard some strange noises at the window. Frightened, he went over to take a look. "Oh!" He shot through the door shouting, "Xiao Ye, Ye Weige, here they come!"

"Who is coming up?" Ye Weige came up to him.

"There . . . at my window . . . coming up!" Zhu Chunxin shouted brokenly. ". . . long ladder. . . ."

"Don't move, wait here in the corridor." Ye Weige took a spear in one hand and a few bricks in the other. Then he rushed into the room like a gust of wind. . . .

A moment later, Ye Weige came out of the room holding his hand over his forehead. Blood was dripping through his fingers. He smiled at Zhu Chunxin: "They retreated, those sons of bitches!"

The blood on his forehead dripped down to his angular mouth and tainted his clean white teeth. Zhu Chunxin abruptly tore off his own shirt and bandaged Ye Weige's wound.

After less than an hour, the alarmed cries of the attackers were heard: "Retreat, quickly retreat. "East Is Red's" main force has arrived!"

"Quickly, quickly, quickly!"

Close combat followed, in which the attackers were sandwiched in between the two forces. Needless to say, the attackers got the worst of it. Lin Fengxiang sneaked out from the toilet after the fighting was over.

"Secretary Zhu," a security officer came to him.

Zhu Chunxin woke from his memories, and found that unknowingly he had been leaning against the old birch tree.

"Secretary Zhu, are you not feeling well?" the security officer asked. "Department Head Li asked whether you had any instructions."

When Zhu Chunxin returned to the pretrial room, the criminal had already been led away. Department Head Li said to Zhu Chunxin with a satisfied smile: "Criminal Ye had a rather good attitude. He basically confessed his crime." Department Head Li pointed at the record saying, "He admitted that during the fighting a student named

Shi Zhihong in the faction attacking the building climbed up a ladder to a second-floor window. When the criminal, Ye, entered the room, Shi Zhihong stood on the windowsill and threw a dagger at him, injuring his forehead. He retaliated by stabbing Shi Zhihong's shoulder with a spear. Fleeing in haste, the latter fell from the second floor. Others were still climbing up the ladder. So he threw down a few bricks but did not know whether anyone had been hurt. He also said that they had been told to fight with words and defend with force. Since the Lao Bao attacked, they had the right to defend with weapons." On saying this, Department Head Li flipped the pages of the file and said: "According to the investigation, the student, Shi Zhihong, was killed, and a worker was crippled under that window."

"Hm." Zhu Chunxin nodded distractedly.

"Criminal Ye and the deceased Shi Zhihong did not know each other, so we can exclude the element of revenge," the department head continued. "But Criminal Ye refused to admit that he was following the Gang of Four and disrupting the Cultural evolution; nor did he admit the motivation for his crime."

"Oh . . ." Zhu Chunxin knotted his brow, troubled and unable to find something appropriate to say. He could not really plead for Ye Hui, nor did he want to chime in with Department Head Li's conclusion. "It is late. Leave the matter till next time. . . . Tomorrow morning we shall analyze it more."

Zhu Chunxin walked out of the main entrance of the district's Public Security Bureau and sank heavily into the soft seat of the car waiting for him. He felt as if his head were bloated, like a round-bottomed basket. His mind was all confused, like a bundle of threads in a hopeless tangle, or like a pool of dirty water fiercely stirred. In particular, a few strange notions flashed in his mind occasionally like neon lights—little generals, benefactor, criminal, revolutionary leading cadre, law. . . . He could not remember clearly how he got out of his car and climbed the stairs of his new home.

"What is the matter, are you sick?" his wife asked him. "Your face is deathly pale. Is it a cold?"

"Perhaps," he answered.

"Have your meal then!"

"No, I want to lie down for awhile."

Zhu Chunxin turned in bed while the notions that had appeared repeatedly during the drive home were still flashing across his mind like a dazzling electric arc. He was turning over in his mind the meaning of his encounter with Ye Weige and the attitude he should take, but the act only tightened the knot in his stomach further.

There was a knock on the door.

"Someone wants to see you," his wife came to his bed to tell him.

"Whatever is the matter—tell them to report to the department concerned. Otherwise, I'll discuss it with them in the afternoon," he said irritably.

"It is an old woman. She insists on seeing you."

"What is her problem?"

"She did not say—all she said was that she was the mother of Ye Hui."

"Oh? Ye Hui—his mother?" Surprised, Zhu Chunxin abruptly climbed out of bed. "Quickly, ask her to come in!"

A frail old worker entered. She looked as if she had reached retirement age. Her kind, honest face had been wrinkled by hard work and worry. She held her large hands awkwardly in front of her chest. Timidly, she stood in the middle of the room and looked at the district's deputy secretary with worried, pleading eyes.

"I am Zhu Chunxin." Zhu Chunxin avoided the old woman worker's gaze, and pulled over a chair. "Sister, please have a seat!"

"Oh, oh, no, thank you. . . ." The old woman worker was a bit overwhelmed by the unexpected favor. "I came from Beining municipality because of Ye Hui's matter. My daughter-in-law telegraphed me. I have only a few words to say. . . . I will say what I have to standing up. You are not well. . . ."

"No, no, no, nothing serious! Please sit down," Zhu Chunxin said kindly.

"Ye Hui committed a crime. . . ." As she said this, the tears were already rolling down the wrinkles on her cheeks. "They arrested and prosecuted my son. That cannot be helped. I am a worker, and we are so happy that the Gang of Four has been smashed. To thoroughly investigate the disorderly elements is a very good idea. Even the investigation fell on my son's head, what could I say? Who told him to go and commit murder!"

"Right," Zhu Chunxin nodded, fixing his gaze on a teacup on the desk. "That is a good attitude, sister." He used the cordial form of address again.

"However, I feel that I still have some honest thoughts to relate to your leadership," the old woman worker said. "I am not sure if they are appropriate. If I say something wrong, your leadership must criticize me. . . ."

"It doesn't matter. Don't worry. Please speak your mind!"

"I think my son does not have a bad nature." Timidly watching Zhu Chunxin's face, the old woman worker decided to make this statement. When she saw that his face twitched a little but showed no sign of reproach, she felt relaxed enough to continue. "When the

Cultural Revolution began, he was a party branch secretary of the second grade in senior middle school.* Some students rose up to seize the headmaster and struggle against the teachers. He was very upset. When he returned home, and told me what happened, he was in tears. He felt as if people had struggled against him instead. Later I heard that he was considered a 'capitalist' and was not allowed to go to Beijing during the Great Linking Up.† He came home and cried. . . ."

At this point, the old woman worker gave a long sigh. "Some class-mates came to comfort him. I also consoled him, but he would not say a word. He spent his time reading newspapers and pamphlets, and then he would look dazed and stare at the ceiling. I was so afraid that he would go crazy. After a few days, he disappeared. Nobody knew where he had gone. His father and I were worried to death—I only have this son. We searched all the wells, woods, and rivers in the area, thinking that he might have killed himself. Then, after ten days or so, he returned. He looked so happy, as if he had been trans-formed. First he apologized to me, saying that he should not have left without saying a word, causing the family such worry. Then he took out a packet from his belt and unfolded it layer by layer. At last, he shook out two souvenir badges of Chairman Mao, the size of a finger-tip, and carefully put one on my shirt. I asked him to wear one too, but he was reluctant for fear that it would be damaged. Carefully, he wrapped it up and kept it close to his chest. He told me that he had secretly gone to Beijing, and had received the greatest education at the command headquarters of the proletariat. He had thought things through, and decided that what he had done in the past was all wrong, that his actions had been revisionist, and that he had been cheated and misled into being a monarchist. 'I was so foolish,' he said. 'How could the son of a worker be a filial descendant of the capitalist class?' He tore up all the 'three-good'‡ certificates he had gotten as a student, saying that they were all 'black cultivation'§ stuff. From then on, he organized something like a fighting detachment, and seldom returned home. I was worried that he would get into trouble and tried to dis-suade him. He pleaded with me, 'Mother, the working class should be the firm support of the Red Guard's little generals. You must sup-port me. You have suffered half your life. Are you willing to see our party and country turn revisionist?' I could not win an argument with

* Eleventh grade.
† When all the Red Guards began traveling around the country, establishing ties with one another and exchanging experiences.
‡ "Three-good" means good in health, learning, and work.
§ Similar to principles outlined in Liu Shaoqi's *How to Be a Good Communist*, which had been branded "black cultivation," *i.e.*, revisionist, elitist, etc.

him, and he blamed me for being muddle-headed. How I wish that I had stopped him then. I only recently learned that he had killed someone. . . ."

The old woman worker wiped her tears, and said apologetically, "Here I am saying all these things! I have no education. . . ."

"No, you put it very well . . . very well." A muscle on Zhu Chunxin's pale face kept twitching. He was not annoyed at the old woman worker's long-winded account. On the contrary her wordy account was pounding his heart like a heavy hammer, making him feel that he was being tried on the stand of the accused. He had committed no crime. This was a trial of his conscience!

"Ye Hui's father passed away three years ago. Ye Hui married not quite a year ago, and his wife is expecting a baby very soon. For the last few days, my daughter-in-law has been crying. . . ." The old woman worker continued with tears in her eyes, "She asked me to think of a way out, but what could I do?"

Zhu Chunxin turned his head away and quickly wiped his eyes with his handkerchief. Then he turned and said, "Do I understand that you would like to ask the district committee to show leniency to Ye Hui?"

"To be lenient or severe, the judge would not listen to me. I only want to make a few things known to your leadership, since I heard that you, Secretary Zhu, are responsible for this work." The old woman worker thought a little and said: "I remember that during the Cultural Revolution, Ye Hui mentioned you once to me. It seemed that you and he had worked on something together. You probably still remember him. . . ."

"Ye Hui mentioned me?" Zhu Chunxin's ears hummed, and perspiration appeared on his temples. He was worried that Ye Hui had given others a full account of the fighting during that September of 1967. "What did he say about me?" Zhu Chunxin asked.

"It was ten years ago—I have long forgotten!" the old woman worker sighed. "It was something about how he had to risk his life to protect leading cadres like you. . . ." The old woman stood up and nodded apologetically to Zhu Chunxin. "I have disturbed your rest. I should be going."

"Won't you stay here for a little while?" Zhu Chunxin asked.

The woman shook her head: "No, I am going back to Beining tomorrow. This time, I have at least seen my troublesome son for the last time. I have asked for five days' leave. We are very busy with production."

After seeing the old woman worker off, Zhu Chunxin lay down on the bed again. The woman's speech and manner had made him more uncomfortable than ever. "My son is basically not bad. . . ." "What could I do?" "I must risk my life to protect leading cadres like. . . ." Her tearful account kept echoing in his ear. He simply had to get up. Looking at his watch, he realized that it was time to go back to work. So he came back to the office of the district committee by car.

A pile of documents and reports were waiting for his comments. He casually looked at one, but put it down after reading only a little. He was in a very troubled mood. This second encounter with Ye Hui and his conversation with Ye Hui's mother had disrupted his life—he couldn't work and he couldn't think. For the first time, he felt that he was not the only victim of the Gang of Four: when he was pushed into the trap, he had dragged this innocent, lovable young man with him. Aside from feeling ashamed and remorseful, he had also developed an annoying cowardice, just like a bad element who has been released after being paraded through the streets. He imagined that the official staff persons greeting him politely were wearing sarcastic smiles. When he saw two cadres discussing something, he felt that they were discussing his behavior during the Cultural Revolution. He was angry at his own abnormal thinking, and wanted to dispel these notions. Yet these thoughts were like disagreeable flies. When he had chased one away, another bunch came! Crossly, he pushed the documents aside.

The party committee secretary came in to inform him that at 2:30 that afternoon the conference of progressive representatives on the "Two Learnings"* on the finance and trade fronts was conducting its closing ceremony. His participation was required. After the conference there would be an unofficial party. At 4 o'clock the organization department had invited him to participate in an analysis of the appointments and removals of cadres. Also, an "advanced experience" reporting group† from another area would be going home in the afternoon, and he would have to greet them. Then, the province's investigation team on city traffic also needed to be greeted. . . . And . . . There were a dozen more of these tasks. Before, he would have moved his strong body around, lifted his square chin, and efficiently managed these affairs with seriousness, self-confidence, and a great deal of energy. But today, he declined them all. "Here is a meeting . . . there is some group or other, tiring people out . . . greeting and entertaining with such fanfare! This style of doing things is terrible!" He was grumbling to his secretary. Suddenly he had an urge—to go and talk to Ye Hui.

* Learning from Dazhai Brigade and Daqing Oil Field which at the time were models in agriculture and industry.
† A group that would report on its advanced political experience.

When the car stopped in front of the district's Public Security Bureau, Zhu Chunxin was hesitant again. What am I here for? he asked himself. Am I coming to show sympathy and pity for my brave defender of that year? Or am I here to do some patch-up work out of fear that Ye Hui might reveal my not-too-honorable deeds? Also no. Am I here to tell Ye Hui that I am sorry? Again no. He actually forgot the reason that had made him decide to come. As he was contradicting his intentions, he entered the gate. It could have been for all of these reasons, or it might not have been for any of them. It might have been the average of their total that had brought him.

First he went to the Bureau's party committee to explain that he wanted to talk to a few disorderly elements whose cases had been established in order to understand the situation further. It happened that the bureau was conducting a meeting, and the appropriate personnel were not there to accompany him. Zhu Chunxin felt that it would be more convenient for him to act by himself. All he demanded were a couple of public security officers to escort the criminals back and forth. He asked for an office for his meetings. After a few words with a criminal charged with beating, vandalism, and looting, he sent for Ye Hui.

Ye Hui entered. He wore the same clothes he had worn that morning, and the same expression—neither excited nor startled. Smiling, he stood before Zhu Chunxin.

"Do sit, Ye Hui." He was going to rise slightly in a greeting, but involuntarily he stood up instead. "Shall we talk?"

"I was already examined this morning." Ye Hui smiled a little.

"No, I am now acting as an old comrade, an old acquaintance. Let's chat a bit . . . casually."

"You flatter me. We only spent a night togther. This is our second encounter . . . you see, in the Public Security Bureau!" Ye Hui laughed. "This is not a place for old comrades or old acquaintances to chat."

"I haven't seen you since the fighting. But you left a deep impression on me."

"I nearly died from not having taken immediate care of my injury. After I recuperated for a few months in bed, the two factions joined, and the revolutionary committees were set up.* I went to the countryside. I never expected that we would meet again."

Zhu Chunxin felt that he was at a loss for words with which to reply to this young man, so he changed the topic: "During the Cultural Revolution, owing to the negative disruptions of the Gang of Four,

* Provisional organs of power set up on all levels in 1969 that included representatives from the army, the party, and mass revolutionary organizations.

many people, including myself, committed that kind of mistake. We must learn from experience and raise our political consciousness. We still believe in education. . . ."

"The forms of the crime are different; the forms of the 'education' are also different," Ye Hui interrupted Zhu Chunxin smiling. "You committed a mistake, but you can justifiably and forcefully accuse Lin Biao and the Gang of Four of having persecuted you. I committed a mistake, but I have to admit I followed Lin Biao and the Gang of Four in undermining the Cultural Revolution."

Zhu Chunxin stood up, speechless, and paced back and forth. The more he was afraid of being touched, the more he was touched. He felt that Ye Hui's every sentence was hitting him where he was most vulnerable.

"Do you mean that you are not being treated fairly?" Zhu Chunxin asked suddenly. "I am willing . . ."

"No . . ."

"Let me finish." Zhu Chunxin stopped him, saying, "I am willing to stand up and shoulder all the responsibility for that fighting in September of 1967."

"You can do what you like, but it does not affect my having to be responsible for my own crime. I am willing to accept whatever punishment is given me, because I committed a crime. I have never tried to cover it up. The victim, Shi Zhihong, was also a brave young man. It was I who did him in. I do not need anyone's sympathy or pity. This punishment, even though it seems high, is the price I shall pay for learning."

"I know you bear a grudge against me."

"No," Ye Hui's chest heaved, betraying his emotion. "I only hate Lin Biao and the Gang of Four, because you are a victim too. I have reason to criticize you, but I also have a liking for you. Since you can admit that you have not been totally correct, you are honest and you have conscience. Some cadres did some dishonorable things during the Cultural Revolution, and were also cruelly persecuted by Lin Biao and the Gang of Four. However, when they were rehabilitated and restored to their positions, they would not mention anything about their past mistakes, except the honor of having been persecuted. . . ."

Zhu Chunxin felt his face burning; he felt terrible inside. He suddenly thought of something: "I remember that ten years ago you were called Ye Weige."

"Yes," Ye Hui replied.

"This morning, why did you not admit to having used that name?"

"That name had nothing to do with the nature of my crime or with this case." Ye Hui's face suddenly clouded over with pain. "Ye

Weige was a name I chose during the Cultural Revolution. It was the mark of my immaturity and shame. I want to reject it totally. . . ."

"How is the discussion going?" Two leading cadres from the Public Security Bureau and Department Head Li walked into the room and greeted Zhu Chunxin.

"It is all right," Zhu Chunxin commented lightly. Originally he had wanted to convey to Ye Hui his concern for Ye's family situation. Now it seemed that it would not be convenient. He took a look at Ye Hui, and in an indecisive tone said, "I guess our conversation is over."

"Secretary Zhu, please come to the receiving room to take a rest," Department Head Li said respectfully. Then, after giving Ye Hui a stern look, he called toward the door, "Lead the criminal away!"

Zhu Chunxin shivered suddenly, and his face turned pale. In his heart, he kept repeating the word: "criminal?"

> from *Shanghai Wenxue* (*Shanghai Literature*)
> April, 1979

The Get-Together
GAN TIESHENG

With the passing of the autumnal equinox, it was by turns rainy and cold. The potatoes were harvested from the fields. The big green grasshoppers, whose clacking noises are only heard in autumn, had soared up from the fields and glided down again. Another year was just about over.

It was at this time that I got a letter from her, sent to the little mountain village where I was team-hitching.*

September, 1975

Xiong Chang:

Do come to our village. On the last day of September, we are planning a jolly get-together. Banish all unhappy thoughts, and come.

I miss you.

Qiuxia

I did not write back. I even repressed all thoughts of her so as to make the coming meeting more "delicious." It wasn't easy! After all, my classmates—my fellow team-hitchers—had all dispersed, leaving me all alone. I had hoped to enter the university this year, but had once again been eliminated owing to problems with my family background. Then my bunch of egg-laying hens caught the chicken pest

---

* Sent to join a rural production team.

and died off one after the other; only my big strong rooster survived, but his characteristic clarion call was reduced to a pathetic croak. When the autumn wind blew, and the leaves scuttled, he would awaken from his lethargy and charge about panic-stricken in search of his mates. That woeful sound was enough to make one weep. . . .

I was enduring, desperately holding out—I did not write or think about her.

At last, the last day of September arrived! I was sure that she would be waiting for me at the gate of the compound. Why not? For one thing, she loved me. For another, of the thirty-odd team-hitching youth, only five or six remained, and half of them were permanently absent in Beijing while another two just roamed about. A couple of girls were all that were left in the once bustling compound! Thirdly, she had also failed to make it in to the university. In a word, our situations were too identical!

And yet, all there was to greet me at the gate were bunches of weeds, blowing in the wind. From within came frolicking noises! I walked through the doorway and was struck dumb: a girl dressed in a pink sweater was shrieking with laughter, stuffing a handful of chicken feathers into the mouth of a young fellow who had fallen on the grass. The fellow kept rolling to get away, while seven or eight young people looked on, clapping and hollering and laughing.

The girl caught sight of me. She walked over to me, wiping away her tears of laughter, and said: "Oh, he is here. What is this? You didn't bring a thing? Come here to scrounge for food, have you? Off with you! Go get some wine!"

It was she—Qiuxia! Tiny teardrops still clung to her long eyelashes.

"I am not going!" I said laughing, but hating her a little inside.

"In that case, I shall have to dispense with courtesy!" she said in her loud, clear voice to those around, beckoning them with a waving handful of feathers.

The crowd closed in on me, rubbing their hands and rolling up their sleeves. Ah ha! They were the "long departed." They were the heroes "of great renown" in our county: Huo Bo, nicknamed Niuer,* had once carted off all the old belongings left behind by educated youth who had left the village, and auctioned them off in front of the County Educated Youth Office! Tall Wang Cheng once shook the county by traveling all around the country without a penny to his name! The two girls—Xiao Xiu and Xiao Lan—even the person least familiar with them could tell you ten exploits of each! The others—

---

* Second Ox.

chess champion Wang Guoxiang and Yao Ben the tailor—now they could pass for the well-behaved. . . .

"Oh, haven't seen you for ages! The absolute dregs have surfaced; the bottom of the barrel has been scraped!" I clasped my hands in greeting to all.

The pink woolen shirt flashed, and Qiuxia was at my side.

"You spoilsport! I am telling you, if you break the taboo again, I'll throw you out!"

The rowdy crowd gathered around, but with a haughty wave of her hand Qiuxia stopped them all. She dragged me away from the crowd and said in a low voice: "The few remaining hitchers in the county are all extremely sensitive. It is best not to touch on issues concerning our situation. We badly need some fun!"

The kitchen was filled with the aroma of meat. She pointed at the wok big enough to cook a meal for thirty, and said: "Ten chickens—how about it? You've never treated yourself this way?"

I was suddenly overwhelmed with tenderness. I wanted to have a few private words with her. But that rowdy Niuer came into the room, followed by Guoxiang and Wang Cheng. They stuck next to the chicken pot, as if the soup had cast a spell over them.

"Shall I get wine to go with this?" Reluctantly, I grabbed a five-catty jug. "Bring some money."

We went into her dormitory. She gave me a furtive glance as she pulled money from under her pillow.

"You must have noticed! Let's not be so intimate. . . ."

"Come on, what does it matter?" I protested.

"Of course it matters!"

"What?"

"People will be jealous, or it will trigger old memories . . . you understand? Let us have a happy get-together, to wash off the unpleasant. . . ."

"It can't be washed away, nor is there any need to! You show such Buddha-like compassion for the others, but who cares about us?" I grabbed the outstretched hand that was giving me the money, and conveniently pulled her onto my lap.

Like an agitated cat, she darted away, and said with annoyance, "How can you be so insensitive! Selfish devil!"

The door shut. Then I heard her laughter in the crowd.

Anyway, I could not get excited anymore.

I had to admit that using a plastic sheet to cover bed boards for a table was quite a sophisticated idea. Yet I yawned. My gaze listlessly rested on the bowl of wine. I took a mouthful, and it was as if I had swallowed a hot, stinging little dragon. Wine, sweet potato wine—

light purple—never had I tasted such stuff in Beijing. It was really strong! Who had covered the lamp shade with a piece of green gauze, saying that it signified freedom and joy? What a fantasy! I suppose I was still all right. The green gauze reflected in the wine was like water weeds, floating, floating—so much like water tinted red by the setting sun! It reminded me of the reservoir near their village. There, Qiuxia and I had swum . . . the green algae getting tangled up with my legs—how awful. And what about the shallow banks? Stepping on that soft, sticky warm mud. Bah, that sickening feeling was so much like this "feast." I turned up the volume of the radio at the head of the bed to its loudest. Li Yuhe was singing ". . . lofty aspirations and great ideals are surging high . . ." I changed the channel— it was "Long Jiang Xiong." There, the debate was heated over the issue of "sacrificing the pawn to save the chariot."* Another channel. Oh, finally, there was a voice: ". . . Confucianism . . . Confucian scholar . . . Old Man Kong . . . Capitalist roaders . . ." My head swam. I was just about to block my ears when Xiao Xiu screamed angrily: "Can't you shut that off?!"

"Spare us!" The gang yelled at me. I wanted to enjoy myself too. I turned the radio off.

"Ahh . . ." I yawned again.

"Six six six wa!"

"Three horses ah!"

"Five bright heads ya!"†

"Hey, we are happy, right!"

"Cheers!"

The room was filled with smoke. Someone tired of drinking. A match was struck—the wine was lit. The light blue flame caused a wave of exclamations. The bowl cracked. Blue flame raced along the table. Confusion. Suddenly everyone became a firefighter. Xiao Lan leaned her head against Wang Cheng's shoulder and said in an affectedly delicate tone: "Oh, I am fainting . . ."

Qiuxia's pink figure flashed around. "Eat, do eat." She served food to one. "Drink, do drink." She poured wine for another. "Don't be in a daze, be merry!" she whispered to chess champion Wang Guoxiang in a soft voice. And so Guoxiang woke up with a start, shouting: "Cheers! How come I blanked out?" Thanks to her efforts, witty conservation, humorous stories, and hilarious gossip, the party livened up again. But who was quietly sighing, "Every festival day, you miss your dear ones even more." No matter how carefully the voice dodged the crowd, the sadness and anxiety somehow crept into everybody's

* Pieces in a Chinese chess game.

† Chinese drinking game.

eyes. And so again the pink flash of a figure moved around again. She narrowed her eyes into a smile, shook her head, and said with sympathy in her voice: "Drink, drink, eat! Let's play the drinking game! Niuer, do start!"

She was attentive to everyone but me. Pouring wine and serving food, she walked past me as if I were not there.

I could not tolerate it any longer. Quietly I stood up, quietly I pulled open the door, and quietly I slipped outside.

Gazing into the dark blue evening, I had the urge to shout songs to the stars! But I could only take a few deep breaths of the clear, cold air. Suddenly, the door opened. Judging from the breathing and those familiar steps, I knew that Qiuxia was standing right behind me.

"Don't you feel that what you are shouldering is too heavy?" I asked. "How could you think up such a cruel game? You are urging the prisoners to dance by cracking a whip!"

"Nobody thinks of it the way you do," she said in a low voice.

"I cannot tolerate . . . all this," I said.

We were silent. There was the sound of autumn insects weeping in solitude.

"You should tolerate it. You should help me." Her tone carried a note of sad pleading.

"I . . . want to return to my village."

She did not say anything. A moment later, I could tell that she was heading toward the door.

"Qiuxia!" I turned, and dashed to her side. "Let's join each other! I shall come to your village, or you come to ours."

She was undecided. "Then we would have to go through so much— start a new network of personal relationships, give dinners, hand out gifts. . . .* You know, I am so fed up with all of that . . . though it is awfully lonely here." She coughed. "Why bring that up again? Let's not talk about this, at least no tonight. Do come in."

"Then I shall go," I stubbornly insisted.

In the moonlight, she stared severely, straight into my eyes. Then she determinedly pulled open the door and went inside.

I had gone beyond the door of the compound, but I returned.

Inside, Qiuxia was vigorously beating the table with a chicken claw. "Quiet! Quiet! I propose that each of us tell about the happiest thing that has happened in his life. Nobody is spared! If it is good, we will give three toasts; if not, the person must empty six cups!"

The atmosphere in the house suddenly became like an examination hall—nervous, solemn, quiet.

---

* All of which would have to be done in order to facilitate getting official permission for a transfer.

Xiao Lan's eyes sparkled with a glowing memory. When asked to speak, she declined, saying: "Happiness can't be spoken of." Guoxiang was picking his brain to decide on the best of numerous happy incidents. After much hesitation, he gestured, smiled, and said: "Nothing could be more exciting than knocking the loser's head after a game of chess—thump, thump, thump—all it takes is three knocks to make a huge bump on the head." Niuer, the fellow who did not care much about anything, talked about a romance he'd had when he was twenty, acting out the affectionate gaze and smile of the girl in his memory. One didn't know whether to laugh or cry at this kind of acting. Watching his strange act, and the premature wrinkles on that thin, dark face, I could not help but shiver.

"Where is she now?" Qiuxia was always so concerned about others. Niuer's face was twisted. He stared at tailor Yao Ben, and in a muddled voice said: "Where? It . . . doesn't matter. . . . Some people don't even have as much as this memory!"

Yao Ben hastily held up the bowl of wine. "Oh . . . I have lived for a quarter of a century. 'Sewing wedding clothes for others' is my pleasure. . . . Forget it, I have nothing interesting to say." He gulped down two mouthfuls, and began to retaliate: "However, I do want to hear about present happiness. Niuer, when you were auctioning off others' leftovers in the county, your heart must have been. . . ."

"You broke the taboo!" Qiuxia interrupted Yao Ben with a bang on the table. This, however, did not stop the onset of silence. Obviously, it was again Qiuxia who, afraid that this mood would spread, blurted out in a loud, incongruous voice:

"All right, I shall talk about present happiness! You all know that I love to read at the dam of the reservoir. Several days ago, I was reading alone on the dam. I discovered a squirrel-like animal climbing skillfully on the dam wall, just like Pidefu* speeding on his motorcycle. I stared at it blankly, because it reminded me of life: if you are not skillful, you will drown, fall to your death. . . . Suddenly I heard loud shouts: 'Miss, miss—' I lifted my head, it was the old fellow who was tending sheep over the hill. Shouting, he ran over desperately: 'Miss, miss—' 'What is it?' I asked. Panting, he said: 'Miss, miss . . . I heard that on the plain a girl hitcher drowned herself in a well . . . I, I wanted to mention this to you . . . She was so foolish, so young to take her own life. . . .' I suddenly realized he was afraid that I was going to jump! Instantly, my heart swelled with emotion, that during such a desolate autumn there could be a stranger who cared about me. . . ."

* Famous acrobat.

Silence. Nobody said a word. I stared at her intensely, my temples throbbing.

Qiuxia took a cigarette, but before lighting it she suddenly spat it on the ground, yelling, "Damn! I broke the taboo! I shall drink six cups!"

She scooped up the wine cups, filling one after another, and then drank each down in one gulp.

"Are you out of your mind?" I went forward and snatched the cup away.

"You'd better stay away from me!" Without looking at me, she grabbed the cup again.

I was embarrassed. But I still tried to take her cup away.

"What do you think you are doing?!" She glared at me.

"I shall drink for you!"

"Can happiness be substituted? Young man, be prepared to talk about your own happiness! Nobody can substitute for anyone else! Right?" She turned and asked the others loudly. She was getting drunk.

"Certainly." "The role of the sorrowful ghost fits him well." "Drink to get drunk!" "It is not your turn yet to be chivalrous." "Who needs you to help drink the stuff!" "Make him talk!"

I was anxious. I did feel that I could help her! No, I was not going to talk! I did not have anything I felt happy about! I refused to beat my face until it was swollen to look plump! I did not want to lash out under the pretense of drunkenness! I . . . I was just going to yell when I caught sight of Qiuxia's face deliberately hidden behind the wine cup to block it from the others' line of vision. The look she gave me was so full of pleading, so full of painful patience, of a pure, self-sacrificing glow.

She was asking for help from me with her eyes! I would be together with her, and shoulder the responsibility for generating fun! But with this kind of party, what could I do? I returned to my seat, downcast. . . .

Time dragged on this way to a tasteless end, like that green light filling the whole room. The feast was dying down; the wine was nearly exhausted. Qiuxia looked miserable. She realized that her efforts had been wasted; she was disappointed, sad.

When Niuer grabbed the last piece of chicken breast, I said, "Wait!"

"What for?"

"See how much wine is left?"

Niuer emptied the wine jug—exactly a full bowl!

"The chicken breast belongs to whoever gulps down this bowl!" I said.

"Is this shriveled piece of breast worth a week's headache? You don't even know how to bet!"

Sure enough, nobody took the bowl of wine.

"Didn't you want to get drunk anyway?" I teased Niuer.

" 'A thousand glasses are not enough for bosom friends.' That is an old saying. Somehow it does have a point." Niuer glanced at Qiuxia. "Man is solid; fire, insubstantial. To put up a front, to create an atmosphere artificially, is self-defeating. . . ."

"Bet! Let's bet!" Abruptly, I interrupted Niuer, "Whoever empties this bowl in one gulp, I . . . I will help him transfer back to Beijing!"

The room was silent for a moment. Then they clamored: "Ha, what big talk!" "Bragging isn't taxed!" "Having a fantasy, are you?" Obviously, they did not believe my words.

"It is true. I bribed a channel. The people promised to arrange it all. I will let whoever drinks this bowl of wine have my chance. What about it? Nobody dares to take me on? I'll count to five: one, two, three." I raised my voice, pretending to be resolute: "A chance missed, and that's it! Four—"

"Wait!" Niuer rushed forward, "He is finally speaking the truth after a few drinks—I shall drink it! It would be great to be able to drink heartily and then be transferred back to Beijing! Only a fool would not do it!"

"But there is one condition. There," I lifted the grate on the windowsill, "take this to the graveyard, straight inside, and put it on the tenth grave. If I don't help you transfer to Beijing, you can lynch me!"

Niuer made a face, and to the others said, "This bet of his is really weird! Let me tell you, this bet goes beyond the limit. There won't be anyone. . . ."

Abruptly, Qiuxia pushed Niuer aside, and with a solemn air lifted the bowl, took a deep breath, and let the wine gush down her throat. She boldly flashed the bottom of the bowl, wiped her mouth, and, amidst cheers, grabbed the grate, pretending to balance herself without much effort, and walked out of the house: "Wait till I come back before you take a torch to look for this—this . . . gra—grate . . ."

The crowd that remained, barely suppressing its laughter and curiosity, stealthily followed her. I took Niuer into the shadows, and spoke a few words to him. He then announced to the others: "The compound is empty—I shall stay and watch." He left.

A village night. The moon was so desolate. The rustling wind accompanied distant barking. Qiuxia dragged a long shadow with her, humming some tunes to keep up her courage and occasionally burping. She walked through a patch of melons, wound her way around a wheat field, jumped over a ditch. Beyond was the graveyard.

She leaned against an old willow tree at the edge of the graveyard, looked back at the road she had taken, gave a long sigh, and headed on.

An owl suddenly cried—it sounded like a child. The crowd that had scattered to hide now quickly came together. It was so creepy: the swaying tree shadows over the graves, the flashing light on the tombstones, a moist rotten smell, made everyone hear his pulse throb.

Suddenly, big Wang Cheng and Yao Ben yelled; Xiao Xiu and Xiao Lan covered their faces and fell paralyzed to the ground. A strange white figure sprang out from the dark graveyard and lightly and noiselessly danced around! Qiuxia made a startled noise and turned around to run. Instead, she stumbled headfirst into the ditch that went through the graveyard. The strange creature took a few leaps to the edge of the ditch, and cried with a hoarse voice:

Cats and rabbits are dancing together,
They step one, two, one.
Cats and rabbits are dancing together,
They step one, two, one.

I rushed over and pulled off the white bedsheet: "Enough! Niuer!"

Niuer howled with laughter: "Marvelous! Absolutely marvelous! Dear fellow, incredible! You are now spared from the crime of lying!"

I pulled Qiuxia from the ditch.

"Aiy, I am scared to death. I am really scared to death!" Devastated, she fell weakly into my lap.

I half carried her toward the house. The crowd gathered around Niuer, who was choking with laughter and giving an account of his stirring game.

Suddenly Qiuxia started to vomit. I stroked her back. Finally, she let out a few miserable cries and quietly wept. But immediately she restrained herself, only to lift her head up weakly, looking for the moonlight. Tears flowed silently down her cheeks.

I said, "You must feel wretched. Let it all out. You will feel better afterwards."

But she shook her head, straining her neck to look back at the excited, chattering crowd. "They were all, all very happy, weren't they?" she asked.

"No, more than that! Simply exhilarated!" I said with annoyance. I refused to turn my head to look at them.

"Cold, I am cold. I am really cold . . ." She folded her arms around her trembling shoulders.

My heart tightened, and an immense sadness surged up in me. I hastily took hold of my jacket—but a sweater had been thrown around Qiuxia, followed by a patched blue jacket, and then a third. . . . They had quietly gathered around.

With a calm look that covered her misery and anxiety, Qiuxia gazed into Xiao Lan's frightened eyes: "I am not cold . . . really! Now, now . . . you . . . you, you had fun, right?" She tried to act composed, struggling to pull the clothes from her body to return to them, but her trembling hand only clutched her own pigtail. Xiao Xiu rushed into Qiuxia's lap with a loud wail and broke down crying. Then they wept together. Niuer sank heavily onto the ground and punched his own head. Then he fiercely tore at his hair. Big Wang Cheng leaned his face on the rough old bark of the willow. I slowly lifted my head. The moon, through my tear-filled eyes, was a ball of angry fire. . . .

Soon enough, another September arrived. We gathered together again, not at their compound but on the hill near our village. It was drizzling that day. Xiao Lan and I stood before the newly planted willow—staring at her grave. She had died. She had been alone, reading on the dam, and somehow had fallen and drowned. I buried her there. I tied some wild autumn flowers into a bundle, and placed it in front of her grave. The colorful flowers were covered with rain, like tears, like mourning. Xiao Lan looked at the soaked tombstone and over and over said: "It will pass, everything will pass eventually, but nothing will be forgotten!"

Through the misty ranges of Taihang Mountain in the distant horizon, in the rustling autumn chill, a tint of light blue suggesting a gleam of hope stretched over the peak of the hills. "It will pass! Over there it is already clear. Can it be far from here?" I said. Xiao Lan gave me a silent glance. She did not say anything, but with sincere yearning she watched the patch of blue with its suggestion of hope.

That was the last day of September, 1976—only a few days before the fall of those four historic criminals.

from *Beijing Wenyi* (*Beijing Literature and Art*)
February, 1980

Appendix

The Activists

To suggest the full spectrum of the Mao Generation's discontent, we include here an essay by, and an article about, young political activists from the democracy movement of 1978–79. Most of the New Realism writers confine their "activism" to writing literature that exposes the faults of the political system, leaving it to others to find solutions. Or, if they propose a solution, it is that those in power reform themselves. In contrast, the young activists represented below see the system itself as structurally flawed, present a program for reform, and have worked actively to bring about change.

The reforms these writers suggest concern democracy and legality. They seek democratic reform, because although in China's socialist system, policy decisions sent down as directives to the masses are supposed to be based on information and suggestions sent up to the party leadership by the masses, in reality, the flow of communication has only been one way: the masses have participated in carrying out policies, but not in making them. They want legal reforms because although the Chinese constitution guarantees certain rights, including freedom of speech, in practice, these rights exist in name only and have been systematically violated.

In "Proletarian Dictatorship Is a Humanitarian Dictatorship," Wang Xizhe, one of the most outspoken of the democracy movement activists, argues that what the Chinese government calls socialism violates the humanitarian assumptions of Marxist theory. His essay attacks decision-making based on untested ("unscientific") axioms rather than on information gathered from the masses. Through his criticism of the present system, Wang Xizhe points to what he feels a proper socialist system should be; in this sense, his critique is a theoretical program for reform.

"Proletarian Dictatorship Is a Humanitarian Dictatorship" has never been published in China; its thesis was too critical to be tolerated by official circles even during the height of the liberal period following the fall of the Gang of Four. The translation that follows is an abridgement of the essay as it first appeared in the Hong Kong journal, *The Seventies.*

"China's New Generation of Politicians," by Wei Ming, is an article based on a series of interviews with four participants in the 1980 elections for people's representative. In 1980, for the first time in the history of socialist China, competitive elections (as opposed to elections in which voters merely ratify a list of candidates) were allowed. Although the elections were held only for the position of people's representative at the county district levels or below, the young people who participated saw them as a significant step toward more mass participation in the decision-making process. The campaign took place at Beijing University, which has traditionally been the center of political and intellectual acitivity in China. Wei Ming's article appears here in abridged form.

Proletarian Dictatorship Is a Humanitarian Dictatorship
WANG XIZHE

The Historical Roots of the Totalitarianism of the Gang of Four

The basis for our claim that a proletarian dictatorship is a humanitarian one lies in Marx. . . .

However, for a long time past—in the hands of Kang Sheng,* Lin Biao, the Gang of Four, and the like—our proletarian dictatorship has become a most inhumane, merciless, pitiless, cruel thing. . . . They would not give Comrade Liu Shaoqi the proper treatment for his illness, their reason being that class struggle is cruel and merciless; they mixed sand in with Comrade He Long's food and gave him no water to drink with the reason that class struggle is totally beyond any considerations of humanity; they could even cut the windpipe of Communists who refused to bow down, with the excuse that "If we can cut the windpipe of chickens and ducks, then why not those of counterrevolutionaries?" Before the knife of the proletarian dictatorship there is no difference between poultry and people. Here we shall not

---

* A high state and party official (appointed one of the five vice-chairmen under Mao in 1973) associated with the Gang of Four. During the trial of the Gang of Four, sixteen persons were accused in all: ten of these were alive. Six, including Kang Sheng, were denounced posthumously.

attempt to list the beatings, struggle sessions, hunger, cold, and humiliations suffered by thousands upon thousands of people besides Liu Shaoqi, He Long, and Zhang Zhixin—all in the name of the benevolent "Dictatorship of the Proletariat."

As we know, neither the proletarian dictatorship of the Soviet Union nor that of China was born of the highly developed material and spiritual civilization of capitalism. Quite the contrary, they were built on the wastes of the barbaric Russian Tsarist autocracy and the even more barbaric Chinese Asian landlord autocracy. The Russian Bolsheviks and the Chinese Communists had to struggle to try to overthrow these dictatorships. . . . In order to survive and develop, the Communists (especially the C.C.P.) almost *had* to use all weapons used by the enemy. The Guomindang (KMT) used a party-run army (hence the origin of the warlords) to suppress the Communists; in response, the Communists had to build a party-run army of their own. The KMT used a secret service (from whence came police terror) to suppress the Communists, whereupon the Communists had no choice but to set up their own secret service in response. The ruthless injury wrought by the KMT on all levels of Communist Party organization meant that they had to militarize—turn into a machine—making it impossible for the broad masses of party members, or even the party Congress, or even the Plenary Party Central Committee, to hear entirely truthful reports on party matters. Neither could they thoroughly discuss, in a democratic way, the party's policies and strategies nor could they democratically elect their leaders. Thus we find a state of affairs in which the Communists, using the weapons of their enemies, made steady gains against the autocracy—although, at the same time, a price was exacted for every gain, and the Communists inevitably became tainted by the autocratic tradition.

All this was necessary, inevitable. Nonetheless, in the early days of a proletarian dictatorship founded on the ruins of such a feudal autocracy, it was necessary and inevitable that Communists would use the weapons of autocracy. Lenin explained, "In order to hasten the westernization of barbaric Russia more effectively than Peter did, we do not scruple to use dictatorial methods; in opposing the powers of barbarism, we do not refuse the use of barbaric methods of struggle." Mao explained it thus: "Do unto them as they do unto you." That's what we do; we do unto imperialism and its lackeys, Jiang Jieshi* and his reactionaries, as they do unto us.

* Chiang Kaishek.

Does Marxism Concern Itself with Humanitarianism?

Here there are two questions. First, should Zhu Xi's* Lex Talionis serve as a guiding principle of the proletarian dictatorship? Second, is the use of "barbaric methods of struggle" an essential policy of the proletarian dictatorship or not?

The question is, in fact, Should Communists, who represent, in theory, the most progressive, most civilized social force, gradually eradicate the marks branded on them by an autocratic historical tradition?

In China [this question] was never even raised. For a long time now, in the eyes of the people, it has gone almost without saying that the dictatorship of the proletariat is one drenched in blood, cruel and inhuman. Before Liberation, the landlords and capitalists oppressed us; why should we not now oppress *them* in the same way? These villains treated us with such cruelty, why should we not deal with them with the same cruelty? Thus, one had to be cruel and dispassionate to the "class enemy"—whether real or imagined—and inhumanity became a social virtue to be emulated. . . . Furthermore, the crueller they are, the less humanity they show, and the more they are shown to have a firm "proletarian" class stand. In order to justify theoretically this widespread barbarity, theorists decided that humanitarianism was a patently bourgeois virtue, and that Marxism did not concern itself with humanitarianism. . . .

Since Marxists do not concern themselves with humanitarianism, all manner of cruelty and viciousness may be committed in the name of the "Dictatorship of the Proletariat," all with an easy conscience and innocence. And yet this statement that "Marxism is not concerned with humanitarianism," which is so hard to take on an emotional plane—can it be correct on a theoretical plane?

Here we must delve into the roots of the matter—and remember just what Marx's communist doctrine was all about.

We shall not quote from Marx's famous *The Economic Philosophical Manuscripts of 1844,* nor from *The Holy Family,* as some people would dismiss these as the immature works of Marx in his youthful days. But in his work *The German Ideology,* which came after his criticism of Ludwig Feuerbach, Marx described his basic communist tenets as follows:

> One of the most important principles in which communism differs from all reactionary socialism is the following actual belief, which is based on the study of human nature: that differences in the brain and intelligence in no way entail differences in requirements of the stomach and physical

* Zhu Xi was a philosopher of the Sung Dynasty (960–1279 A.D.).

body; hence, the incorrect principle "to each according to his ability," which is based on our present system, should—because this principle is narrowly defined in consumption—be replaced by a principle of "to each according to his needs." In other words, differences in activity and labor should not entail any inequality or privilege in the sphere of possession and consumption.

How can one claim that Marxism does not concern itself with humanitarianism?

Is the Standard of Value People or Productive Forces?

We often say a communist society—which has neither exploitation nor oppression—is the ideal human society. But what is our basis for saying that the most ideal human society is the one without exploitation or oppression? What is our basis for saying that the most rational system of distribution should be according to need, which takes no account of capacity for labor? What is our basis for saying that the purpose of human existence is none other than the all-around development of human capabilities? If these communist beliefs do not arise from the study of human nature, then where do they come from?

Those theorists who feel disgust at every mention of the word "man" refuse to acknowledge this. They claim that communist tenets can only emerge from the necessary development of the productive forces. . . .

Even some brilliant theorists have taken this view. Comrade Wang Ruoshui,* for one, says: "The criterion for judging a society is not whether or not it is in accord with human nature, but whether or not it is suited to the development of the productive forces."

Maybe so. Then how are we to account for the fact that Marx and Engels never showed the least bit of sympathy for the slave owners, landlords, and capitalists who had at one time stood for new relations of production? Was not the exploitative social system that they represented precisely the one that was best able, at one time, to promote the development of the productive forces? Conversely, how are we to account for the way in which Marx and Engels praised the early struggles of slaves, serfs, and workers against their exploiters? When, in fulfillment of the role allotted them by history, exploiters set about exploiting the laboring people in what was then the only mode capable of developing the productive forces, from what basis did Marx and Engels proceed to praise rebellions—from that of Spartacus to that of the weavers of Lyon and Silesia?

According to Marx, the capitalist classes are "destined to create

* Editor of the *People's Daily*.

the material basis for the new world." So, of course, it is very revolutionary of the capitalists to do their utmost to develop the forces of production. By Comrade Wang Ruoshui's standards, these capitalists must all be good people since they are developing the productive forces, and we must not be concerned with "whether or not it is in accord with human nature."

Since it is so, it follows naturally that while slavery or serfdom remain systems that best serve the development of the productive forces, one has no right whatever to criticize them; and, furthermore, one has no standard by which they may be judged. (For on what basis can one say that the life led by slaves and serfs was not the happiest, fullest, and best suited to the human nature of the time?) Hence, so long as we can show that modern imperialism can still develop the productive forces at high speed, we must pay respect to imperialism, no matter how much the workers' blood flows to maintain it.

If we still persist in these standards, we naturally arrive at the following conclusion: in order to develop the socialist forces of production and to protect this "socialism," the needless sacrifice of a few more people or the slaughter of a few more innocent people is of quite negligible importance.

What is Human Nature?

. . . In the domain of history, Marx's chief concern was always man. In his view, it is not the need for productive forces that determines man's value; on the contrary, the rationality of the productive forces should be determined by the values of man.

We have seen above that while the capitalists did their utmost to develop the productive forces, these forces caused injury to the workers' health and defiled human nature. Therefore, they had to be condemned—this was Marx's logic. As Marx saw it, mankind has to "eliminate the material and social conditions that require the enslavement of man in order that he may develop his potential." After these old social conditions are destroyed, new social conditions will be established wherein "socialized man, united producers, shall regulate their material interaction with nature in a rational way, set it under their joint control, and not permit it to govern over itself as a blind force. [They] will carry on this material interaction with the minimum expenditure of effort, under conditions unashamedly best suited to their human nature."

Thus we find that Marx considered that the mode of production existing under capitalist conditions had to be condemned, and that the standard he used was that of human nature. (The view cited here dates from 1845.)

What, then, *is* human nature? According to Marx, it is that human quality, founded on his fundamental activity—labor—that shows itself in the desire to develop freely and fully. Man's value lies precisely in his ability to create, through this free and full development, his own infinite variety.

Two Criteria for Judging the Rationality of a Society

Thus there are two criteria by which to judge the rationality of societies, past and present—a horizontal measure and a vertical measure.

A society that does not conform to human nature, or indeed runs contrary to human nature, violates it; it oppresses people, exploits people, alienates man from his labor power and the fruits of his labor, makes him a slave to his own labor power and its products, makes him suffer an animal-like existence. Such a society is inhumane, and under all circumstances praises should be sung of any attempt on the part of the laboring people to oppose it. Socialist society is a prototype humanitarian society, but it still does not completely abolish alienation within social relations, and may in fact restore and develop such alienation. Only the environment for existence provided by communism (where "the development of human potential is an end in itself—a true realm of freedom") is best suited to human life. In such a world "the free development of each man is the condition for the free development of all men." Man reaches a destiny seemingly more in accord with human nature on a higher plane. Thus, our fight for communism is really a fight for thorough humanitarianism.

However, ever since the demise of primitive communist society, the successive societies in history have all been oppressive, exploitative, and injurious to man; they have all run contrary to human nature, and men have instinctively fought against them, enacting scene after scene of moving tragedy. But, whether it is the egalitarian utopia of the small producer farmer or the "communist" utopia of the early handicraft factory workers, these could still never replace the existing anti-human-nature societies. Why is this?

In actual fact—Marx and Engels tell us—man has never obtained freedom within the limits imposed by his ideals, but only within the limits imposed by the existing productive forces. . . .

The Basic Features of Human Nature

. . . It is not that human nature becomes class nature after human beings enter a class society; on the contrary, ever since there has been any surplus in human products, there has been a proportion of "human beings" who do not labor themselves but who live by exploitation and oppression of other people (i.e., they indirectly feed on other humans). This precisely shows that they have lost their humanity. This is a type of regression. It is an expression of a remnant bestiality. Thus, the history of human evolution is in actual fact the history of the struggle between man's humanity and remnant bestiality. Within society, this struggle is externalized as class struggle. . . .

So the Marxist idea that the proletariat must liberate the whole of mankind implies that the proletariat must liberate not only itself but the capitalist who represents the last exploiting class, so that the capitalist may recover his humanity. . . .

The History of Mankind Is the History of Societies' Incessant Mutilation of Human Nature

It is an almost inconceivable reversal that, in class society, it is those inhuman "humans," devoid of humanity, who enjoy the fruits of man's labor, who "hold a monopoly on development," and always seem so civilized; whereas those vested with humanity, the laboring people, lead an inhuman life, and thus "lose all potential for development" and always seem so barbarous. In order to destroy this inhuman, upside-down society, progressive thinkers and leaders are forever devising schemes to liberate mankind. However . . . it is only utopia, outlined by the pioneer thinkers of the proletariat in recent times, that approaches the essence of the problem, which is that private property must be abolished. From More and his "Island of the New Moon" to Campanella and his "Sun City" to Robert Owen and his "labor communes," we see that mankind's attempt to humanitarianize his own society is gradually becoming more scientific and less utopian, along with the increasing possibilities provided by man's economic conditions. . . . Marx and Engels not only helped to make socialism scientific rather than utopian, they also made humanitarianism a science and not a dream! Marx himself told us,

". . . From the moment the working class movement became reality, all manner of utopias disappeared. However, this was not because the working class gave up the ideals sought after by the utopians, but because they had found the means to accomplish these ideals. . . ."

The Humanitarian Nature of the Dictatorship of the Proletariat

The humanitarian nature of the dictatorship of the proletariat shows itself in two ways.

On the one hand, because this is a transitional society, there exist various classes and struggles among them. Classes cannot be eliminated by bayonets (except for parasitic ones), nor can they be eliminated by going beyond the limits of the level of productive forces and merely using laws to announce the transfer of the ownership rights of the means of production. Classes can only be eliminated by a tremendous wealth in material production. So long as society is still bound by the old division of labor, thus retaining the basis for generating classes; so long as in this society some of the people live in freedom and a majority of the people live in need; then even though this society uses law a hundred times to announce that classes are eliminated, the existence of classes is still a material fact.

We know, since the disintegration of mankind's primitive communism, that class struggles up to today—that is, the struggles that classes have conducted to compete for society's wealth—have all been most cruel, most barbaric, most inhumane (though the trend is moving toward the more humane and more civilized). . . .

Under the dictatorship of the proletariat, the various classes and strata can negotiate democratically the distribution of social wealth. There will be conflicts, but these can be resolved through the mediation of law (coded by the proletariat and based on the opinion of the vast majority). There will be violence, but it is only a backup for the proletariat in defense of the will of the majority. Its use will be strictly limited; its function will progressively decrease. . . .

Even with the criminal elements, one should still use civilized, humane methods to reform them. In the social relationships of this type of dictatorship of the proletariat (actually it is the people's democratic dictatorship), people can develop mutual loving emotions.

A second way in which the humanitarian nature of the dictatorship of the proletariat shows itself is by the following: the working class and all working people will gradually be able to *transform* the mode of work inherited from the capitalist modes of production that is injurious to the workers' health and make it suited to human nature.

The eight-hour workday, noon rests, exercises, breaks in work time, as well as work security, social security, prevention of occupational disease, rotation of work that involves health hazards, et cetera—all these are manifestations of this humanitarianism. Under the condition of socialism, the raising of productivity should only

entail falling labor intensity. All of these humane features following the development of the socialist economy will increase, will
become more perfect, and will make the lives of laboring people
richer and happier. Now, some Western friends have discovered
China's noon rest. They seem to think that it is a barrier to China's
Four Modernizations. They say, Isn't the bottleneck of China's Four
Modernizations not the calcification of the economic system and the
bureaucratization of the political system but the Chinese workers'
rest that is apart from the rest that comes after a day's work? One
cannot say that this is the bias of the capitalist mode of production.
But in the eyes of the capitalist, their machines—their invariable capital—are everything; as for the workers' health, it is as valueless as
the industrial wastes that are dumped in the sea by the machines. . . .
This right to rest of the Chinese worker is precisely the result of
bloody struggles of the proletariat; it is precisely the realization of
the humane quality of the dictatorship of the proletariat.

   In Western intellectual circles today, a call for human values is increasingly being heard. This is a reflection of the crisis in capitalism, under which man faces the danger of being swallowed up by
machines. . . .
   History shows that the "charisma" that socialism holds for the
whole world lies not in its having brought a highly rich material life
to the people (though this is, of course, something it brings). Its charisma springs, first and foremost, from its being a humanitarian society—given which, the people feel that there is reason, and warmth;
feel themselves human; and therefore wish conscientiously to immerse themselves in the society and offer all they have for its advancement.

Why the Dictatorship of the Proletariat
Became an Irony of History

Having made a study of the humanitarianism that should exist under
the dictatorship of the proletariat, we must explain why it is that
under socialism there appeared such powers, as are represented by
Lin Biao and the Gang of Four, who so abominate socialist humanitarianism.
   As we said before, in Russia and China, the proletariat dictatorship in its early period had to learn certain "barbaric measures" from
its enemies. However, the law of dialectics requires that during the
course of its development, it is inevitable that interest groups will

emerge that foster the prolonged existence of barbaric measures. Such are the powers of darkness, as represented by Lin Biao and the Gang of Four. They represent not only the struggles of human bestiality but also the brand of totalitarianism that has besmirched Communists. The Cultural Revolution gave them a chance to stir up trouble. Raising the flag of Marxism-Leninism against revisionism, they malignantly developed some wrong theories and practices on the dictatorship of the proletariat since Stalin's time. They deceived the masses, sharpened social contradictions, disrupted the society's normal order of production. . . .

We should understand that the only political means of preventing a reemergence of such powers of darkness as Lin Biao and the Gang of Four is to continue to push the proletariat dictatorship in the direction of democracy and humanitarianism. . . .

Abridged from *Qishi Niandai* (*The Seventies*) June, 1981
Translated by Michael Crook

China's New Generation of Politicians
WEI MING
Profiles of Beijing University students
who participated in the elections

The Twenty-Two-Year-Old "April Fifth" Hero—Wang Juntao

In November, 1980, a young man of twenty-two stood on the platform during a political question-and-answer meeting and dared to announce publicly that if there were a democratic election for a minister's post or even for premier, he would not hesitate to participate. His remarks caused an uproar in the large crowd. This fellow was wild. . . . He was a student in the nuclear physics department, but he wasn't applying himself to his studies in order to work directly for the Four Modernizations. Instead, he was barging into politics. He was simply not doing what he should.

. . . This young man presented an "explosive" topic: "Comrade Mao Zedong was a revolutionary inspired by Marxism, but not a Marxist." This instantly aroused a mass reaction. People immediately stood up to argue with him. After the meeting, some hurried home to write essays. . . .

Yet, during the primary elections of December 3, out of thirty candidates nominated from all departments (in which seventeen actively sought election) this "besieged" young man received the second highest number of votes, and became one of the three formal candidates. . . .

The formal election was set for December 11, when two out of three would be elected the people's representatives for Beijing municipality's Haidian district.

At first glance, this tough, workerlike young man was not a bit outstanding. Nevertheless, he was definitely an outstanding student at a top university and had quite an "illustrious" background: alternate committee member of the National Party Youth League, the "April Fifth" hero who had been arrested in the 1976 Tiananmen Incident. . . . So we sat in the headquarters of his "election committee"—a bedroom somehow squeezed out of the dormitory. Next to some unused bed frames covered with dust, two of his schoolmates in the election group were counting the primary votes. Yet, after a few questions and answers, Wang Juntao's eyes became animated and glowing, and he opened up his heart. . . . Out of the corner of that innocent, straightforward, self-confident mouth flashed the look of a twenty-two-year-old young adult.

Everybody says Wang Juntao is "full of vim and vigor." This powerful little steel cannon was born in Nanjing and grew up in a military quarter of Beijing. That was a special, closed world of Chinese society, one made up of military staff and their families. At the time of the Cultural Revolution, he was only eight, but he was organized. All day he fought with neighbors, practicing how to smash other people's windows. He was the second of four brothers and sisters in the family. His father was a teacher of theory in the Institute of Military Affairs. Not long after the Cultural Revolution started, he was away for long periods, supporting the movement, and so could not directly influence his children's education. However, the theoretical readings he left at home gave them a start.

According to this mischievous second child, his mother did not have much education. She only kept a close watch on him to see that he did his household chores, and did not get into trouble outside. Nevertheless, in the fourth grade, he began to enjoy reading classical novels like *The Monkey King* and *Water Margin*. But during those years, surely those books hadn't been for sale? "Ha," boldly and assuredly, he curled his lip in disagreement. "Who says they weren't! Our military quarters had them. All came from libraries that had been ransacked and closed. Some had been confiscated from people's homes!"

He has always been a good student, and he is particularly interested in the humanities. . . . He cannot understand why many of his schoolmates in the humanities who are particularly active thinkers have surprisingly become more muddleheaded as they study. Then why has he gone to the university, and even joined the science department? He replies that he hopes to discipline his thinking with training in the natural sciences, because in the world today social sciences are more and more permeated with, and bombarded by, the natural sciences. . . .

This strong-willed, honest, straightforward young man was jailed in 1976. At the time, he was in tenth grade. Because he was too innocent and naïve, he mentioned unsuspectingly in a political report that he had been to Tiananmen Square during the Qingming Festival. As soon as the report was handed to the teachers of the school, he was thrown into jail. In his jail cell, there were twenty criminal offenders and four political prisoners. He became the leader of them all. He was not released until the fall of the Gang of Four. He was then sent off to work in Shangzhuang Commune in Beijing's Haidian district until he was admitted into the university in 1978. During his time in the rural areas he came into contact with many poor farmers, and discovered that some of them lived in worse conditions than cattle in other countries. The greatest force of repression was actually the low-level cadres. Yet the farmers still said: "The scriptures are still good scriptures, they are just distorted by monks with crooked mouths." This chilled him. That extremely repressive mood of the rural area was a provocation to someone who was ambitious to work and who was used to being active. Therefore, his belief that China had to be reformed got stronger and stronger. This led to his being a strong supporter of, and participant in, Xidan Democracy Wall and to his promotion as the youngest deputy chief on the editorial committee of the theoretical mass journal *Beijing Spring*.

Though supposedly such things have all been banned and closed down, the people behind them can still be regarded as hidden reserves of youthful strength. They have no power or money. Yet energy that cannot be seen or grasped is buried in, and radiates from, so many sharp and exploring minds, so many hearts ready for sacrifice. It was no coincidence that twenty-two-year-old Wang Juntao was more mature and sensitive in his political thinking than many young people of similar age, and that he had made an impression in Beijing University's democratic elections. This had something to do with his having friends around him who shared his concerns.

He admits that he believes in scientific socialism, but at the same time he strongly advocates breaking out of traditional social science paradigms to examine the Chinese reality. In October, 1978, it seemed natural for him to be elected to the Central Committee of the party Youth League, given his good background and his being one of the April Fifth heroes. As early as the time when he was in the countryside as an educated youth, he had applied to be admitted to the party. After his entry into Beijing University, he had applied again. But as soon as he participated in running *Beijing Spring*, he was dismissed from his former post as the chief branch secretary of the Youth League in the department. The higher officials said with displeasure: "You ask to be admitted to the party, and yet you seek to be independent of it. . . ."

In China, university students in both the humanities and science must take political courses including the history of the Communist Party, Marxism-Leninist philosophy, and political economy. In every examination on politics this student, who believes in his own point of view, and who does not wish to repeat other people's thinking, often gives many "reactionary answers," and is regarded as a "typical believer in idealism. . . ."

He believes that when the nation faces its moment of decision, every reformer must be strong; he must not hesitate, must not consider the costs and benefits to himself. He proclaimed in his statement that in participating in this election, his first priority is to push forward China's democratization. This is because this election is "the first to try to build an electoral system that fits China's conditions." On the other hand, the group he represents has made the transition from having believed in the glorious, beautiful history of the older generation to "having learned to doubt and be critical." Moreover, he wants to make it clear to people that this generation will also learn to create and construct. At the same time, as the first group of young people to have come forward for a campaign election, it is very important to set the tone. He must represent the standards of Beijing University and must to a certain extent be a reflection of this generation.

During the election campaign, he put up a poster, a long essay that covered the walls of two dormitory buildings. . . . The essay pointed out: "History is so interesting; in abolishing and criticizing Democracy Wall, it at the same time accepts Democracy Wall's principal thinking." The essay also reflected the aspirations of some young people who had fully tasted the pain of deception and disappointment. Unable to go to school and unable to find work, they have totally deserted Stalinist or Maoist "socialism." They pursue the socialism that acknowledges the value of humanity, the meaning of humanity, and the rights of humanity. They eagerly hope for the creation of new values, styles of living, and models of society.

However, Wang Juntao feels deeply that throughout Chinese history it has not been easy for people to understand reformists. For example, when he took part in running *Beijing Spring*, people in general sneered at it and spread rumors that it was "officially" run; they did not know that his family was threatening to cut off relations with him so as not to be implicated. He disagrees with the kind of opinions that placed the Communist Party in opposition to reforms. He believes that "the existence of a reformist faction within the Chinese Communist Party is the historical precondition for the Chinese people to move with steady steps toward reforming the political and economic system. The party should be in the vanguard of democratization. . . ."

As a student of nuclear physics, what does he intend to do after graduation? He intends to make a career of what he has learned, "fulfill a legitimate obligation to society," and use his time away from work to continue thinking and exploring. In the dormitory room that he shares with five others, he sleeps in the upper section of a bunk bed. The rumpled bedding looks the same day or night. The young man says, "I feel only that there is too little time. I feel energetic enough though."

The Politically Zealous Philosopher—Hu Ping

Although the voters who supported Wang Juntao appreciate his uprightness, outspokenness, and boldness, they probably regret his lack of maturity and theoretical sophistication. Another candidate, however, compensated for these deficiencies. He is Hu Ping, a graduate student in the philosophy department, specializing in European philosophy and history. When Wang Juntao was in the second grade, Hu Ping was at the other end of the educational hierarchy, in his third year of senior high school. Unlike Wang Juntao, who was barely affected by the remaining ripples of the Cultural Revolution, Hu Ping experienced its entire course.

But if you have read his political essays or heard his speeches, you would have to admit that this apparently gentle, frail scholar from Sichuan province has tremendous inner strength. His thinking is tight, sharp, and logical, and he has deeply and thoroughly explored social and political questions.

Everyone was impressed by his quick responses in the question-and-answer meeting. He was good at identifying the central point of the questioner, often first clarifying muddled points: "Hmm, the question should be put this way . . ." And then casually he would give a simple, to-the-point answer.

He had spent a few years in Beijing during childhood, and so had picked up the standard accent. Afterward he returned to Chengdu for his primary and secondary schooling, where he did very well. He had wanted to go into the sciences, but, like many Chinese secondary school students of this period, when the Cultural Revolution began he submitted to the banner of the humanities.* In 1978, he applied to participate in the national recruitment examinations for research students. After only a few days he also participated in the university entrance examinations that year. In that examination he scored first in the humanities for Sichuan province. Beijing University also admitted him as a research student in European philosophy and history.

His parents were ordinary people. During the Cultural Revolution, he worked for five years in the countryside, in the town of Dukou of Sichuan province, bordering Yunnan. The living standard of that rural area was about average for China except that, since the weather was particularly hot, working there was very harsh. . . . After he returned to Chengdu he did not have a steady job for a long time. Once in a while he was a temporary worker; sometimes he was a substitute teacher. . . .

Outwardly, Hu Ping's experience—going to the countryside, returning to the city, and going back to school—was similar to that of many young people, but he was regarded as having had the roughest time among his group of schoolmates. Maybe it was because his family had overseas ties, and his father had a politically problematical background. His life has not been easy, and thus his perceptions of social problems are deep. Hu Ping did not wish to talk too much about the past. He only said lightly: "Am I not sitting here today? I cannot say that I have not been able to salvage anything from my past experience."

Now, many Chinese youths of the same age and experience have become silent, even demoralized. The majority of them are still concerned about politics and the fate of China, yet they no longer have the courage and enthusiasm to get involved personally. The intellectuals, particularly, feel chilled in their hearts at the ignorance caused by the low cultural level of the majority of the masses, who do not consider the long-term effect, and at many of those in power who are illiterate to a certain extent and often unreasonable. Therefore, they do not want to brave the currents, but would rather retreat a step

---

* Scientists and technocrats were especially vulnerable and often persecuted in this period for being "expert" at the expense of being "revolutionary."

and be sympathizers of the revolution. Some people say the fact that thirty-three-year-old Hu Ping still has so much energy is because he isn't married yet and doesn't have the burdens of a family. Hu Ping rebuffed such a view with a lighthearted smile. . . .

This month or so of participating in the election contest, though frantically busy, was really interesting for him. All of a sudden, he had become friends with so many people, and, moreover, he had found cause for hope in Chinese youth. As soon as his election proclamation was posted, many students from other departments unexpectedly came over to volunteer their help on the "election contest committee."

Hu Ping's emergence in the election, like Wang Juntao's, was no accident. The fact that he had received more than two thousand eight hundred votes in the primaries and had come in first was mainly due to his profound insights on political discussions. This side of his intellectual explorations was not achieved in a day. A while ago, during the period of Democracy Wall, he had had dealings with the Beijing mass publication *Wotu* (*Fertile Soil*), and had published essays in it. Among these was a long essay entitled "On the Freedom of Speech," which he posted in this election. He quoted a saying of the inventor of the lever, Archimedes: "Give me a fulcrum, and I can raise the world." He believed that in politics, freedom of speech was just this kind of fulcrum.

He was also aware that the power of a people's representative in a district of Beijing was limited, but that the main thing was to see how the representatives work. He said: "A small drama can always be played big! Like this small election contest in Beijing University— isn't it very meaningful?" He came from Sichuan, and so he particularly cherished Beijing University's very special position in the national sphere.

He appreciated those candidates who first stood forward to participate in the election campaigns, such as Wang Juntao, Fang Zhiyuan, and Xiashen. Their proclamation at the very outset started things off at a relatively high level. . . . Hu Ping was one week late. He did not feel isolated or fearful, because he believed that in an environment such as Beijing University his suggestions would be understood. He respected all the other candidates, believing that history had given this generation a common base. All that was lacking was exchange and mutual understanding, and therefore they could not join further in common cause. Everyone was very self-confident, because each one's conclusions had been tempered by struggle, and had not been merely recited from books. But Hu Ping hoped that everyone could go further toward grasping the intellectual substance of human society. One must stand on giants' shoulders in order to see further. One should not be divergent and in isolation "pull one's bootstraps up from nothing," or walk again the paths others have walked.

Because of this, he hoped that this democratic election contest at Beijing University would be able to leave something enduring and meaningful. He planned to edit a publication that would continue the enthusiasm of the discussion of issues during the time of the election contests. He, of course, had not forgotten the abortive attempt a year ago of a joint literary publication entitled *This Generation* by the students of Chinese departments at thirteen universities. But he was quite optimistic about the future. He felt that with the support of so many votes, plus official sanction, there was room to have some influence. . . .

The Future Politician—Zhang Wei

If Wang Juntao attracted voters with his selfless spirit, and Hu Ping with the depth of his theory, then the third formal candidate, Zhang Wei, won votes with his experienced style. Zhang Wei was the chairman of Beijing University's student union. At first, people asked him not to run. He was already doing well in the official track: he held important positions, among them deputy chairman of the Federation of Students in Beijing municipality, and this summer he had been a leader for a group of student representatives visiting Japan. As "one who had already gained benefits," why on earth was he competing for this insignificant post as district representative? For a young man who intended to go on to political office, to experience a genuine democratic movement was definitely good practice.

Obviously, Zhang Wei's different "official posts" sometimes worked against his favor. According to some, the school initially did not wish him to participate in the election contest, in order to show that the higher levels did not support students going into politics. The newspapers had avoided discussion of such a big event for a long time. . . . He nevertheless came forward and revealed his support of democratic movements. . . .

. . . He has a self-confident demeanor, in the style of a politician. When he led a group to visit Japan this year, he would on different occasions make appropriate impromptu talks. This ability is rare among China's foreign-service staff, let alone in a twenty-six-year-old young man who was visiting outside his country for the first time. He is realistic, rational, quick, and convincing.

He grew up in a warm, democratic family. . . . Their mother was a head nurse in a hospital, and their father an administrative cadre. During the Cultural Revolution, like many other families, the parents were each sent off to the countryside or to peripheral regions. He then took care of himself and his younger siblings in Wuhan. Because their father was always circling around the whirlpool of political movements, the children were naturally more concerned about these matters.

He has always been a well-behaved student, an outstanding student cadre, well liked by his teachers. After graduation from secondary school, he was trained in a teacher's training college for half a year and then assigned to a two-thousand-student secondary school to be a language teacher. Soon afterward, he also became that school's party Youth League secretary. In 1975, on his twenty-first birthday, he became the deputy chairman of the school's revolutionary committee (equivalent to deputy headmaster). After the fall of the Gang of Four, he was promoted to deputy section chief of the secondary school education section of the Education Bureau. His vita shows that he rose high and smoothly at a young age, but he repeatedly emphasized that his achievements were not due to obedience and chiming in with others. On the contrary, he said he had achieved so much by being tough and firm. For example, in early 1976, the school's party secretary was placed under pressure from higher levels, and dared not conduct memorial services for Zhou Enlai. This young deputy chairman came forward to prepare for memorial activities. After the April Fifth incident, the whole country was enveloped in white terror. He was assigned to investigate those in his unit responsible for being counterrevolutionary. So he easily brushed off his own "crimes." . . . He has either used the power of his own position or he has ridden the changing moods of the country. From another point of view, these kinds of experiences affected his mode of thinking and his views, and made him quite different in temperament from other young people his age.

During the election contest, some voters posted wall posters claiming that people like Zhang Wei were qualified to be district head, even premier, but were somehow not suitable to be people's representative. It was because he has always been the mediator between the masses and the leadership, someone who promoted compromise between the two sides.

Zhang Wei professed that he advocates reforms, as long as they are not too radical, because China can no longer endure instability. . . . When he was asked in the debate what his favorite motto was, he quick-wittedly said: "No matter if it is a white cat or a black cat, the 'meow' is useless; you still have to catch the mouse!"*

Zhang Wei was competing to be the people's representative in the Haidian district of Beijing, a district that included more than just Beijing University. The election form of other people's representatives in the district was different from Beijing University's. There was a great gap between the thinking of other candidates and the students at the University. . . . Presently, some people outside were saying that Beijing University students had been propped up by their full stomachs, and wondered whether or not financial aid had been allocated too generously.

Zhang Wei hoped to be able to unite middle-level cadres who were fluctuating and weighing advantages and disadvantages to conduct reforms. This group should not be slighted; without their support, and only a few powerless hot-blooded youth jumping about to rely on, nothing could be achieved. . . .

Zhang Wei indicated that one must fully make use of the country's present reformist atmosphere. If it were missed without anyone's making an effort, who knew when a similar opportunity would arise again? All his analysis was based on this: with the present situation in China, it was utterly unrealistic to hope for full democratic political participation, from the masses to the leaders, from the bottom to the top, in running the country. . . . Therefore, he hoped to proceed from reality point by point to do what could be done now.

He hoped that people outside the country would not see the reform movements in the country as a process of "liberalization" (Here, "liberalization" means to move away from the leadership of the Communist Party.) . . . Moreover, he felt that people outside the country should not overestimate the strength of the reformist force, because in reality the difficulties they faced were numerous. The recent atmosphere at Beijing University was only a beginning. But Beijing University's position in the country was special. Half a century ago the May Fourth Movement began in Beijing University. Yet many of its goals and directions have still not been realized today. People are still struggling for them.

Zhang Wei is a student in the economics department. His academic thesis for the year was about the employment problem of Chinese youth. When he graduates at the end of 1981, he would like to participate in practical economic work. After attaining some results within

* A play on a motto made famous by Deng Xiaoping: "It doesn't matter if the cat is black or white—as long as it catches the mouse."

the department or the district, he would use this experience to say something. Ultimately he would like to go into politics. From this solid, competent young man, people might be able to get a glimpse of what China's future politicians will be like.

The Pioneer Who Dared to Bang His Head Against the Wall—Fang Zhiyuan

Then what was the situation for the fourteen candidates who lost in the primary? Early on the third day following the results of the primary, I visited Fang Zhiyuan of the Department of International Politics. He lost to the third elected candidate, Zhang Wei, by only 107 votes. . . . According to the polls, the opinion of him was that he was sincere. I really could not believe that this humble, gentle young man who ground his teeth when he spoke could have been, as he claimed, the "local bully" among his teen-age schoolmates, who drank and fought, et cetera.

When asked about what had been gained in this election contest, his first statement was: "The election has been successful. . . ." It came truly from his own heart. . . . Some regretted that he had lost by so few votes, and came to console him. But Fang Zhiyuan politely declined their condolences.

He was the first person at Beijing University to consider running in the election . . . He later joined with Wang Juntao to take action. On November 3, the two of them took the first step by posting their election speeches. The two disagreed on specific points, but their general direction was the same—to push democratic elections in Beijing University, to make them a model. Therefore, he was not concerned about whether he would be elected or not. . . . According to the experience of history, "democracy" in the past had always been "decreed as a gift." If the leaders changed their minds, they could immediately turn around and take "democracy" back. He was psychologically prepared for the worst.

During the election contest activities, four apparently neutral reporting teams appeared at Beijing University: "Election Contest Moves" of the Philosophy Department, "Election Contest Short Waves" of the Chinese Department, "Election Contest Observation" of the Law Department, and "A Page in History" of the History Department. One time, "Election Contest Short Waves" asked about the political, economic, historical, artistic, and religious works the candidates liked and had read. Fang Zhiyuan honestly put *The Romance of the Three*

*Kingdoms** in the section on literature. Nevertheless, honesty is strength. He is a glorious loser.

He was born in Beijing and grew up in Dalian. When the Cultural Revolution began, he had just graduated from primary school. Not long afterward, the whole family moved to Guangzhou, and he attended middle school there. His father was a naval technician who had defected from the Kuomintang before Liberation, and his mother was an activist in the "antihunger, anti-civil war" student movements in the late forties. Later she was a reporter and a teacher of foreign languages. At the end of 1974, in Guangzhou, Fang Zhiyuan read a wall poster written by Li Yizhe on socialist democracy and legality. He tried to argue with it, but found himself unable to. The viewpoint of the wall poster was firm and unbeatable. Finally, he changed over to Li Yizhe side.

After graduation from middle school, he became a worker in a ship repair factory of the Marine Transportation Bureau. He applied to enter university seven times in seven years, but every time he was rejected because he had failed the check on his political background. (Though his father had defected to the Communists, and had later joined the party, the problem of his background had not been cleared.) At the time, some people advised him not to waste his energy, but he was stubborn. He knew that in front of him was a wall; if he did not bang it with his head, the wall would never crumble. In 1978, he was admitted to Beijing University. In 1979, before and after the rise of Democracy Wall in Xidan, mass publications mushroomed all over the country. He became the contact for Guangzhou's *People's Voice* and made many young friends, among them Wang Juntao and Hu Ping.

People say that since May Fourth Beijing University has always had a special tradition. . . . The people somehow sense that here is an important center of political thought in the country. Its movements matter, and thus generate a strong sense of mission. He treasures the experience of this election. The election toughened the masses. The habit of democracy could not be cultivated overnight. . . .

Beijing University students initiated the setting up of a group to edit materials on the democratic elections—to gather all the candidates' speeches, political opinions, posters, taped interviews, messages from the audience at debates, answers to reporters, et cetera—and planned to organize them as historical documents. After the primary, Fang Zhiyuan wrote an article for this group about his memories of the process of the election contest at Beijing University. In

* As "feudal" literature, this traditional Chinese classic would have been considered counterrevolutionary.

the article there appeared this sentence: "In physics things appear small from far away but big from close up. Historical events are just the opposite. As time passes, people will discover the historical significance of what we are creating at this moment."

Abridged from *Qishi Niandai* (*The Seventies*)
February, 1981